D1526301

A LITTLE GROUP OF WILLFUL MEN

Kennikat Press

National University Publications

Series in American Studies

General Editor
James P. Shenton
Professor of History, Columbia University

THOMAS W. RYLEY

A LITTLE GROUP
OF WILLFUL MEN

*A STUDY OF
CONGRESSIONAL–PRESIDENTIAL
AUTHORITY*

National University Publications
KENNIKAT PRESS • 1975
Port Washington, N.Y. • London

Manufactured in the United States of America

Published by
Kennikat Press Corp.
Port Washington, N.Y./London

Library of Congress Cataloging in Publication Data

Ryley, Thomas W.   1931–
   A little group of willful men.

   (National university publications)
   Bibliography: p. 192
   Includes index.
   1. United States—Politics and government—1913–1921.
   2. United States—Foreign relations—1913–1921.
   3. European War, 1914–1918—United States. I. Title.
E780.R94   320.9′73′0913   74-80591
ISBN 0-8046-9088-X

TO MY WIFE AND CHILDREN

CONTENTS

PREFACE

Although this study deals with the United States Senate in the days before World War I, it is not intended as another attempt to explore the already overworked questions of why the United States entered the war, or whether it should have. Nor is it designed to be an attempt to chronicle all the events between the outbreak of the war in Europe and the declaration of war by the United States. Rather, the focus is on the Senate, on the attempts of the antiwar faction within it to fight policies and practices they believed were leading the nation into war, and on their perception of the proper role of the Congress in shaping foreign policy.

There are several people whom I would like to thank in connection with the preparation of this book. Their assistance has made the writing and editing of it much easier. In particular, I would like to thank some of my colleagues at New York City Community College who read all or part of the manuscript and offered helpful suggestions and comments: Edward Kaplan, Thomas Karfunkel, Wayne McCullers, Robert Montgomery, Henry Esterly, and Timothy Driscoll.

I would also like to thank the New York City Community College library staff for their help: Edward Mapp, chief librarian, Darrow Wood, and John Howard.

The deepest debt of all is owed to my wife Mary, not only for her endless typing efforts but for her patience, toleration, and moral support.

T.W.R.

Baldwin, N.Y.

A LITTLE GROUP OF WILLFUL MEN

THE SENATE OF THE SIXTY-FOURTH CONGRESS

Democrats

Henry Ashurst	(Ariz.)	Francis Newlands	(Nev.)
John Bankhead	(Ala.)	James O'Gorman	(N.Y.)
John Beckham	(Ky.)	Lee Overman	(N.C.)
Robert Broussard	(La.)	Robert Owen	(Okla.)
Nathan Bryan	(Fla.)	James Phelan	(Calif.)
George Chamberlain	(Oreg.)	Key Pittman	(Nev.)
William Chilton	(W.Va.)	Atlee Pomerene	(Ohio)
Charles Culberson	(Tex.)	Joseph Randsdell	(La.)
Henry DuPont	(Del.)	James Reed	(Mo.)
Duncan Fletcher	(Fla.)	Joseph Robinson	(Ark.)
Thomas Gore	(Okla.)	Willard Saulsbury	(Del.)
Thomas Hardwick	(Ga.)	John Schafroth	(Colo.)
Gilbert Hitchcock	(Nebr.)	Morris Sheppard	(Tex.)
Henry Hollis	(N.H.)	John Shields	(Tenn.)
William Hughes	(N.J.)	Furnifold Simmons	(N.C.)
Paul Husting	(Wis.)	Ellison D. Smith	(S.C.)
Ollie James	(Ky.)	Hoke Smith	(Ga.)
Charles Johnson	(Maine)	J. W. Smith	(Md.)
Edward Johnson	(S.Dak.)	Marcus Smith	(Ariz.)
John Kern	(Ind.)	William Stone	(Mo.)
William F. Kirby	(Ark.)	Claude Swanson	(Va.)
Harry Lane	(Oreg.)	Charles Thomas	(Colo.)
Luke Lea	(Tenn.)	William Thompson	(Kans.)
Blair Lee	(Md.)	Ben Tillman	(S.C.)
J. Hamilton Lewis	(Ill.)	Oscar Underwood	(Ala.)
Thomas Martin	(Va.)	James K. Vardaman	(Miss.)
James Martine	(N.J.)	Thomas Walsh	(Mont.)
Henry Myers	(Mont.)	John Sharp Williams	(Miss.)

Republicans

James Brady	(Idaho)	Henry C. Lodge	(Mass.)
Frank Brandegee	(Conn.)	Porter McCumber	(N.Dak.)
William Borah	(Idaho)	George McLean	(Conn.)
Thomas Catron	(N.Mex.)	Knute Nelson	(Minn.)
Moses Clapp	(Minn.)	George Norris	(Nebr.)
Clarence Clark	(Wyo.)	George Oliver	(Pa.)
LeBaron Colt	(R.I.)	Carroll Page	(Vt.)
Albert Cummins	(Iowa)	Boies Penrose	(Pa.)
Charles Curtis	(Kans.)	Miles Poindexter	(Wash.)
William Dillingham	(Vt.)	Lawrence Sherman	(Ill.)
Albert Fall	(N.Mex.)	Wm. Alden Smith	(Mich.)
Bert Fernald	(Maine)	Reed Smoot	(Utah)
Jacob Gallinger	(N.H.)	Thomas Sterling	(S.Dak.)
Nathan Goff	(W.Va.)	George Sutherland	(Utah)
Asle J. Gronna	(N.Dak.)	Charles Townsend	(Mich.)
Warren Harding	(Ohio)	James Wadsworth	(N.Y.)
Wesley Jones	(Wash.)	Francis Warren	(Wyo.)
William Kenyon	(Iowa)	James Watson	(Ind.)
Robert LaFollette	(Wis.)	John Weeks	(Mass.)
Henry Lippitt	(R.I.)	John Works	(Calif.)

1

A LITTLE GROUP OF WILLFUL MEN: CONGRESS AND FOREIGN POLICY

The termination of the last session of the 64th Congress . . . disclosed a situation unparalleled in the history of the country, perhaps unparalleled in the history of any modern country. In the immediate presence of a crisis fraught with a more subtle . . . possibilit[y] of national danger . . . the Congress has been unable to act either to safeguard the country or vindicate the elementary rights of its citizens. . . . More than 500 of the 531 members of the two houses were ready and anxious to act; the House . . . had acted by an overwhelming majority; but the Senate was unable to act because a little group of eleven Senators . . . determined that it should not.

The Senate has no rules by which debate can be limited or brought to an end . . . by which dilatory tactics of any kind can be prevented. A single member can stand in the way. . . . The result . . . is a paralysis of the legislative and executive branches of government.

The inability of the Senate to act has rendered some of the most necessary legislation impossible at a time when the need of it was most pressing and most evident. . . . It would not cure the difficulty to call the Sixty-fifth Congress into extraordinary session. The paralysis of the Senate would remain. . . . The Senate cannot act unless its leaders obtain unanimous consent. Its majority is powerless, helpless. . . .

Although as a matter of fact, the nation and the representatives . . . stand in back of the Executive with unprecedented unanimity . . . the impression made abroad will . . . be that it is not so and the other governments may act as they please without fear that this government will do anything. . . . We cannot explain. The explanation is incredible. The Senate of the United States is the only legislative body in the world which cannot act when its majority is ready for action. A little group of willful men, representing no opinion but their own, have rendered the great government of the United States helpless and contemptible.

The remedy . . . the only remedy is that the rules of the Senate be altered so that it can act. The country can be relied on to draw the moral. I believe that

3

the Senate can be relied on to supply the means of action and save the country from disaster.[1]

If there is any one statement of Woodrow Wilson's which has survived, it is this one, his castigation of a group of United States senators who filibustered to death a bill which would have permitted him to arm American merchant vessels in March of 1917. Certainly many of his speeches were more memorable, many of his proposals more controversial and far-reaching, but this brief statement, issued shortly after he took the oath of office as president for a second term, has become part of the American legend.

The statement cast eleven (or twelve, for the exact number is open to some question) senators into the sort of calumny reserved for those who defy the will of a nation bent on a particular course of action. What those seven Republicans, who joined with Democrats in 1868 refusing to remove Andrew Johnson from office, had been two generations earlier to an aroused public, these men would be in 1917. They were traitors to many Americans alarmed by what they believed to be violations of neutral rights, and to be threats to the nation posed by the recently revealed plot to align Mexico and Japan against the United States as proposed in the Zimmermann Note.

American senators had opposed popular measures at other times, and had not, for the most part, suffered any serious consequences. Nor, for that matter, had there been any great criticism of the thirteen members of the House of Representatives who had voted against the Armed Ship measure when it came before that body. But what made the action of these senators deplorable in the eyes of many was that by filibustering (and at this point it must be mentioned that all who were accused of having obstructed the bill by a filibuster did not, upon analysis, do so) they incurred the charge of having prevented the passage of what was considered to be a bill vital to the defense of American rights. This made their crime all the greater than having merely opposed an otherwise popular measure.

There are a number of extremely significant aspects to the Armed Ship filibuster of 1917. Perhaps of the greatest long-range consequence is that this filibuster provided the impetus for the curbing of that unique practice, a practice that had been part of the lifestyle of the Senate for many years. The upper chamber had long cherished this right, although periodically some senators would raise the question of the right of a minority to obstruct in this fashion.

However, the cry for altering Senate rules in the light of what had happened here—the prevention of a bill that appeared to have the urgency of this one—was too much for them to overlook. In a matter of days a practice that dated back many years was eliminated, and with only three dissenting votes a modified set of procedures was installed.[2]

Second, and perhaps also of great significance, is that this dispute represented a clash between the executive and the legislative branches as to where the initiative in foreign policy rested—with the executive asserting primary responsibility in this area and many legislators claiming the right of the Congress to partnership. To be sure, those legislators who were the most vocal in claiming this right were those who found themselves in opposition to the president on the substantive aspects of policy. Others who were in sympathy with the chief executive's position would generally support his right to be the sole determiner of foreign policy. But the issue was joined, no matter what the motivation.

This debate had gone on before in American history, although not to the extent that it has in recent years. It would be waged over the Versailles Treaty fight a few years after the Armed Ship debate; it would be a major issue in the 1960s as the United States fought what can probably be accurately described as the most unpopular war in its history. It was in the aftermath of this latter conflict that the Congress passed the most significant restraint ever placed by the legislative branch on a chief executive's ability to conduct foreign policy. In 1973 it voted, over the president's veto, a measure limiting the amount of time that American troops may be committed to battle without the approval of the Congress. But it took an extremely unpopular war, which had gone on for over eight years, as well as a significant lack of confidence in the particular chief executive as a result of revelations of misconduct in his administration, to bring not only the Congress but the American public around to the point where they could accept this.

For the Armed Ship Bill was not simply a measure that would have permitted the president to arm merchant vessels. Had it passed, it would have authorized the president to take even further steps in the defense of American commerce—even perhaps to conducting an undeclared naval war in the Atlantic. To the senators who opposed the bill, this was its most ominous aspect, for it would have given the president what seemed to them to be an unprecedented grant of power and an assumption that he had the sanction of Congress to do as he wished. Perhaps today, with the Gulf of Tonkin Resolution and the Eisenhower Doctrine, such a grant seems minimal, but to the dissenters in 1917 it represented the ultimate in arrogation of power to the executive branch and would,

5

they argued, take from the Congress in theory, if not in fact, the one power that it believed it had in foreign affairs, that of declaring war.

The filibuster then, was an attempt to withhold this sanction, but it came at a time when it appeared that anything less than a complete defense of American rights was treasonable. It occurred against a background of a tradition that had seen the Congress, even in the days of weak presidents, generally assume a secondary role in foreign policy and rarely exercise the options it had to affect said policy. To many Americans in 1917 a protest against the right of the president to conduct international affairs as he saw fit seemed contrary to the nation's tradition.

Particularly throughout most of the nineteenth century, when the United States was absorbed primarily with domestic problems, this secondary role of Congress in foreign policy was evident. Even in the matter of the ratification of treaties, the Senate, which alone possesses this power, rarely asserted itself. Of 928 treaties submitted to it prior to 1934, it rejected only fifteen, the most prominent, of course, being the Treaty of Versailles.[3] Otherwise, the upper chamber generally acquiesced in pacts made by the executive.

Occasionally the Senate might amend treaties, as in 1794 when it struck out a clause pertaining to the West Indies trade from Jay's Treaty, or might completely mutilate them as with the first Hay-Paunceforte Treaty in 1900, causing the other nation (Britain) to say that the agreement was void.

Similarly, the Senate had rarely asserted its prerogative of rejecting diplomatic personnel as a means of trying to influence American foreign policy. In 1826 it did hold up, until it was too late for the United States to participate in a meaningful manner, the approval of two representatives to be sent to the Panama Conference of Western Hemisphere nations.

The use of the power of the purse was rarely employed by the Congress as a means of having a voice in foreign policy, though a delay in approving funds for the Panama Conference was one such instance. The House of Representatives did indicate in 1867 that it would refuse to appropriate the moneys to complete the purchase of the Virgin Islands from Denmark, but before the issue came to a test President Grant withdrew the treaty from the Senate, which had indicated a reluctance to act on the matter. For the most part, the House accepted the arguments employed by Hamilton and others in 1794—that once an agreement is ratified, the nation is bound to accept the financial commitments growing out of the arrangement.

A LITTLE GROUP OF WILLFUL MEN

The view that the executive and legislative branches are "partners" in foreign policy making was never accepted by the executive. This was perhaps most dramatically demonstrated by the rejection, by Secretary of State William Seward in 1864, of the assertion by the Congress that it was a coequal in this area—an assertion that arose over the concern of the legislature that the United States was taking too tolerant a view of the efforts of France to set up a client state in Mexico during the period of the American Civil War. Once again the question was raised by legislators who disagreed with the executive branch's policy, as Lincoln and Seward, concerned to keep the European nations neutral, had not pressed France for what was a clear violation of the Monroe Doctrine.[4] Ironically, this incident would be cited by an antiwar senator in 1916 as being as example of a time when the Congress had "asserted" itself in the area of foreign policy and had rejected the traditional approach. However, he neglected to inform his colleagues that despite the legislature's brave little manifesto, no acquiescence had been made by the executive in its interpretation of partnership.

Where the executive branch has attempted to make a partner of the legislature, it has done so for a reason. Thus it was that Polk laid the Oregon boundary dispute before the Senate in 1846, hoping to get the sentiment of that body (he was originally disposed to reject it); when the Senate indicated its approval, he accepted its advice. In 1893 Cleveland, confronted with the vexing Hawaiian annexation question in light of revelations that American officials had played a major role in the revolution, put the issue to the Congress, promising to abide by any reasonable solution. The Congress advised him that it was its wish neither to annex, nor to assist the old government to return to power, but rather, in effect, to maintain the status quo. Cleveland accepted this course of action.[5]

Similarly, the executive had rarely felt itself obliged to accept Congressional "instructions" in dealing with foreign policy problems. One time in which it did feel so obliged was in the late 1880s when Secretary of State Blaine indicated that, in dealing with the pelagic sealing question, he considered himself "instructed" by the congressional mandate of March 1889 directing the United States to seize vessels which had gone into American waters around the Bering Sea to slaughter seals. It put him in a dubious legal position, which Britain, one of the other disputants, would not accept, and the ultimate resolution of the matter did not please most Americans.[6]

One area in which the Congress had held the initiative was that of declaring war. In two of the three instances in which the United States went to war with a foreign nation prior to 1917, the Congress, despite its usually recessive role in foreign policy, took the initiative boldly and "pushed" a war that the chief executive at the time was either reluctant about or averse to. There were other instances in which adroit diplomacy by the executive branch cooled the war fever, as when Secretary of State Fish was able to resolve the *Alabama* incident without bowing to the more belligerent faction in Congress, and in the crises in the early 1890s with Italy and Chile, in which there was a strong clamor for war, both in and out of the legislature.

It might be advisable, therefore, to look briefly at those incidents in which the United States went to war, particularly analyzing the nature of the opposition to war within the Congress. The opposition in each of these instances is identifiable—as identifiable as the 1917 dissent will be shown to be—although in only one of these cases might it be said that the allegation of treason was thrown at those in the Congress who were reluctant to commit the nation to battle.

In the first of these, the War of 1812, provoked by such men as Henry Clay and John C. Calhoun, the legislature took a more belligerent view towards the situation than did the president and tended to force the issue. In fact, critics of American involvement in 1812 would have done well to have called it "Mr. Clay's war" rather than "Mr. Madison's war," for it was the Congress, particularly the war hawks in the House, that created the greatest demand for it in that year. Madison tended to be less than eager for war with Britain, but as the movement built up in the Congress it made a more belligerent tone necessary and eventually the request for a declaration of war. Ironically, on the eve of the war the British made concessions which, had they been known to the American government, might have averted the conflict.

The agitation for war was strongest in the West, and it was not over neutral rights or impressment of seamen, for as most historians agree today, the real causes of American involvement had little to do with British maritime practices. Rather, it was expansionism and the Indian problem that caused the interest in that part of the country most eager for war as the voting distribution on the war resolution shows. Opposition to involvement was greatest in the East, particularly in the seacoast regions. New England was particularly opposed to a war with Britain. On a partisan basis, opposition was strongest among the Federalists and among moderate Republicans from the eastern areas.[7]

Resentment over the war in New England led to the abortive Hartford Convention, and the involvement of many antiwar Federalists spelled the end of that party's political life. The party was on the downgrade. Opposition to a war ostensibly to protect American rights hastened the demise.

The war in 1898 over the matter of Cuban independence has several similarities to 1812—a relatively weak president, a more aggressive Congress, and concessions on the eve of a declaration of war by the other nation involved. McKinley was perhaps even less disposed to ask for a declaration of war than had been Madison, but he too found the initiative being taken from him by the Congress, which acted perhaps as aggressively in the area of foreign policy as did any legislature in the nineteenth century. As early as 1896 it attempted to prod Cleveland with a resolution urging that the United States government recognize the revolutionary government of Cuba, a move that the chief executive rejected.

As public opinion hardened over what the newspapers reported in Cuba, the Congress became even more belligerent. McKinley's orientation was, as Cleveland's had been, to remain above the matter, to adopt a course of strict neutrality in what was essentially a civil dispute. He was backed in this by the leadership of his party, including the Speaker of the House, Reed, and most of the business interests who had supported him for the presidency. However, the "backbenchers" in the Senate and the House were in revolt, and as the level of resentment grew, so did McKinley's demands on Spain.

The strong populist sections of the West viewed intervention with the greatest interest. Intervention was prompted by a number of considerations—pseudohumanitarianism, a certain amount of anti-Catholicism, and possibly even the view that the war might help bring America to the silver standard. The demand for war became so strong there that William Jennings Bryan, later to be an outspoken opponent of involvement in World War I but at this time the nominal leader of the western agrarians, took up the cry for intervention.[8]

In April, unable to resolve the situation through diplomacy and unable to resist the pressure any longer, McKinley asked the Congress for the power to take whatever steps might be necessary to bring about a free Cuba. The legislature happily complied, and when Spain regarded this action as a declaration of war, the United States responded that indeed war had existed ever since the passage of this legislation. The Senate had gone even further during the consideration of McKinley's proposal; it had voted recognition of Cuba, a clear infringement on executive prerogatives, but this action was blocked in the House. On partisan lines, most of the dissenting legislators were Republican, chiefly from the Northeast.[9]

9

But if Congress had taken the initiative away from two weak presidents and had forced the issue in these cases, the reverse was true in 1846. At this time a stronger president, Polk, as part of his plan to expand American possessions, was able to force a war on an apathetic Congress.

The expansionism of this period was not universally popular. The conventional view that it was opposed most strongly in New England because of the slavery implications is only partially the case. Frederick Merk points up that there was uniform opposition within the Whig party to the idea of war. There was also opposition among most northern Democrats and many southern Democrats, including Calhoun. In fact, probably no major political figure of that period was sympathetic to the idea of a war with Mexico for any reason.

However, Polk was able to stampede the Congress by creating the sort of provocative incident that would compel some sort of immediate action on its part without its looking at the circumstances or even the implications. The debates were brief. Much later a young congressman from Illinois, Abraham Lincoln, would dare the president to name the spot on American soil where the blood had been shed that would require that the United States go to war. But for the moment there was little by way of question, as only fourteen antislavery northerners, including John Quincy Adams, voted against it in the House, and only two opposed the resolution in the Senate. Calhoun did not vote and Webster stayed away. But the vote in no way reflected any enthusiasm for war.

Merk, in his analysis of American dissent in this conflict, suggests that the Whigs failed to contest the war because they did not wish to be known as an antiwar party and thus possibly suffer the fate of the Federalists in 1812.[10] The real antiwar sentiment manifested itself after the declaration, reflected by Lincoln's statement, the famous speech by the noted Whig orator Thomas Corwin against the war, and eventually the Wilmot Proviso, which, had it passed, would have forbidden the extension of slavery into areas taken during the course or as a result of the war.

The emphasis in this study of the Armed Ship proposal and its fate is on the Senate of the Sixty-fourth Congress. This is not to suggest that the measure was greeted with enthusiasm in the House, nor for that matter were other presidential actions regarding the European war reived warmly. In fact, at several points prior to entry into the war in April 1917 there would appear to have been greater resistance to diplomatic belligerency in the House than in the Senate.

It would be the Senate that would deal with the Treaty of Versailles, another matter in which the relative roles of the executive branch and the Senate would be at issue. While it would be a different Senate, the Sixty-sixth, it would contain some of the names that will be prominent on ensuing pages.

In one sense, the Senate was operating under several very distinct disadvantages in dealing with the president at this time. This was true not only of those senators whom one may identify as being major or minor figures within the antiwar bloc, but of all legislators as well, regardless of how they felt about the issue. First, the president has an advantage over Congress in any disagreement, whether it be in foreign or domestic matters. He has greater access to the media, which in 1917 was almost uniformly pro-Allies, pro-British, prointervention, or prowar, depending upon how one wishes to interpret the question. A greater public forum was provided to the president than to any senator or group of senators of any period. This is no less true today. In addition, a president has the potent weapon of patronage at his disposal. As we shall subsequently note, Wilson used this power liberally in pushing for his foreign and domestic programs.

And finally the expertise that legislators had in foreign affairs of this period, particularly in European government and politics, was limited. This is not to suggest that those in the executive branch were expert. Perhaps some critics of congressional behavior in recent years might contend that nothing has changed over the last five and a half decades, and that legislators today have as limited an understanding of foreign affairs. But in 1917 the problem was even more acute than today, as the Congress had been focusing almost entirely on domestic matters and had abdicated much of the direction in foreign policy to the executive. As freely admitted by members of the Senate, the complexities of the problems confronting America abroad were not truly understood. The attention of most senators in foreign policy matters centered around the problems in Latin America where some expertise was evident, and around problems in the Pacific.

The character of this particular Senate must also be considered. The enactment of the Seventeenth Amendment had brought about a considerable turnover in the upper chamber, as direct election of senators eliminated some of those who had been chosen through the old methods and could not be under the new one. Junior legislators are frequently at a disadvantage in dealing with the president and even in dealing with their seniors. Of the twelve men charged with obstructionism in the

Armed Ship fight, eight were in their first term.

Francis Russell, in his biography of Harding, writes of the Senate of the Sixty-fourth Congress that it was a body with few men of any reputation and stature. This was not a Senate such as the ones that had featured the luminaries of the middle years of the nineteenth century, but a body perhaps symbolized more by men like Bert Fernald, John Beckham, Thomas Catron, Henry Lippitt, William Chilton, James Phelan, and J. W. Smith. There were titans, however, like Lodge and LaFollette and perhaps John Sharp Williams, as well as others who were early in their Senate careers and whose fame lay in the future, George Norris, William Borah, Thomas Walsh, Joe Robinson, Charles Curtis, Henry Ashurst, and Warren Harding. But for the most part, it was the Fernalds, not the Lodges, who symbolized the Senate of the Sixty-Fourth Congress.[11]

2

THE PROTAGONISTS

Wilson and the Executive Branch

There have been a number of attempts to analyze Woodrow Wilson's attitude towards the war in Europe. To some he is a hero, a man who truly tried to keep the United States out of the war while reacting to threats presented by Germany. To others, usually referred to as the "revisionist" historians, he is a villainous anglophile who took a biased position early in the war and moved closer and closer each day towards the point at which American involvement became inevitable.

Certainly, whatever interpretation one wishes to place upon his behavior, it should be noted that Wilson was more sympathetic to the Allied position; although perhaps for the pro-Allied faction this point was disputable. However, Wilson, in being more willing to accept the Allied point of view than that of Germany, was not reacting solely on the basis of his own personal pro-British bias. He was mirroring the sentiments of the American people, for once the war broke out and Americans became aware of the dimensions of the conflict and of the issues involved, public opinion generally tended to side with Britain and France. Only a relatively small segment of the American people, in particular some German-Americans, openly aligned themselves on the side of Germany and the Central Powers.[1]

For the most part, those Americans who were not sympathetic to the Allies generally called for the United States to pursue a policy of "absolute neutrality." This phrase meant that the nation should try to follow a course of action that involved being "above the battle" and neutral in thought as well as in action. Wilson's early statements in 1914, as those of most other prominent citizens, urged this policy on Americans. Even Theodore Roosevelt, never one to back away from a conflict, opined that it would be best for the United States to stay away from this war.[2]

However, the absolute neutrality, or "neutralism," that Wilson advocated when the war broke out was beginning to erode by late 1914, and by early 1915 the restraints that many Americans had placed on themselves were thrown off. The reaction in the United States to the German submarine menace, the violation of Belgian neutrality, all reported dutifully by a press that was generally pro-Allies, reflected the end of neutrality in thought. Wilson found himself obliged to condemn Germany for a number of actions, not the least of which was her refusal to recognize the rights of American citizens to travel on the vessels of belligerents. By this condemnation, he abandoned absolute neutrality.

Wilson well knew that the European war must have an effect on the United States. He therefore began several efforts, through Colonel House, to try to bring the fighting to a close by using the good offices of this nation. However, his perception of the terms upon which the war should be terminated and the peace conference begun tended to reflect the war aims of the British and their Allies. By 1915, he had begun to accept the validity of their war goals with almost no reservations.

In short, neutrality in thought and in action was not the policy of the United States for any appreciable period of time after the outbreak of hostilities in Europe. Given the publicity about the war, it was impossible for the people of the United States not to develop a biased attitude towards this particular conflict and thus, not to insist that their government respond more vigorously to a war for the preservation of civilization. Nor was it consistent with any aspect of Wilson's personality to be neutral in any conflict in which the contending forces seemed to him to be so diametrically opposed as these did as early as 1915. He told friends that he saw the Allies fighting "beasts," a statement that suggests that he had already made up his mind about where the forces of good and of evil were in this war.[3]

Most commonly referred to, in an attempt to analyze Wilson's attitudes during the period 1914 to 1917, is the pro-British orientation which had grown out of his love for England. Wilson admired the British people, their history, their literature, their form of government, their land and so it is not surprising that he would be inclined to accept their analysis of international affairs. Since he was not too well informed about European politics, and most American ambassadors in Europe at this time were relatively incompetent and their information of little value, he would naturally be forced to lean for an interpretation of events in the direction of a nation towards which he felt some affinity.[4]

However, Wilson was not the only anglophile in his administration. He frequently had to be a tempering agent in his own official family, as some cabinet ministers who felt even more strongly about the nature of the war than he did called for the United States to be more belligerent. As late as March 1917 many of them were grumbling about what they regarded as his lack of enthusiasm for "positive action."

Within the cabinet men such as Secretary of the Treasury William Gibbs McAdoo, Secretary of Commerce William Redfield, Secretary of the Interior Franklin K. Lane, and Secretary of State Robert Lansing (after 1915; before that, State Department Counselor) were strongly pro-British and pro-Allies. The State Department was heavily infiltrated with pro-British figures such as Frank Polk, who succeeded Lansing as counselor, as were the overseas embassies, where the best-known example is Walter Hines Page, the North Carolinian who was ambassador to Great Britain. Much has been made of Page's apparently total enchantment with Britisn leaders and the Britisn explanation for the war and the effect that this had on American foreign policy. Wilson was aware of Page's bias and had begun to try to work around him long before America actually entered the war.[5]

Arthur Link has pointed out that at almost every significant level of American society there was strong support for the British and Allied position. This included the writers William Dean Howells and Booth Tarkington, educators President Butler of Columbia and President Hibben of Princeton, the financial leader J. P. Morgan, and leaders of the opposition party such as Roosevelt, ex-President Taft, Henry Stimson, Senator Elihu Root of New York (who left the Senate before the Sixty-Fourth Congress), and Senator Henry Cabot Lodge of Massachusetts. Most of the major newspapers, save the Hearst publications, were inclined toward Britain and her Allies.[6]

Even within his private circle of advisers, Wilson was surrounded with pro-British sentiment. There was his secretary Joe Tumulty, despite his Irish ancestry, and his close friend and confidant Colonel Edward House. The latter has been a favorite target for revisionist historians who see him as a shadowy figure in American diplomacy of this period and who wonder about his relationship with Wilson. His position as a private diplomatic agent outside the usual ambassadorial channels might be better understood now by a nation that has experienced Franklin Roosevelt

and Hopkins, and Nixon and Kissinger (before the latter's appointment
as secretary of state).

There were a few men around Wilson who did not include towards the
Britisn position, although this is not to imply that they were anti-British.
Secretary of State (until 1915) William Jennings Bryan, who will be discussed in more detail, and Secretary of the Navy Josephus Daniels were
the two men in his cabinet who leaned more to the position of absolute
neutrality. One or two others, including Postmaster General Albert
Burleson, were not strong advocates of belligerency toward Germany.

What must be mentioned about Wilson, however, in connection with
his pro-British bias, is not so much the substantive consequences that
might arise from it—for as we have seen he was hardly alone in favoring
the British position—but rather, the implications of the respect and admiration he had for British institutions. These feelings would have a
decided effect on how he believed foreign policy ought to be formulated.
Almost every writer who has dealt with Wilson has stressed his fascination
with the British political system and his belief that it was superior to the
American.

His best-known work, *Congressional Government,* was an indictment
of the American system, which he characterized as weak, dominated by
the legislature (particularly the House of Representatives), and parochial.
It was not a system, in his opinion, that would permit a nation to grapple
with its problems effectively.[7]

Wilson's intellectual tradition was British. As one writer has noted,
he had a romantic idea of British statecraft. His heroes were the products
of the British system, Gladstone, Burke, Bright, Bagehot, and Macaulay,
not American statesmen of a similar period.[8] He believed that the
cabinet system of government tended to produce a higher type of
leader.

Still another writer has commented that Wilson wanted to alert the
United States to the merits of the British system.[9] He could not fuse
the executive and legislative branches, given the nature of the Constitution, but he could adapt whatever he might from the British to the American system. Perhaps the most visible sign of this effort was his revival
of the tradition, in disuse since Jefferson's day, of having the president
address Congress in person rather than send his messages to be read. He
was one of the first modern presidents to formulate a complete legislative program and guide it through Congress, and he attempted to use the
caucus system to bring all Democrats into line behind his proposals.[10]
In addition, when frustrated by the Congress he would "take his case
to the people" as does a British prime minister who, balked by Parliament,

dissolves it and calls for new elections. He believed that party government, as understood in the parliamentary concept, was the key to the solution of American ills, and to the extent that he could as president he attempted to bring it about. In the field of foreign policy, where the Constitution gives broad prerogatives to the president, he emphasized it to an even greater extent.

In short, Wilson chose to think of himself as a prime minister, cut from the English mold but stuck in the American system of government. He used his cabinet members as a liaison with the legislature in the pursuit of party government.[11] He insisted, as head of the party, that his lead should be followed by all members of the party in the Congress. Therefore, any deviation from the policy would be punished by patronage denial, by denunciation, or even by going to the American public to urge the dissident's defeat in the primaries.

Wilson laid down his thoughts in this matter very well in a letter to a senator who had clashed with him on a number of issues and who, perhaps not comprehending the president's perception of his office, wrote to him expressing the hope that there would be no hard feelings over it. The reply, which Arthur Link, perhaps the most thorough and thoughtful biographer of Wilson, characterizes as an "illuminating" revelation of his views on such matters as party responsibility and executive-legislative relations, reads in summary:

There are no reasons why there cannot be differences of opinion between the president and legislators. However, party government demands that the legislators put aside their own personal misgivings once the chief executive and the legislative leaders have made up their minds on a course of action. There cannot be effective government in the United States if a few men can join with the opposition to defeat a measure upon which the leadership of their party has already made up its mind, even if the individual legislator feels very strongly about the matter.[12]

It was illuminating indeed, and probably quite shocking and incomprehensible to the legislator in question (who apparently was not convinced, because he continued to be one of the more fractious members of the president's party). But it reveals Wilson's thoughts on the presidency and offers clues to his views of his own personal stewardship; and in particular it indicates why the twenty-eighth president of the United States could view his prerogatives in foreign policy the way he did, and would react to the obstruction of his proposals as he did.

Bryan

William Jennings Bryan was certainly not what Wilson had in mind for a cabinet member when he thought about party government.[13] In all probability, had he known that the world was going to be plunged into a major war and the United States drawn eventually into it, he would not have chosen him to be secretary of state, for in such a delicate position it would have been better for the president to have had someone closer to his own views and more subservient to him as well. But the circumstances of the Democratic National Convention of 1912 made it imperative that the chief executive recognize the three-time Democratic standard bearer in some way. And so Wilson chose him for the most prestigious cabinet portfolio, despite the unfamiliarity of the Commoner with international issues; his lack of knowledge there probably exceeded that of the president.

It was not uncommon throughout much of American history for men such as Bryan to be made secretary of state since compromise choices frequently became president and some of the more dominant losers had to settle for the lesser position. An interesting thesis could be developed around the question of whether or not these men constituted a more select group of individuals than did chief executives—at least prior to 1930. The situation was made particularly difficult for Wilson since Bryan represented a significant number of Democrats who looked to him for leadership more than they did the president. Wilson was a relative newcomer on the national scene, whereas his secretary of state had a loyal following, not only in the nation as a whole but in the Congress. The chief executive knew this and he was well aware that there was a sizable faction of southern and western Democrats, many of them associated with the agrarian reform, or populist movement, who held the same view of the war as Bryan.

As secretary of state, Bryan was both in his element and out of his depth. He found a natural outlet for his missionary zeal in the various arbitration treaties with Latin American states, but he lacked any enthusiasm for and expertise in the general affairs of state. State Department personnel looked down on him, and the more international-minded eastern members of Wilson's cabinet scoffed at many of his views. But more than anything else, Bryan was overmatched in his efforts to persuade Wilson that the response of the United States to the war in Europe should be absolute neutrality, not the type of neutrality that he believed he saw developing in the United States early in the war.

The extent of his disagreement with Wilson did not become evident to many people until after he left the cabinet—less than a year after the war began. However, during the short time that he served as secretary of state after the outbreak of hostilities, he represented the view that the Unites States should avoid even the slightest evidence of favoritism towards either side in the conflict. Both he and Wilson talked of "absolute neutrality"—and both meant it. But Bryan's definition was completely different.

For in support of his definition of absolute neutrality, he went so far as to argue that the United States should even be cautious about condemning alleged atrocities in the war, should prevent any banking loans to belligerents, should keep its citizens off the warships of warring states, and should refrain from pushing Germany too strongly on the matter of unrestricted submarine warfare. For he believed that once neutrality was compromised, there was a strong possibility of war.

Curiously, there was one area in the matter of neutrality where Bryan differed from most of the antiwar people: he did not oppose the shipment of munitions to the belligerents. He argued that an embargo on munitions would be an unneutral act, since the bulk of the weapons would be going to Britain. Therefore, this could only be considered as an act aimed against her, and thus unneutral. The logic of this argument escaped such antiwar legislators as Chairman Stone of the Senate Foreign Relations Committee, who held to the contrary.[14]

There was, however, one important field of agreement between Bryan and Wilson. Each could foresee the United States playing the role of the peacemaker. Each hoped that the nation would be able to play that part and they would be instrumental in the efforts. The difference lay in Bryan's opinion that the pro-Allied sentiments he saw becoming reflected in the administration's policies towards the war were destroying that possibility.

His departure was preordained. At such a crucial juncture Wilson could not have anyone around him who was not totally sympathetic to his views. He was aware of the political implications of the secretary's resignation. However. two strong men, with determined views of how policy should be conducted, could not remain part of the same decision-making apparatus—assuming that Bryan was ever really part of it. The *Lusitania* incident, which brought about his resignation, was simply the catalyst.[15] Bryan had been losing the fight for a foreign policy that incorporated his interpretation of neutrality almost from the moment that the first shot was fired.

Bryan was not, as many would assert, a pacifist. Very few men in public life would meet the strict definition of that word. He had endorsed the war with Spain in 1898 and had gone riding off as a colonel with the Nebraska militia in what hardly seemed to be a pacific act. Similarly, although he opposed a war resolution in 1917 up to the very end, he supported efforts to prosecute the conflict once America entered. Nor was he an isolationist in the strict sense of the word, for as noted, he was not unwilling to see the United States play the role of the peacemaker. And while not its most enthusiastic champion, he endorsed the concept of the League of Nations.

Bryan was a neutralist, one who believed that the United States had no legitimate role to play in the war. But he sought to extend this position beyond the point where it was fashionable in administration circles, and, indeed, in much of the country.

The Antiwar Senators

Members of the progressive Republican bloc made up the largest single segment of antiwar sentiment in the Senate during the period before the war. It is necessary, therefore to examine the most prominent of these. Robert M. LaFollette, senior senator from Wisconsin, a man whose fame transcends the Armed Ship filibuster and debate over the war, and who remains one of the more important political figures of the twentieth century, was the acknowledged leader.[16] Unlike Bryan, who supported the war once the United States became formally involved, the Wisconsinite continued to agitate against various forms of prosecuting the conflict and nearly lost his seat in the Senate because of his strong adherence to an antiwar position. He was not, as alleged at the time, pro-German, but a reading of his speeches and articles suggests that he seemed to feel that he had to singlehandedly ensure a balanced debate.

LaFollette's view was that the United States, in order to guarantee its neutrality, had to rule out any bias towards the war. Even more than Bryan, who was handicapped initially by his cabinet position, LaFollette stressed the many unneutral aspects of early United States diplomacy, which had the effect, he charged, of developing an American economic interest in the war. He maintained that the social progress he believed had been accomplished in America would be undone by involvement in the conflict; the "special interests," his favorite target, would use the excuse of war to undermine progressive legislation. He would point to the arguments of the shipping interests against his Seaman's bill as proof of this thesis.

LaFollette was not unwilling to see the United States play a mediator's

role. He was unqualified in his praise of Wilson when he sensed the
president's efforts to stay out of the war and become a force for peace.
He strongly endorsed the president's "peace without victory" speech.[17]
But this was one of the last favorable statements made by LaFollette
about Wilson—or for that matter about any other American president,
regardless of party. Even before 1914 he had little good to say about the
nation's political leaders and their policies. He had been a loner in
politics through most of his life, from the time he was elected as a
county attorney in Wisconsin, a position he sought without the approval
of the local Republican organization, through three terms in the House
of Representatives, a term as governor, and eighteen years in the United
States Senate until his last, quixotic fight, as an independent candidate
for president in 1924.

LaFollette's term as governor from 1901 to 1905 was considered to
be a model for progressive reformers. Unlike many other products of
the populist revolt of the late nineteenth century, he was not simply
another demagogic rabble-rouser with no practical program, no admin-
istrative ability, and no remote idea of what to do with power once
achieved. In addition to his successes as governor, he established one of
the most potent political machines of the early twentieth century, one
that assured his election to the Senate for as long as he wanted and
guaranteed office for his two sons, as senator and governor, long after
his death. Boies Penrose, the Republican "boss" of Pennsylvania, once
grumbled that LaFollette had a better grip on his own state than did
most of the "power brokers" he railed against.[18]

After his famous abortive candidacy in 1912 for the Republican
presidential nomination, which began with promise when progressive
Republicans rallied to him as an alternative to Taft but disintegrated
because of the disenchantment of eastern reformers, his own physical
collapse, and the return of Theodore Roosevelt to active politics, LaFollette, to all intents and purposes, left the Republican party. He remained
an independent for the rest of his life and never again backed a presidential candidate. His Progressive party in Wisconsin became his vehicle,
and the independence that he had manifested became formalized.

LaFollette left a significant legacy. He had only a few years left in
public life after 1917 and his battle to keep America out of the war. His
political career was largely behind him. Few of his fights were winning
ones; he lost far more than he won, and his letters reveal the bitterness
with which he accepted defeat. He was vain, frequently obstinate,
theatrical, vindictive, and rigid, and succeeded in alienating almost all
his colleagues in the Senate, regardless of political persuasion. But as a

symbol of the progressive era, as a spokesman for agrarian reform, and as a fighter for social justice, LaFollette probably put a greater stamp on American political life than did most of his more successful brethern.

Equally prominent as a reformer in domestic matters and as an opponent of American involvement in the European war was George W. Norris of Nebraska. There is a curious mystique surrounding Norris,[19] strongest among Democrats and independents, in spite of his almost life-long Republican affiliations. He was the recipient of an endorsement from one Democratic president, Franklin D. Roosevelt, who broke tradition and backed him as an independent in 1936. Still another Democratic chief executive, John F. Kennedy, featured him as one of his *Profiles in Courage*. A Democratic senator, Richard Neuberger of Oregon (now deceased), is perhaps his most sympathetic biographer. But among Republicans there is little adulation of Norris, for although he always classified himself (until 1936) as one of them, they got little support and much criticism from him during the last thirty years of his political life. He finally switched to an independent candidacy as a last act of political defiance, not only of party but also of the norms of political behavior. If there is a guidebook to the art of survival in politics, Norris probably never read it, because he managed to break most rules during the course of his career.

Like LaFollette, Norris came out of the agrarian reform movement. Initially he was a regular Republican, who rarely questioned the leadership of his party, and remained such through his first few terms in the House of Representatives. Then in 1910 he bolted and led the attack on the Speaker of the House, Joe Cannon, and the autocratic way in which the chamber was run, an attack which culminated in the reform of the rules of the House.[20] This made him a marked man in official Republican circles, and when he moved to the Senate in 1912 he found the regular party leaders cold and unresponsive. He spent most of his career in the upper chamber as an outsider.

Norris became identified with the progressive Republican caucus in the Senate and was soon acknowledged as a leader of that group. He supported most of the major reforms in the days before the war, and was also one of the few members of his party to support the nomination of Louis Brandeis for the Supreme Court. He was one of the first senators to take a somewhat jaundiced view of what some regarded as biased diplomacy on the part of the United States early in the European conflict, and he strongly criticized the Wilson administration for its policies during the period prior to American involvement.

The Nebraskan has become somewhat of a folk hero to many Americans, and perhaps his reputation in recent years has become even more favorable than LaFollette's. Some of this is probably attributable to his long political survival and his presence as a mentor to younger progressives in the twenties and thirties. He was possibly not all that the legend would have him be. Although he was somewhat of an internationalist late in life, his early career reveals a considerable xenophobia. One student of the early twentieth century, James Holt, points out in his study of congressional politics that by frequently bolting the Republican party to support Democrats and independents, Norris (with others) was driving the party into the hands of the conservatives.[21] In balance, however, and considering these "faults," he must still be measured as one of the more important figures of his time.

LaFollette and Norris are perhaps the only two Republican dissenters whose names are familiar to most serious students of American history. However, five other progressive Republicans joined with them in most of their battles against belligerent diplomacy and preparedness and stood with them against the Armed Ship Bill. The other five Republican "willful men" were Albert Cummins and William Kenyon of Iowa, Moses Clapp of Minnesota, Asle J. Gronna of North Dakota, and John Works of California.

Cummins did achieve some degree of fame, for during much of his Senate career he aspired to the presidency. On two occasions he formally announced for the office, although his candidacy never attracted much support.[22] This obsession is frequently cited as the reason that the Iowan, who came to the Senate in 1908 with a reputation as a radical with strong opinions about the railroad trusts and other corporate monopolies would become increasingly conservative in his old age and eventually (after the Armed Ship filibuster) move into the inner circles of senatorial power and privilege.

In short, Cummins had traveled the full circle from being one of those progressive leaders who had led the opposition to the Payne-Aldrich tariff to being a respectable and conservative stand-patter. Whether he had changed or whether the times had changed, is immaterial. What seems clear is the existence of a fundamentally conservative streak in one of the most radical of the early agrarian fire-eaters. And there is little to indicate that he ever recanted his early associations or that he saw any contradiction between his behavior in the first two decades of the twentieth century and that of the last years of his life.

His diverse talents were recognized by most of his colleagues. As governor of Iowa, he had become famous for the proposal which advocated eliminating duties on all articles manufactured by the trusts. He was considered to be one of the best-informed members of the Senate on the railroad question. He was known as a man with a quick and incisive mind and as a superb parliamentarian. But he lacked the ability to rouse an audience at a time when oratory was important in politics, which perhaps explains why his candidacy never attracted much attention, even among his fellows. The speaking ability of a LaFollette might have given him a chance. Without it he had none.[23]

He made his first bid for the office in 1912, after having first agreed to support LaFollette. When the Wisconsonite announced his own candidacy, Cummins remained in the trenches, something which LaFollette later said did not surprise him because he was always doubtful of the Iowan's profession of support.[24] Later, when Cummins became a candidate for the presidency in his own right, he said that it was only to hold Iowa for LaFollette. He garnered only half of the votes of his native state's delegation. During the general election of that year, he kept a low profile, endorsing Roosevelt quietly, but finding time during the height of the campaign to take an extended trip to Europe.

In 1916 his advocacy of a middle ground between the two wings of his party was attributed to his renewed quest for the office. After indicating to Borah of Idaho that he, Borah, would make a better candidate,[25] the Iowan entered the race himself, hoping to mollify the conservative elements of his party by voting for "some" preparedness and by voting against the nomination of Brandeis. He won a few easy primaries, but then was soundly defeated by Charles Evans Hughes in Oregon and could count only eighty delegates pledged to him when the convention met.

When he joined with LaFollette and Norris and the others in the Armed Ship filibuster, it was the last act of political apostasy in his career. Never after 1917, as he drew steadily into the more respectable and conservative circles of the Republican party would he be associated with an unpopular cause.

But if Cummins's presidential star was setting in 1917, that of his junior colleague William Kenyon was rising.[26] At forty-eight the youngest of the dissenting senators, Kenyon was regarded as a distinct possibility for a future place on his party's national ticket. Although an opponent of the Armed Ship Bill, he subsequently supported the war effort and thus gained one of Wilson's two endorsements of Republican senators in 1918.[27]

He was the product of a small-town environment, as were the other Republican dissenters. He was licensed to practice law at twenty-one, was a city attorney at twenty-three, a judge at thirty-one, and finally a successful attorney in private practice when he had to leave public service to earn more than was available through such service. Later he returned to public service as an antitrust lawyer, winning two of the major decisions in that area during the Taft administration. In 1912, after the death of Jonathan Dolliver, he was appointed to the Senate. where he immediately aligned himself with the progressive caucus.

Although noted as a reformer in domestic affairs, and as a neutralist in foreign policy, he acquired perhaps even more fame initially for his interest in the prohibition movement. Many reformers were "dry," but few were as deeply committed to the cause. A religious man, with deeply rooted scruples about personal conduct, both public and private, ingrained in his personality, he believed strongly that the enforcement of Prohibition was one way to improve American society.

These personality traits, as well as an apparently growing revulsion against certain aspects of political life, caused Kenyon to become extremely restive in the Senate. Vice President Marshall noted that the Iowan was frustrated by life there and was constantly at odds with the veterans and the "inner corps" of the upper chamber. He observed that when Kenyon finally decided to leave for the federal judiciary, it probably served his peace of mind.[28]

Two of the remaining Republican opponents of the Armed Ship Bill, Asle J. Gronna of North Dakota and Moses Clapp of Minnesota, emerge from records of this period as quiet, plodding men, living in the shadows of the more exciting and brilliant figures. They had somewhat parallel careers. Both began as conservative, machine-oriented politicians like Norris, and both began to back off from their conservatism early in their careers so that, by the time they retired, they were looked upon as radicals and the more stand-pat elements cheered their departure.[29]

Gronna, one of the two Armed Ship Bill dissenters who were not lawyers, started out with the McKenzie machine which dominated North Dakota politics for many years. A businessman, farmer and banker before entering political life, he went to the House of Representatives early in the twentieth century and there began his evolution into a progressive. An ally of Norris in the fight against Cannon, by the time he went to the Senate in 1911, his awareness of the growing discontent in the Midwest had caused him to break not only with the machine but with conservatism as well. He supported most of the major domestic goals of the progressive period.

When the war in Europe began to eclipse domestic issues, Gronna was one of the first to call for absolute neutrality and continued, with LaFollette and Norris, to oppose many of Wilson's proposals for prosecuting the war after the declaration. In doing so, he believed, and perhaps quite accurately, that he was reflecting the views of the small farmers of North Dakota. He continually stressed the point that if given the chance in a national referendum, the American people would reject involvement in a war.[30]

It is because of his associations with the leaders of the progressive movement that Gronna is frequently considered as little more than a follower of the more dominant figures of that period. There is some truth to the allegation, for Gronna was not a good speaker and not a brilliant innovator, but it fails to take into account that on at least one matter, he followed a decidedly different course from that of most reformers of the period. The records of most as loyal party men were spotty, but the North Dakotan, despite frequent efforts to overthrow the leadership of his party, always returned to the fold for the general elections. In 1912 he was one of the first to enlist for LaFollette and one of the last to desert him and then, when most of his colleagues either bolted to Roosevelt or Wilson or maintained an obviously public neutrality, Gronna supported Taft on the principle of party loyalty. This was to be the policy for his entire political career.[31]

Moses Clapp of Minnesota had been in the Senate the longest of any of the Republican dissenters to the Armed Ship Bill, and the debate over this bill would be the last of his career. He had been defeated in the Republican primary in 1916 by Frank Kellogg, later to become secretary of state under Coolidge.

Clapp began his career as a Republican regular, conforming to the leadership of his party and accepting its tenets. But he began to shift his position after reaching the Senate so that by the end of the first decade of the twentieth century he was completely identified with the reform faction. He supported judicial reform, the direct primary, the recall of judges, the income tax, tariff reduction, and railroad controls. Despite his long service in the Senate and his support for progressive causes, he never achieved the sort of leadership role in the movement that others who came after him did. He was a studious, observant man, with a deep sensitivity to the problems of the farmers, but not a man with leadership attributes.

This was perhaps just as well, for progressive Republicans did not need another leader but a unifier and a compromiser. Claude Bowers, in his biography of Beveridge, suggests that this talent of Clapp's was especially noteworthy during the reformer's fight against the Payne-Aldrich Tariff.[32]

In 1912 Clapp was in the forefront of the movement within the party to unseat Taft, and when this effort failed he supported Roosevelt in the general election. He never formally affiliated with the Progressive party, however, and kept his relationship with it nominal. He returned to the Republican fold in 1914 and remained until the end of his career.

By 1915 he had become known as one of the leading critics of belligerency in diplomacy. However, this contributed only partially to his defeat for renomination in 1916. His career in the Senate ended because he was spending less and less time in Minnesota and was out of touch with his constituents, in spite of his self-professed and well-advertised role as champion of the small farmer.[33] The presence of another antiwar progressive, Congressman Charles Lindbergh, in the primary field also hurt his chances. When the "Black Eagle of Fergus Falls" was defeated, the *New York Times* celebrated it as a major victory, stating that the Senate would be richer for his departure, as his talents were mainly oratorical. Clapp was no intellectual, or even a leader among reformers, but this still was an unkind description of a decent and honorable man who had fought diligently and honestly for what he believed.[34]

The last Republican dissenter, John Works of California, was also ending his Senate career with the Armed Ship debate.[35] Works was 70, and his departure was voluntary. The California progressives, whose support had been crucial to his selection in 1910, had become disenchanted with him for a variety of reasons, and had he not elected to step down, he probably could not have been reelected.

Works was a midwesterner who had moved to the west coast as a young man, after having achieved a considerable reputation in his native state of Indiana. He served during the Civil War, fighting in a number of major battles, although he was but a lad of fifteen. He returned from the war to study for the bar. After being admitted to practice, he wrote a number of **law** books for the state and served a term in the state legislature before deciding to move on. In California he was as highly regarded as he had been in Indiana, being elected to the superior court of the state and later to the state supreme court.

He also began to dabble in California Republican politics, identifying with the progressive elements of that party, although he never was one of its leaders. In fact, George Mowry's excellent monograph on progressivism in California makes scant mention of him. Although his role was minor, his reputation was such that when he indicated that he wanted the Senate seat in 1910, the reformers were obliged to go along or risk losing the spot to a conservative.[36]

In one term in the Senate, he distinguished himself only by his interest in Christian Science, his concern over Japanese threats to California, and his fears about the war in Europe and "presidential despotism." Historian John Milton Cooper has observed that his antiwar stance was largely a product of his religious beliefs. He notes that, as with Bryan, religious allegories kept cropping up in his analysis of international affairs. After leaving the Senate in 1917 (he was succeeded by Hiram Johnson), he continued his fight against the war. He joined the American Council for Democracy and Terms of Peace and wrote articles whose main thesis was that the United States had gone to war to profit munitions makers and not for the preservation of democracy as it had advertised.[37]

Several other Republicans expressed reservations about involvement in the European war and opposed some of the actions that might tend to suggest a greater American commitment to one of the two sides. They either changed their views prior to the Armed Ship debate or at least chose not to challenge that measure. One senator, Wesley Jones of Washington, would be accused in some circles as having been part of the filibuster, yet his inclusion was largely because of his defense of the right of extended debate.[38] He was a middle-of-the-road Republican, who like Works, had been raised in the Midwest. Another, Porter McCumber of North Dakota, like Gronna, was sensitive to the antiwar feeling in his state, but unlike Gronna tended to vote conservatively on most economic issues.

The list might also include Charles Townsend and William Alden Smith of Michigan, the latter a member of the Foreign Relations Committee of the Senate, Charles Curtis of Kansas, who was particularly critical of preparedness, and Lawrence Sherman of Illinois, described as a maverick Republican who could not be easily classified as either a progressive or a conservative.

The Democratic antiwar group is a little more difficult to classify. First, almost all Democrats were subject in some degree to pressure from Wilson, and thus their voting patterns did not always reflect their feelings. Second, there were at least two major bases for antiwar sentiment within the party: the resentment over British maritime practices and their impact on southern industry, and the economic interpretation of the war, prevalent among a number of midwestern legislators, including those close to Bryan, some of them products of the populist movement. A few legislators objected to belligerent diplomacy on both counts.

Two opponents of the Armed Ship Bill might belong to this last category, Vardaman and Kirby. James K. Vardaman of Mississippi was a highly skilled practitioner of racial politics, and any discussion of him must begin with the caveat that he was a real person, not some figure created by a playwright's caricature of a southern senator.[39] He usually dressed all in white, wore his hair long, and was fond of posing for portraits with his hand tucked inside his coat. While campaigning, he would frequently make his entry into the small towns in the backwoods of Mississippi, his natural constituency, on a wagon drawn by eight white oxen, where he would regale his followers with biblical and literary quotations by which he would justify his opposition to any sort of racial equality and to big business.[40]

The opposition to business was a secondary issue, for Vardaman knew that his chief weapon was his ability to rally his rednecked constituents on the race question. He would vow to go to Washington to fight for repeal of the Reconstruction amendments, which he said were at the root of the problems of the small farmers of Mississippi. He would argue against education for Negroes except in the manual skills, against giving them the right to vote, against drafting them into the army, against anything that might even come close to putting them on an equal footing with whites. Widely read in racist literature, he opposed enfranchising Orientals for similar reasons. He believed that race played a major role in determining the character of a nation, and believing all but the white race to be inferior, he argued that restriction was necessary for the survival of the United States. Interestingly, however, he had a rather noteworthy record of supporting Indian rights and he also opposed the anti-Semitism which characterized many southern politicians of that time, in fact using his newspaper to rebut much of it.[41]

Vardaman began his career in the Mississippi state legislature. After a brief interruption for service in the Spanish-American War, he returned to politics and eventually became a rather undistinguished governor of his state. In 1910, he was an unsuccessful candidate for the United States Senate in a contest enlivened by the announcement of Theodore Bilbo, one of his allies, that he (Bilbo) had accepted a bribe to vote (in the state legislature) for another.[42] Vardaman eventually won his Senate seat in 1912. His record of support of the President's domestic program was consistent, but he never achieved much popularity with Wilson. Vardaman's support of Oscar Underwood for the presidency was responsible for the coolness, while his long-time rival in state politics, John Sharp Williams, backed the eventual winner and had the key to White House patronage.[43]

It was not, however, his relations with Wilson, but more his populist heritage and concern over the cotton crisis of 1915–16 that caused him to take antiwar positions. There is ample evidence that, these matters aside, Vardaman was genuinely against war in principle. It is perhaps hard to believe that a man who would seem to have so few political virtues by contemporary standards would put his career on the line by standing against the president and most of the country over a matter of principle, but this appears to be the case. His defeat in the primaries of 1918 was another one celebrated by the *Times*.[44]

Little is known of William Fosgate Kirby of Arkansas, who was only in the first months of a term to which he had been appointed. He had been an ally of the populist Governor Jeff Davis and had served as his attorney general. But while he was an unknown, his course of behavior clearly stamps him as a populist. His speeches, opposing the severing of diplomatic relations with Germany, the Armed Ship Bill, and other measures relating to the war, are replete with populist rhetoric.[45]

There are several other antiwar Democrats from the Deep South, Southwest and Middle West, who, like some of the Republicans noted earlier, did not oppose the Armed Ship Bill. Some of these men were perhaps also more concerned about the cotton problem than they were with the economic interpretation of the war, particularly the two senators from Georgia, Hoke Smith and Thomas Hardwick. Smith was noted for his antagonism to Britain as a result of the cotton crisis; he and Vardaman stood virtually alone in urging an arms embargo until Britain rescinded her stand on the declaration of cotton as a contraband.[46] As the matter eased somewhat, Smith began to take a more moderate position, although some of the bitterness remained. Hardwick, Smith's junior in government service (Smith had been secretary of the interior in Cleveland's second administration), had not yet come around to a more moderate position (he was the legislator to whom Wilson had written the letter referred to earlier outlining the president's perception of party government) and he was still regarded as one of the more vocal antiwar voices in 1917. He has a rather dubious place in history; he is perhaps best remembered for an incident during the "red scare." A bomb was received in the mail which on exploding blew the hands off one of his servants.[47]

There are some other senators from the majority party who might also be listed in the antiwar category: Robert Owen of Oklahoma, one of the first senators from that state, part Indian, and considered to be an expert in the field of money and banking problems, former governor Charles Thomas of Colorado, and Henry Ashurst of Arizona. The last, who would be the final survivor of the Sixty-fourth Senate, was also one of the first senators from his state and is the author of *A Many-Colored Toga,* a journal he kept which is valuable for the insights it gives into the characters and events of this era. A progressive, the Arizonan was one of the best orators in the Senate and considered to be one of its more literate members.[48]

One of the better-known populists could not be classified as an antiwar voice, however. "Pitchfork" Ben Tillman of South Carolina, the first of the rednecks, was no longer breathing the fire that had marked his earlier career in Congress. As chairman of the powerful Naval Affairs Committee of the Senate, the one-eyed Civil War veteran was more interested in picking off projects for his home state and unlikely to do anything that might offend the president.[49]

The list of antiwar figures would have to include Thomas Gore of Oklahoma,[50] although at the time of the Armed Ship debate and of the war resolution, he was ill and away from the Senate. Therefore, the Oklahoma populist, who had been blind since boyhood, could not be officially recorded on either issue. He never sent word that he would have been opposed to the war resolution. As for the Armed Ship Bill, one can only speculate; his biographer notes that he was apparently not only away from the Senate but so ill as to be out of touch with events and thus probably not even aware that the issue had been raised.[51]

Since Gore had been a severe critic of the march towards war, it would not be unreasonable to suggest that he would have joined in the dissent on the Armed Ship Bill. Had he chosen to assist the filibuster, he would have been of no minor value, because he was experienced at this kind of activity.[52]

There is one other antiwar Bryanite who must be mentioned, although New Jersey could hardly be said to lie in the middle of Bryan country. James Martine of that state was thought of as being closer to the Nebraskan than to the president, notwithstanding Wilson's intervention on his behalf in 1910 against the bosses, a stand that sent him to the Senate and the former Princeton president into the national spotlight. The New Jerseyan had not always pleased the chief executive with his Senate service, and Wilson backed a rival in the Democratic primaries of 1916. Martine won, but lost the general election.[53]

Four other antiwar Democrats had little connection with Bryan, cotton, or populism. Three of them were among the dissenters to the Armed Ship Bill, James O'Gorman of New York, Harry Lane of Oregon, and William Joel Stone of Missouri. The fourth, although thought of as one of the most vocal champions of neutrality, would emerge as the principal advocate of the Armed Ship Bill, Gilbert Hitchcock of Nebraska. At one time Hitchcock had been an ally of the ex-secretary of state, but now the two were the heads of rival factions in the Democratic party of Nebraska. This intraparty friction would have national implications. A newspaper publisher, Hitchcock was the second ranking member of the Senate Foreign Relations Committee.[54]

Of these three "willful men," O'Gorman stands out in the sense that there appears to be nothing that connects him to any of the other dissenters.[55] He was a one-term senator, and his antiwar stance at this time is usually explained by his ancestry, his close ties to the Irish-American community, and his sensitivity to the Irish question. He represented the view of many Irish-Americans at this time that anything that would help Britain would damage the cause of independence for Ireland.

O'Gorman's brief service in the Senate was undistinguished (he too was ending his career with the Armed Ship debate), and his fame is largely based on the manner in which he reached the upper chamber. He was the compromise choice of the New York state legislature in 1910 after the young turks, including Franklin Roosevelt, balked at the original Tammany choice.[56] Once in the Senate, O'Gorman tended to be as responsive to Tammany as the first choice probably would have been, an expected position since he had been a machine stalwart most of his political life. Roosevelt would later express dissatisfaction with O'Gorman and would say that he regretted going along in 1910 with the compromise.[57] The man he had helped send to the Senate fought Wilson on a number of matters, apart from foreign policy, including the Federal Reserve plan. Some attribute his subsequent backing of the measure to the appointment of his son-in-law Dudley Field Malone as Collector of the Port of New York.[58]

His record, on balance, was far more responsible and moderate than his critics would have one believe. He avoided some of the more disreputable elements among Irish-American activists, and as for his absorption with the Irish question, one need only look at debates over that issue to note how many other legislators, with only minimal Irish constituencies, tried to win friends by embracing the cause of Irish independence.

But if O'Gorman is difficult to classify, Harry Lane may well be impossible. The few pictures we get of him, mostly from secondary sources like books on Norris and LaFollette, show the picture of a witty and gentle humanist, deeply committed to the cause of peace and concerned over the course of action America was taking.[59] The stories about him, only a few of which can be noted here, are in many instances probably more reflections of the feelings of his colleagues about him than anything else. For example, Norris, who was probably closer to him than anyone else in the Senate, recounted in his eulogy that Lane, a doctor by profession, had destroyed all his bills before his death, lest someone try to collect them.[60] Then there are the anecdotes; Lane circulating a petition to let some Gila monsters loose on the Senate floor because a bite of one of these creatures paralyzed the vocal chords; commenting that his tenure as director of an Oregon mental institution prepared him for service in the Senate; and predicting that a recently deceased millionaire would be met at the gates of Heaven by St. Peter brandishing a baseball bat.[61]

Probably the best-known story concerns his actions during the last hours of the Armed Ship debate. Hearing that some senators were armed and planning to rough up LaFollette, information that is generally accepted as being accurate, Lane reportedly procured a rat-tail file to defend the Wisconsinite in the event of an attack.[62]

Lane differs from his associates in the Armed Ship filibuster in one other interesting respect, apart from his profession. He was the only one born into wealth and position and into a political family. His grandfather Joseph Lane had been a senator from Oregon. He had the advantages of good schooling and a more ready entrance into politics than perhaps any of the others. In 1904 he won his first elective office, mayor of Portland, where in two terms he established a reputation for civic honesty and eliminated much of the corruption in that city. He went to the Senate in 1913, but served only part of the term to which he was elected. His record there was not particularly distinguished, although the brevity of his service no doubt accounts for this.

His support of Wilson in most of his New Freedom measures and in the early days of the European war, when he believed that the chief executive was set on keeping the country out of the conflict, marks him as a progressive. However, by 1916, Lane, an iconoclast, was becoming concerned, not only over the possibility of war but over Wilson's gradual accretion of power and obvious desire to take all decision making unto himself. Thus it was that he broke with the president in the early months of 1917.

Regardless of how much of the legend of Harry Lane one wishes to believe, there is more than enough to substantiate the view that he was one of the most unusual individuals ever to sit in the United States Senate.

He was formally unchurched—a heresy in and of itself in American politics—and he derided and mocked much of the pomp and ritual attendant upon government. It is not hard to understand the affection that such men as LaFollette and Norris held for him—they were political nonconformists—but Lane's nonconformity was something that went beyond politics and to the roots of his personality. That such a man would sit in the United States Senate at this period is surprising and in defiance of most of the rules by which legislators are chosen.

Finally, there is William Joel Stone, who, as chairman of the Foreign Relations Committee, must be considered separately. What marks Stone as different from the rest is that he was the only one of the antiwar bloc in the Senate who spoke from a position of power.[63] The others who tended towards neutralism, on both sides of the aisle, were outsiders in the upper chamber as far as power and access to power were concerned, but Stone, at one point, could be described by Josephus Daniels as the senator closest to Wilson.[64]

Stone was certainly not a pacifist; in fact, during earlier crises he outdid even some of the most ardent war hawks in his demands for action. At one point during the controversies with Mexico, he would demand retaliation for Mexican actions, lamenting the fact that some Americans seemed unwilling to risk war when it was necessary to protect life and property.[65]

However, he was not quite so ready to risk America going to war in the case of the conflict in Europe. He did not believe that American citizens should ride on the vessels of belligerents, since their deaths might serve as a provocation to war. He opposed loans and the shipment of arms to belligerents. He believed that the United States should stay out of the European war, regardless of how its citizens viewed the nature of the issues that they felt were at stake.

But Stone was a loyal party man. As his biographer emphasizes frequently throughout the story of his life, he regarded himself as a Democrat, first, last, and always;[66] therefore he did not always criticize the administration openly on these matters. In fact, some of those who would join him in opposition to the Armed Ship Bill would be unaware right up to the moment he spoke against the bill that he was going to oppose it. They knew that many times in the past he had put aside his personal reservations to back the president.

For Stone took the view that as the chairman of the Foreign Relations Committee, he was "the president's man." Had there been any sort of revolt against Wilson's policies in the Senate, or against his perception of his role in foreign affairs, it would have to start with the Missourian. But in all instances up to the Armed Ship debate, Stone took the position that he wanted to give the president a free hand, and he used all his political power to quash budding rebellions against presidential leadership. For while he might disagree with the president about certain matters concerning the war in Europe, he initially agreed with the chief executive on the need to keep the formulation of policy in the White House.

Stone would extract a price from Wilson early in 1916—that the Senate would be consulted before any steps which might lead to war would be taken. It was not until he found himself completely out of agreement with the president that he challenged executive domination in foreign policy making. Had he chosen to make his stand earlier, the situation would surely have been altered.[67]

Because of Stone's status in the Senate, and his previous record of support for the president, there was considerable speculation on the reasons for his actions in March 1917. Some have chosen to attribute his behavior to his relationships with German-American groups back in Missouri. This opinion is discounted by his biographer.[68] Further, even without this interpretation of his actions one would find it hard to believe that as seasoned a politician would risk what he did for a distinct minority of his constituents. While he did have good ties with German-American groups, having gone to see them on Wilson's behalf in 1916, he was by no means their captive. A more reasonable explanation would seem to be that Stone believed in the idea of absolute neutrality, and could support Wilson when he felt that the president's action did not veer too far from that position. However, once Wilson took the action of asking for the authority to arm merchant ships and to pursue other means of fighting the submarine menace, Stone could no longer view these acts within any context of neutrality.[69]

Whatever his motives, Stone is still a rather unlikely candidate for the martyrdom that has come to the antiwar senators. His career was far removed from that of LaFollette or Norris. At one time thought of as a progressive Democrat, he had become increasingly conservative as his career continued. His tenure as governor of Missouri had been racked with scandal, a point that newspapers delighted in reminding the public about after the filibuster, when he was one of the most hated men in the nation. He was never personally charged with anything, but the nickname Gumshoe Bill, which stuck with him through the rest of his life, was given him because of the ease with which he avoided implication.

The stories about Stone, which can only be capsuled here, include the suggestion that he once advised people to make contributions under false names to avoid inquiry as to their source, that he used his influence to gain favors for friends, and finally, in an incident which has almost comic-opera overtones, that he appeared (while in private law practice) before a state body as a lobbyist, representing something called the Missouri Health Society. The society was a small, exclusive organization—only three members and all of them by an odd coincidence employees in Stone's office.[70]

Whatever his problems in Missouri, he was sent on to the Senate in 1903 after several terms in the House. In 1912 he became chairman of the Foreign Relations Committee and one of the most influential men in the chamber. He also acquired the reputation of being one of the shrewdest men in the Senate; when loyal Wilsonians contemplated ousting him as chairman of the Foreign Relations Committee after the filibuster, they wisely decided against it, once the first flush of excitement had passed. Even a discredited William Joel Stone was a difficult man to deal with.[71]

In a previous chapter there was an attempt to identify the general character of antiwar sentiment in the Congress prior to the three major foreign wars of the nineteenth century. It is now appropriate to examine the men who constituted the antiwar bloc in the Senate to try to ascertain what conclusions might be made about the character of senatorial opposition in 1917.

In general, the nature of antiwar sentiment in the Senate tended to follow the national trend. There are some studies which point up that the more vocal noninvolvement voices came from the Middle West, from Germanic areas, as well as from areas dominated by ethnic groups whose ties to the nation of their ancestry were strong. There were, of course, also the Socialists, certain women's groups, some left-wing labor unions, and pacifists.

Opposition to the war in the Senate was most noticeable among the reformers from the Middle West, the Southwest, and the plains area. Most of them were products of the rural small towns of the Middle West in the latter part of the nineteenth century, where they had grown up, received what little education they had been able to obtain, had (in most instances) begun the practice of law, and indeed where they spent practically all their lives prior to being elected to Congress. They had little knowledge of the world much beyond their country or state. They tended to view international affairs with a marked insularity.

Many of them represented constituencies in which there were considerable blocs of those ethnic groups adhering more to the neutralist position. This point has been most effectively demonstrated by John Milton Cooper, whose excellent study of American isolationism of this period suggests that ethnicity had a strong relationship to antiwar stances by legislators. His focus is the House of Representatives, since the smaller districts (than the Senate's) are more easily analyzed. [72]

The composite portrait is that of a rural progressive, probably born into rather humble circumstances, from the Middle West or at least having his roots there, and representing a state with a considerable Germanic or Scandinavian population. Of course, there are some exceptions. Stone began his career as a progressive, but by 1917 he was considered a conservative; Porter McCumber could never have been thought of as a reformer. O'Gorman was from the sidewalks of New York and responsive, as noted previously, to the Irish, not to the German, elements of his constituency. Both Lane and Hitchcock came from fairly well-to-do families. And one cannot ignore the economic impact of the British blockade on shaping antiwar sentiments in southerners such as Hoke Smith.

One senator fitting the description above quite well can not be included in any list of antiwar senators. William Borah, senior Republican senator from Idaho, would emerge in the 1930s as a major spokesman for isolation and neutrality towards the developing war in Europe. However, Borah, while siding with the antiwar bloc on one or two issues, was in general not an advocate of neutrality during this earlier period, and his views on most issues did not coincide with those of other Republican progressives. [73]

The Pro-Ally Faction

It is more difficult to generalize about all those senators who either unequivocally favored the British or Allied position or who inclined towards it and thus would be called interventionists, or perhaps in some instances, unfairly prowar. Most of the Democrats in the Senate tended to subordinate their judgment to that of Wilson. Therefore, in this section it would perhaps be best to concentrate on just two men, one from each party.

Henry Cabot Lodge was the senior Republican senator from Massachusetts, ranking member of the party on the Foreign Relations Committee, and a close friend of Theodore Roosevelt. [74] Running through the descriptive accounts of men who dealt with Lodge are words like "shrewd," "aristocratic," "partisan," "ruthless," and "brilliant." He

37

was possibly one of the most important men ever to sit in the Senate, where he served for 31 years until his death in 1924. Unfortunately, his reputation is that of the "wrecker of the dream"—the League of Nations—an image handed down through history books and even a motion picture, *Wilson*, in which the senator from Massachusetts is portrayed as a classic cinema villain.

However, in his time Lodge was very highly regarded. Of all the men in the Senate, he was acknowledged to be the best informed on foreign policy matters and on European history and politics.[75] He held a doctorate (one of the few things he had in common with Woodrow Wilson), had studied abroad in his youth, so it was not surprising that many Republicans turned to him for advice on matters relating to the European war. He was also the natural leader of his party—the nominal Republican floor leader—Jacob Gallinger of New Hampshire could not rival him for influence—and only men like LaFollette and Norris, progressives, held him in no awe.

The Republican regulars during this period were largely men from the Atlantic seaboard states, where pro-Allied feeling was strong, and many of them were also, like Lodge, ardent nationalists. Included in this category would be Frank Brandegee from Connecticut, one of the best orators in the upper chamber, John Weeks of Massachusetts, a Naval Academy graduate turned businessman, James Wadsworth of New York, son-in-law of John Hay (scion of a noted New York political family, who had succeeded Elihu Root in the Senate), and Boies Penrose, previously identified. Outside the East there were other champions of the pro-Allied position such as Reed Smoot of Utah, a conservative and an elder of the Mormon Church, and Albert Fall of New Mexico, whose interests were in oil and the Mexican situation.[76]

Lodge did not favor intervention from the beginning. In fact, he echoed the sentiments of most prominent Americans in advocating a strict type of neutrality during the first days of the war. However, he did develop a partisan interest in the war very early, and he accepted willingly the British explanation for the conflict and their rationalization for fighting it as they did.[77] But this was not his only concern. He represented the point of view, as a nationalist, that no nation could hold up its head in the family of nations without asserting its right in a vigorous fashion; hence, he was critical of what he called "cowardly diplomacy." He also believed that a nation should be strong militarily; he had always advocated a powerful navy. He could countenance nothing less than a strong build-up of the United States armed forces. Lodge advocated belligerent diplomacy and preparedness because they represented his views about what made a nation strong and respected.

It is true that Lodge hated Wilson—a feeling generously reciprocated—and therefore he lost no chance to excoriate him for failing to live up to his definition of the proper defense of American rights. And he knew that his attacks on the president could not hurt the Republican party's prospects in 1916. However, the excuse of partisanship is only a partial explanation for his conduct, for the Massachusetts senator's ultimate national goals were just as important to him as embarrassing or even defeating Wilson.

Ironically, Lodge would frequently be a strong supporter of the president when the latter's policies were in accord with his. Through most of the key debates between 1914 and 1917, while antiwar senators were challenging the chief executive over diplomatic policies, Lodge stood behind Wilson. In particular, his support of the president in the debate over the Gore-McLemore resolutions was crucial.

Lodge was concerned, as were many of the antiwar senators, about Wilson's apparent attempts to exclude Congress from any meaningful discussions over foreign policy. It is probable that he understood the complexities of executive-legislative relationships better than most of them. But he could put aside partisanship if the issue was one in which he believed. For Lodge, one of the more astute practitioners of politics of that period, knew that a direct challenge to the president would have to wait until the time and the issue were right. They would come in 1919 when he was chairman of the Foreign Relations Committee and more than one-third of the Senate was ready to reject Mr. Wilson's Treaty of Versailles.

On the Democratic side, the most ardent spokesman for the British position was the colorful John Sharp Williams of Mississippi, a product of the elite faction of that state's politics in contrast to Vardaman, who represented the rural element. Williams was a cultured and sophisticated politician, who wrote poetry, and had studied abroad. He was considered by many of his colleagues as virtually the equal of Lodge in the area of European history and politics.[78] It was unusual for any southern senator to be pro-British at this time, given the hostility towards that nation over the cotton question, for as the Mississippian once commented, every politician from that area was expected to be anti-British.[79]

As with other pro-British or pro-Allied spokesmen, Williams's early statements seem to reflect a desire to see the United States stay out of the war. He wrote to a constituent after the outbreak of hostilities that Americans should ensure that the nation remain neutral and that they should remember that they were not German-Americans nor British-Americans, but Americans. Throughout the war he would be critical of the "hyphenated" influence of certain Americans with ancestral ties to one of the European belligerents, and their efforts to coerce governmental policy. However, he tended to concentrate in his criticism on German-Americans, Irish-Americans, and Scandinavian-Americans, not groups tending to favor the Allied side.

By late 1914 Williams's neutrality was weakening, his earlier admonitions forgotten. He made a number of comments that showed that he saw the war as a conflict between the forces of light and the forces of darkness. By 1915 he had become a fervent apologist for the Allied position and was impatient and hostile towards those who still spoke of absolute neutrality.

In most respects Williams remained loyal to Wilson, perhaps more so than did almost any other member of the upper chamber, and rarely criticized his actions publicly. In fact, he usually defended him vigorously. In the fall of 1916, when the Democrats were running on a peace platform, he would say of the president's reelection bid that the chief executive had kept peace withohonor and should be continued in office in order to further that policy.[80]

Most of the time Williams did not have any difficulty squaring his feelings about the war and American policy with his loyalty to the president, although he was one of those senators who did advocate breaking off relations with Germany over the *Lusitania* incident.[81] Mainly, the two were in harmony.

The remainder of the Democrats in the Senate, excepting the neutralists, followed the president without hesitation. The more important of them will be noted in the account of the Armed Ship filibuster and the events leading up to it.

3

THE CONTROVERSY PRIOR TO 1917

1914-16

Several important events in the period between the outbreak of war in
1914 and the severing of diplomatic relations between the United States
and Germany in February of 1917 brought into focus the conflict between the antiwar or neutralist forces in the United States Congress and
the president. The wisdom of the course of action followed by the administration and the legislator's perception of the role of the legislature
in the conduct of foreign policy were questioned. In the first months
of the war, there was little argument. The concept of absolute neutrality
was the policy of the administration, and it was only when there appeared to be a shift in attitudes and policies that some senators began to
challenge the White House.

One of the first issues facing Wilson was the matter of private banking
loans to belligerent nations. Initially, the president took the position
that loans of any nature were out of the question as inconsistent with
the country's policy of neutrality. This stand pleased not only the
neutralist senators but also Bryan, who, as a true populist, regarded
money as the most insidious type of contraband; but by October of
1914 the policy was under fire from banking interests as well as elements
sympathetic to the Allied side.[1] Eventually even Bryan began to rethink
his position on the matter, and shortly afterwards enforcement of this
policy was eased.

First, the position was modified when the president indicated that he
would not oppose the extending of commercial credits; by March of

1915 the policy had been completely reversed. It was then announced that the government would not oppose a $50 million commercial credit loan by the house of Morgan to the French government.[2] LaFollette expressed the concern of many antiwar senators when he complained that the United States could not maintain any semblance of neutrality once the bankers started to supply one side with the material of war. He charged that the nation had begun to underwrite the success of the Allies and was in effect no longer neutral.[3]

The antiwar legislators were also concerned over the refusal of the government to declare an embargo on munitions. Embargo resolutions were introduced into Congress as early as 1914, with Gilbert Hitchcock as sponsor of the matter in the Senate.[4] The resolutions were initially stalled, but the question came up in the upper chamber in early 1915 in the form of an amendment to the controversial ship purchase bill. This set the stage for the first major challenge to the president's conduct of foreign policy.

The ship purchase bill, introduced in December 1914 with Stone as its chief sponsor, would have authorized the United States to purchase those vessels of belligerent nations which were lying idle in American harbors as a result of the naval war. The purchases would, among other things, help to build up America's merchant marine. The proposal immediately ran into trouble when most of the Republicans, led by Lodge, opposed it. The Massachusetts senator, worried about the economic aspects of the proposal, was even more concerned about the diplomatic implications. He feared that the acquisition of German ships by the United States under the terms of this legislation might bring the nation into conflict with Britain.

Regardless of motivation, the Massachusetts senator was determined to make this issue a test of strength. Wilson was equally determined and made support for the measure binding in caucus on all Democrats and clearly indicated that he expected no desertions. The Republicans then decided that they would filibuster; all save four progressives, LaFollette, Norris, Clapp, and Kenyon.[5]

Through January the debate went on, with regular Republicans and some progressives talking at great length. The Democrats fought back, but by February 1 they discovered that some rebels in their ranks would not accept the leadership of their president and of their Senate leaders. Seven (Clarke of Arkansas, Camden of Kentucky, John Bankhead of Alabama, O'Gorman, Hardwick, Vardaman, and Hitchcock) joined with the Republicans to oppose the bill. Link attributes several possible motives to the dissenters; some of them, he says, were concerned over the matter of separation of powers and were trying to rebuke Wilson, while O'Gorman, Vardaman, Hitchcock, and Camden had patronage problems with him.[6]

Lodge was disinterested in their motives for deserting their party; he was happy to have them.[7] Wilson, though furious, refrained from public statement. Stone uttered a vigorous condemnation.[8]

With members of his own party in revolt, Wilson turned to the progressive Republicans, in particular Clapp, Norris, and Kenyon, for help. Clapp rejected the appeal but the others were not initially unfriendly. Their interest in backing the bill seems to have been based primarily on economic considerations. However, Wilson would not agree to certain amendments they wanted; and when he committed an unusually crude error in dealing with Kenyon (after the junior senator from Iowa leaned toward support of the bill, the president appointed his brother a postmaster) all possible support was eroded.[9]

There is little evidence that any of the antiwar senators saw the bill as a threat to peace. None of them seems to have referred to it in that light, and the dialogue does not reflect any such fears. Rather, it was Lodge and others of the faction that was more favorable towards Britain who spoke about the unneutral aspects of the bill. The position of the antiwar advocates was determined more by partisan or economic considerations.

The bill died on February 11, with the progressive Republcans joining in the kill. Wilson would not relent and continued to press the matter through the House. But when it came back to the Senate, even the administration stalwarts were unwilling to go through another fight. It was at this point that Hitchcock introduced his motion to amend the bill with an embargo of munitions proposal.[10]

On February 18 the leaders of both parties agreed to end the matter of the ship purchase bill, but before they could work out their arrangements several amendments to it were voted on. One was Hitchcock's. The amendment was a clear challenge to the president's right to make foreign policy; however, one cannot interpret the vote strictly in terms of the senator's feelings about this, or even about the substantive issue. For the bitterness over the ship purchase bill was still intense, and voting patterns apparently were affected. For example, three Republican regulars, Gallinger, Penrose, and Smoot, supported the principle, and several antiwar Democrats, some of whom like Stone approved of the principle of an embargo, did not. The final vote which tabled the amendment (there was no discussion) was 51−36. (One Democrat, Martine, announced after the vote that he had voted incorrectly in favor of tabling, whereas in fact, he was in favor of the principle.)[11]

The matter had been raised at an unpropitious time, and the vote must be regarded in that light. This is not to suggest that Hitchcock erred in presenting it here; the original resolution had been held up in committee, and the only way he could have gotten it to the floor was by offering it as an amendment to an already pending matter. Had it been raised at a different time, without the tension and resentment over the ship purchase issue, votes could have been lost by the embargo advocates as well as gained.

Thus, the first battle was lost by the antiwar forces in their efforts to curb the president and to reduce the possible provocations to war. However, significant issues were developing in the early months of 1915 that would produce even more dramatic clashes between neutralist forces and the administration. These would be more volatile from the public point of view, for they would stir sentiment to far greater heights than could be aroused by such matters as banking loans to belligerents, and embargoes.

One issue was the United States response to the unrestricted submarine warfare commenced by Germany in retaliation to the British blockade. To most of the antiwar bloc, the more tolerant attitude towards blockades than towards submarines only confirmed their fears that the government viewed British goals more favorably than Germany's. They could not equate the harsh notes to the latter with what seemed to be a bland acceptance of the legitimacy and the morality of the former's practices. It was the resentment over the blockade and the administration's unwillingness to condemn it that created the previously cited antiwar feeling in the South because of the impact that the practice had on their economy.

But even more controversial was the question of United States citizens sailing into the war zone on the vessels of belligerent nations while other belligerents, notably Germany, did not recognize their "neutral" status. This issue would raise the questions of neutral rights and freedom of the seas which would become the rallying cries for many Americans. The antiwar legislators, mindful that sinking ships with American citizens aboard could produce demands for intervention, argued that the nation should keep its people off these vessels, or at least warn them of the possible consequences.

However, the administration was disposed to do neither. Bryan, LaFollette, and others were convinced that continuation of this policy could bring trouble, although Bryan, of course, could not express these feelings publicly.[12]

Germany's program of unrestricted submarine warfare was inaugurated in February 1915, and by March the first incident of concern to the United States took place when the British ship *Fabala* sank, with the loss of one American life. Bryan urged Wilson to be moderate in pressing Germany on this matter, but the note that finally was sent reflected more the hard line urged by Lansing and others. [13] This incident passed, but with the sinking of the *Lusitania* on May 7 1915 off the Irish coast with 128 Americans among her dead, the crisis was brought to a head.

The ship had been warned of a possible submarine attack before leaving New York, for the German government insisted that she carried munitions and thus was a legitimate target of war. This point was maintained also by many antiwar groups in the United States and appears to be confirmed by a recently published book on the subject. [14] LaFollette, convinced that the *Lusitania* carried the forbidden cargo, stressed this point throughout the period before American entry into the war and even afterwards. He would also allege that Wilson knew of this, and eventually his accusations would lead to the motion to expel him from the Senate.

The public outcry alarmed the antiwar bloc; Norris expressed the fear that the pro-British press would exploit the matter to a point where the demand for American involvement would be overwhelming. Stone insisted that the nation view the matter in its proper perspective—a British ship carrying arms and flying the British flag in a war zone. Works contended that the United States was morally at fault, since she had done nothing to discourage her citizens from sailing on such ships. Hoke Smith warned that he would never vote for war over the sinking of a munitions-bearing British ship.

These sentiments suggest that this might have been the time for some action that could express the wish of the Congress that the president do something about American citizens sailing into the war zone on the vessels of belligerents. Many of the senators who were not regarded as being in the antiwar bloc were not yet ready to issue a call for war. One of the more influential Democrats, Thomas Martin of Virginia, reportedly told Wilson that any move towards a declaration of war would be resisted by the Congress. [15]

Despite the concern of many legislators, the public outcry over the *Lusitania* was too strong to attempt any resolution that would call upon the president to retreat from his position that American citizens had the right to travel when and where they wished and that Germany must respect that right. The "murder" of 128 Americans would have probably caused public outrage to be visited on any lawmaker who voted for a proposal that would either warn or legally prevent American citizens from exercising these rights. Nor was Wilson disposed to abandon his stand, as he once again accepted the advice of Lansing and others and sent a strong note to Germany, signed reluctantly by Bryan. The German response was unsatisfactory, provoking one even more strongly worded; this time the secretary of state would not sign it. His stance was that, should the United States continue to take the position implied in the message, it would run the risk of war. He decided therefore to resign; a decision he kept even from his closest advisers such as Ashurst, who would write that he spoke to Bryan only an hour before the resignation and got no hint of the pending move.

His frustration, as noted earlier, was not confined to the *Lusitania* incident or to the question of unrestricted submarine warfare. He had been overruled or bypassed too many times. Reportedly, he told Wilson as the two were discussing the alternatives that he believed that Colonel House rather than the secretary of state had been the dominant figure in shaping American foreign policy and that he did not enjoy Wilson's confidence.[16]

Josephus Daniels would comment later that the departure of Bryan was critical for the antiwar movement; for from this point on, no one of stature around the president would be a voice for caution. The reactions of many of the neutralist senators, particularly LaFollette, O'Gorman, and Works, seemed also to reflect this concern.[17]

It was after this incident that the focus of the antiwar movement moved completely into the Congress. The Hitchcock resolution had only been a skirmish; until May of 1915 most of the neutralist legislators had apparently not been so nearly concerned as they would be after Bryan's resignation. Now they found that not only was the sole strong voice for moderation gone from the president's cabinet, but that the majority of their own colleagues in the Senate were possibly even more inclined towards belligerency than the president.

The immediate peril presented by the *Lusitania* sinking abated when Germany announced, after a series of notes were exchanged over the destruction of another vessel, the *Arabic,* that she would cease unrestricted submarine warfare against passenger vessels. Nothing was said, however, about her policy towards armed merchant vessels on which passengers might be sailing.

Gore-McLemore

The silence of Germany on its attitude toward the sinking of armed merchant vessels and the refusal of the administration either to clarify its stand should such an event take place or to take some action to keep American citizens off such ships, caused concern among neutralist legislators during the latter part of 1916. It appeared to some that the refusal was a covert statement affirming the rights of American citizens to sail when and where they pleased, and many feared the consequences of another sinking in which American lives might be lost.

In early 1916 the first steps were undertaken to put some restraints on policies which might lead to war. In January, Gore, acting apparently at the request of Bryan, introduced two bills. The first would have prohibited passports from being issued for travel on belligerent vessels. The second would have banned these ships from carrying American passengers to or from the United States and would have prevented any American vessel from simultaneously transporting citizens and munitions. There was some support, but the proposals died in committee.[18]

Kenyon introduced a resolution based on a petition circulated by peace groups showing support for the principle of an arms embargo. The Iowan had allegedly been refused a seat on the Senate Foreign Relations Committee by the Republican leadership the previous December, because of his advocacy of this and such ideas as that moneys for defense should come from taxes and munitions, which were unacceptable to the minority party leaders.

Kenyon's embargo resolution was endorsed by a number of other senators including Works, Clapp, Ashurst, Lane, Martine, LaFollette, and Townsend, but it was buried in the Foreign Relations Committee. Antiwar senators had hoped to avoid having it referred there, for they knew what action Stone would probably take, and instead tried to have it sent to the Commerce Committee. This maneuver, initiated by Hitchcock, failed, and off it went to the Foreign Relations Committee, or as LaFollette called this body, "the rubbish room," for he had seen some of his own ideas disappear there earlier.[19]

Wilson was trying to get an answer from Germany about her policy towards armed ships, and was also attempting to defuse the potentially volatile situation by persuading Britain to disarm her merchantmen, which she adamantly refused to do. Then on February 10 1916 Germany gave her answer: she would sink any armed vessels on sight.

The president reversed himself dramatically. He announced that he would no longer press Britain to disarm her merchantmen, that he would hold Germany responsible for any American lives lost. This latter remark was especially disturbing to Stone, who went to see Wilson on February 21 with other congressional leaders.

At that meeting, attended also by Senate majority leader John Kern of Indiana and House Foreign Affairs Committee Chairman Hal Flood of Virginia, the question was put to the president: What would the United States do in the event that a sinking of an armed merchant vessel occurred? Wilson said that he would treat the matter no differently than if the ship were a passenger liner, such as the *Lusitania*, and that if American lives were lost he would hold Germany to account.

Angered, Stone reportedly shouted at him: "Mr. President, would you draw a shutter over my eyes and intellect? You have no right to ask me to follow such a course. It could mean war for my country."[20]

Stone's concern about Wilson's intentions is corroborated by the account of Arthur Mullen, a Democratic committeeman from Nebraska, who reports on a conversation he had had earlier in the year with the Missourian. Allegedly, the latter then told him that he and the president had been talking about the war in Europe and that he was convinced that Wilson meant for the nation to intervene. He reportedly told Mullen also that he was personally against going to war and would continue to fight against it.[21]

The reaction in Congress to Wilson's attitude was immediate. In the House the Foreign Affairs Committee reported out a bill that had been introduced by Representative Jeff McLemore of Texas, withdrawing the protection of the United States from citizens on the vessels of belligerents. Shortly after, Gore introduced a companion piece in the Senate. (When the issue finally came to a vote, the resolutions were "warnings" to stay off these ships, but the implications were clear enough.)

Congressional leaders privately favored the idea, but they worked to head off the revolt in their chambers. Stone was doing so in the Senate because he still apparently believed in leaving the initiative for foreign policy with the president. So were House Speaker Champ Clark, majority floor leader Claude Kitchin of North Carolina, Flood, and others, despite their better judgment, because either they were loyal to Wilson or they feared the consequences if they could not keep their troops in line. Clark predicted that if there were a free vote, it would pass in the House by a large margin.[22]

Wilson was deeply concerned about the strong possibility that his influence in world affairs might be lessened if it could be shown that the legislature was repudiating him on a point he considered to be fundamental. Even a "warning" was an attempt to cut into his exclusive domain, and he wanted no implication that he was not the sole maker of foreign policy.

By the twenty-ninth the worst of the crisis was over. Wilson had ordered Burleson, his liaison with Congress, and the leaders to use all their resources to bring the recalcitrants into line, particularly in the House, where the revolt was more widespread; and they were successful. In addition, he had sent a letter to Stone stating that he would do everything he could to keep the United States out of war, but that he would not surrender America's position as a spokesman for right and morality in international affairs. The former move probably had more influence than the latter, for by the twenty-ninth the president could insist to the House Rules Committee that it "unblock" the McLemore resolution and vote on it.[23]

Wilson wanted a vote on the matter, not a mere statement of confidence, because he still believed that his reputation was at stake. Although many members of both houses would rather have allowed the matter to die, Wilson wanted no less than complete and total victory. The measure was reported out in each chamber and went to the floor for debate and vote.

It came up first in the Senate, where Lodge and Williams led the floor fight against the resolution. The former talked of the need for the president to be free to carry out his constitutional responsibilities, while the latter scoffed at the danger of war, arguing that the real danger lay in the possibility that the president would be hampered in his negotiations with other countries if Congress criticized him.[24] Wilson had for some time been negotiating, through Colonel House, with various belligerents in an effort to secure a negotiated peace, but most of the legislators knew little of this.

During the first day of the debate, Gore made the famous charge, rebutted by most historians, that Stone had said in his presence that Wilson had once indicated that war might not be a bad idea. Although Stone may have thought this, it is very doubtful that he would have had the bad judgment to express it at such a delicate moment and in the presence of one of the president's most vocal critics. He denied the statement on the floor and claimed that there was no truth to it.[25]

On March 3 the resolution came up for a vote. By prearrangement, Senator Ollie James of Kentucky, a Wilson loyalist, moved to table, a motion that was not debatable. Gore, given a chance to perfect his resolution, reworded it in such a way that it appeared to endorse Wilson's point of view, and when the vote started many senators did not know what they were voting on. Smoot asked to be excused from voting for this reason.

49

Ashurst reports that the neutralist senators were annoyed at Gore for his actions. As it was, the vote is probably meaningless as a barometer of sentiment. Fourteen senators voted against tabling: two Democrats—O'Gorman, who was definitely in favor of the principle, and Chamberlain of Oregon—and twelve Republicans—LaFollette, Norris, Gronna, Clapp, Cummins, Works, Sherman, Jones, McCumber, Borah, Gallinger, and Fall. The latter two could probably be said not to favor the principle of the resolution, and the impression is that Borah did not either. Many neutralist senators voted to table, including Hitchcock, Ashurst, Lane, Vardaman, Thomas, and Gore; the latter voted to table his own resolution. He had changed the wording, his biographer reports, and then voted to table because he realized that he could not win and wanted Wilson's victory in this matter to be by default.[26]

Jones had a resolution similar to Gore's but he withdrew it rather than have it suffer a similar fate. McCumber also had a resolution, and his was the one that the neutralist senators would have tried to substitute had the tabling motion failed. Several senators were ready to vote for the principle involved in the original but voted to table because, in Hitchcock's words explaining his own actions, the motion had been twisted out of shape.[27]

The House defeated the McLemore version on March 7, despite Bryan's efforts.[28] The vote, 276–142, is probably a better indication of sentiment, since this was a "pure" motion and not the kind that Gore had substituted at the last minute. There was strong support for it in the Midwestern delegations.

This resolution had offered the best opportunity for Congress to challenge the president's prerogatives during the period prior to the outbreak of war. It failed, not because of Gore's actions, but because its leaders subordinated their judgments to their desires to support the president. But it is quite probable that the measure would have been voted down anyhow, particularly in the Senate, where the Lodge faction opposed it. The attempts of the legislative leaders to put down the uprising took much of the steam out of efforts to curb the president. A narrow victory for the chief executive would have served notice on him that the Congress was going to assert itself. But Wilson's decisive victory convinced many senators and representatives that it would be unwise for them to challenge him in the future.

LaFollette spoke about this a week later. He addressed the Senate at great length, telling them how he feared that the chief executive was now going unchecked in a field in which war was a constant threat. He urged his colleagues to stand up and assert their right to have a voice in the determination of foreign policy, and reminded them of the House of Representatives' rejection of Seward's contention some fifty years earlier that foreign policy was exclusively an executive affair. The senator said he feared that exclusive executive control over foreign affairs would lead to the type of tyranny that characterized the warring nations in Europe and that it was time for the Congress to declare its constitutional authority to prevent that in America.

LaFollette's biographers report that many senators and representatives expressed their private support for his speech and for his stress on the responsibility of the Congress in foreign affairs.[29]

Norris was also alarmed. He insisted that the Congress should assert its responsibility over commerce by banning passengers on munitions-carrying vessels. He noted that there was a federal statute preventing dynamite from being sent on a train carrying passengers, and he urged that this principle be applied to foreign commerce. He also criticized the president's mistaken belief that he was the sole voice in foreign policy making and demanded that the chief executive report to the Congress before taking any further action that might run the risk of war.[30]

War was a very distinct threat in the days following the defeat of the Gore-McLemore resolutions. Their defeat had not resolved the question which precipitated their introduction, and on March 24 the matter arose again when the *Sussex* sank in the English Channel with the loss of eighty lives. Again there was pressure on the president, from Lansing and others, to break relations with Germany.

Wilson's response to the sinking was too weak for some, too strong for others. After an unsatisfactory exchange of notes, he told the guests at a political dinner that the current crisis could well bring about war. On April 19 he went before Congress to tell it that he had sent an ultimatum to Germany, warning her to cease unrestricted submarine warfare or accept the position that the United States would have no alternative but to break off diplomatic relations.

Before addressing Congress, Wilson had conferred with Stone and other legislators who were extremely upset about the crisis. According to Link, the president regretted his commitment to the Missourian that he would confer prior to any drastic actions and was not eager to meet with lawmakers at this point. He sent his most severe note to Germany before meeting with them and then presented them, and later the entire Congress, with a fait accompli. This was probably not the sort of consultation that Stone felt was appropriate.[31]

The Foreign Relations chairman was cautious in his reaction to the president's speech and would appear to be angry at the way he had been treated. Norris reacted strongly to the address, again criticizing Wilson for coming before the Congress after the fact. Kenyon remarked that if war should come out of the crisis, the first persons in the trenches should be those who had caused all the trouble by sailing on the vessels of belligerents.[32]

But there was no real effort by lawmakers to assert any role in shaping foreign policy. For most of the lessons of the Gore-McLemore fight had been learned. Only LaFollette seemed anxious at this time to challenge the president. On April 29 he introduced a resolution into the Senate that would authorize an advisory referendum in the event the president severed diplomatic relations with a foreign nation, and would require the results to be reported to Congress. It was originally referred to the Committee on the Census, but shortly thereafter Stone insisted on having it referred to his own committee. His motion never came to a vote, nor for that matter did LaFollette's proposal. (Some months later the Wisconsin senator would have another resolution before his colleagues—this one calling for a national referendum before war could be declared. It too wound up in one of the Senate's "rubbish rooms.")[33]

LaFollette's gesture, although of small significance, expressed the frustration that he and other antiwar senators felt. However, the crisis passed, as Germany, in what represented a triumph of the civilian over the military faction, decided not to press the United States at this time and on May 1 announced what was to be known as the *Sussex* pledge, the end of unrestricted submarine warfare. Lansing was dubious about the message and told Wilson that he was being handed a "gold brick."[34]

In the period prior to the Democratic convention of 1916, Anglo-American tensions became aggravated because of American resentment over the execution of some leaders of the Easter Rebellion in Ireland. Later in the summer the tensions worsened with the British publication of a blacklist of American firms doing business with Germany. Wilson's anger and suspicion towards England became almost as severe as they had been towards Germany.[35]

Preparedness

The question of the adequacy of America's military establishment was raised as early as the latter months of 1914, while the United States was still, in most people's minds, following a practice of absolute neutrality. Theodore Roosevelt and others who favored the Allied side professed worry about what would happen if the nation had to go to war with defenses so weak. The push for preparedness became stronger after the sinking of the *Lusitania* when, in the minds of many, the possibility of war became more likely. Wilson, noting the growing demand, asked Daniels and Secretary of War Lindley Garrison to assess the state of military readiness and to come up with recommendations.

To the extent that either increasing or decreasing the size of the military and naval appropriations affects foreign policy, this would represent the one area in which antiwar legislators could have the greatest opportunity to assert the role of Congress. There would be no question about the constitutional roles of the chief executive and the legislature in appropriation measures. It appeared to Bryan and his followers in the House of Representatives in the latter months of 1915 when the army and navy boards indicated the need for major increases in the size of the two services that this would be the place to fight the growing war fever.

Antiwar legislators wielded greater power in the House than in the Senate. Floor leader Kitchin had considerable leverage in making appointments to the House committees, and when they were realigned at this time he assigned many like-minded Democrats to the crucial House Military Affairs Committee under Congressman James Hay of Virginia. This committee would be the focal point of the first battle over Garrison's proposal for a major military expansion, including the elimination of the National Guard and the creation of a standing reserve, known as the Continental Army. The committee rejected most of the war secretary's plans.

Link notes that there was probably one other factor that helped the House forces in their efforts. In the latter part of 1915, Wilson was occupied with his marriage to Mrs. Edith Bolling Galt, and thus not as absorbed with politics as he might have been. When the representatives shelved his plan, he took the case for the Continental Army to the people, but it was too late. On February 10 1916 he abandoned the plan, and his war secretary thereupon tendered his resignation.[36]

There was a much different feeling about military preparedness in the Senate. Here Lodge and most of the other Republican regulars were advocates of military preparedness. Most of the Democrats supported a major military build-up (including the chairman of the Military Affairs Committee, Senator George Chamberlain of Oregon). These men were eventually successful in their efforts for a strong bill, and in April the Senate passed a measure that embodied many of the ideas set forth by Garrison. The conference committee report represented a compromise; Wilson was able to persuade the Senate conferees to give up on some of the more enthusiastic proposals and the House conferees to accept some. What emerged was something that both sides could live with—although preparedness advocates complained that it was not nearly strong enough, even though the size of the army had been doubled.[37]

One of the few Senate Democrats to oppose the military build-up was Vardaman. He had originally been a member of the Military Affairs Committee, but had been dropped from it during the reshuffling of committee assignments in the fall of 1915; even had he remained a member, it is doubtful if he could have altered the outcome. Part of his opposition to the original proposal stemmed from his concern over the Continental Army, for he and other southerners feared that it might mean the eventual racial integration of the armed forces. But this aside, he still opposed the concept of preparedness in principle.[38]

Preparedness supporters scored their greatest triumph in the build-up of the navy. At first they were disturbed by the rather modest proposals that Secretary Daniels originally envisioned, and attempted to modify them with a big-navy plan. They failed by a narrow margin in the House, which passed a measure providing for a limited increase in the size of the navy. But in the Senate the preparedness faction, led by Lodge, who was contemptuous of Daniels and his moderate plans, resolved to come out with a strong bill.

Preparedness factions in both houses had an ally in their efforts to expand the navy. Discouraged about Daniels's timidity and pacifism, Under-Secretary Franklin D. Roosevelt gave information to critics of the navy plan and remained on good terms with them, even when they were criticizing his superior. Daniels never pressed the issue with Roosevelt, who usually stopped short of any action that would have warranted his dismissal.[39]

Lodge found a very valuable aide in the person of Senator Claude Swanson of Virginia, who had become a more dominant figure on the Naval Affairs Committee than its nominal chairman. Ben Tillman was apparently more interested at this time in getting the government to build up an armor plate factory in his state. Lodge wrote Theodore Roosevelt that Swanson had been instrumental in persuading the president and the navy secretary to call for a larger build-up than planned and that he (Lodge) had been successful in persuading Daniels to go even beyond that.[40]

The progressive Republicans led the fight against the navy build-up, but they were practically alone. The achievements of House antipreparedness spokesmen were not matched in the upper chamber, as some antiwar senators capitulated completely to the idea of naval preparedness.

Norris was one of the more prominent critics of the bill, charging that the government was employing scare tactics (the Battle of Jutland in early June of 1916 had made some people big-navy conscious) and lamented that the tax burden to pay for this would be placed on the ordinary citizen.[41] He challenged the bill with an amendment that would have postponed any battleship construction until the president had attempted an arbitration treaty, but could get only limited support.[42]

LaFollette tried to amend the bill to provide that no warship could be used to collect debts from any foreign nation (he was worried about the situation in Mexico, which had become serious again). Attacked for trying to tie the president's hands, he charged that the business interests were behind the measure, but he too could get only limited support.[43]

Cummins, while indicating that he favored a naval build-up (and keeping an eye on the presidential race), tried to limit the size of the expansion, but only fourteen senators, including the seven progressive Republicans, voted for this. On final passage, July 21, only eight senators voted against the bill: LaFollette, Norris, Gronna, Clapp, Works, Thomas, Vardaman, and Curtis—antiwar positions notwithstanding.[44]

In the conference committee the Senate members were successful, as Wilson supported the upper chamber's version over the more limited House bill. The House accepted the compromise, with regret on the part of some of its leaders, and on August 15 the Senate measure was adopted.

The progressives were able to salvage some minor victories by placing some items in the revenue bill of 1916 that would ensure that the bulk of the tax burden for financing this new build-up would fall on the upper economic classes. Here, the antiwar progressives would have the support of many who were unhesitating supporters of Wilson in the area of foreign policy. The bill, passed on September 6, provided for a strong levy against the rich.[45]

In general, the Senate had a poor record in trying to curb the president by cutting down on his preparedness program. Many of the legislators who were critical of him for his failure to consult with them and who were critical of belligerent diplomacy, voted without question to increase the American military capability. Only a few senators apart from the progressive Republicans showed any consistency in opposing the program.

Summer 1916-February 1917

The renomination of Woodrow Wilson was expected, but what surprised some Democrats was the tremendous emphasis they would have to place on the peace issue. The keynote speech by ex-Governor Martin Glynn of New York, the famous "he kept us out of war" address, sounded the theme for the campaign. Of perhaps even greater note was the fact that the greatest reception at the convention was for William Jennings Bryan, who was there not as a delegate but as a journalist. The former secretary made it clear to his followers that he was supporting Wilson all the way.[46]

Wilson would have preferred to run on his domestic record and did not care for the campaign slogan. He reportedly told Daniels the following year that his being credited with keeping the nation out of war was ridiculous—one torpedo from a "little German U-boat lieutenant" and the war would come.[47] But in the Middle West, where Bryan barnstormed preaching the gospel of peace (and Prohibition), the theme was welcomed. Senator Thomas Walsh of Montana, managing the campaign there, told state leaders to use it to the hilt.[48]

Stone played a major role in the convention and in the campaign. He helped write the platform plank on foreign policy and went among German-American leaders to stress the president's desire for nonintervention. He reminded them of the pro-Allied orientation of men such as Theodore Roosevelt, who had enlisted in the cause of the Republican nominee Charles Evans Hughes, and further informed them of Hughes's "Welsh" ancestry.[49]

Actually, Stone was not alone. While both sides decried bowing down and catering to the ethnic, or "hyphen," vote, they sought it eagerly; as the leaders issued the pious proclamations stating that all Americans had interests as Americans, their aides moved quietly around with appeals based on national origins.

The election is famous as the closest one of the twentieth century; the final outcome was not known for several days. As most know, Hughes retired on election eve thinking he had won because of his showing in the East. However, when all the results were in, Wilson, who had run exceptionally well in the Midwest and West, was the victor. The implications are mixed, but Wilson appears to have profited from the peace issue, particularly in the Germanic and Scandinavian areas, although there were other factors present here as well.[50]

LaFollette was reelected, endorsing neither candidate, although there is considerable evidence that he supported Wilson. Specifically, one might note the warm welcome given John Sharp Williams when the Mississippian ventured into the northland of Wisconsin to urge the reelection of the president.[51] Gilbert Hitchcock was also reelected, his faction having defeated Bryan's in the battle for the Democratic endorsements. Wilson, incidentally, had appointed a key Bryan aide to an important patronage post during the middle of the primary, something which could not have been pleasing to the senior senator from Nebraska.[52]

It was in the background of this election that the president decided to make one last try to resolve the war in Europe. He told Lansing and the House that he was going to try to bring the belligerents to the peace table. Both scoffed at this as impossible. But Wilson pressed ahead to prepare a message that would be the first step in his new peace plan.

The note was sent on December 18 at a time when the Germans, impressed by military successes, had already secretly decided to resume unrestricted submarine warfare unless a peace conference could be arranged on favorable terms. The note asked both sides to state their war aims and also indicated that the United States recognized its international obligations in this situation and would be willing to cooperate in an international organization to secure the peace. However, the two sides would first have to end the fighting.

It was the reference to a commitment by the United States to help end the fighting that caused the controversy in the Senate. Borah complained that this would mean that the United States would be committing itself to the defense of any small nation needing protection and would render the Monroe Doctrine meaningless. Still others, most particularly Lodge, believed that Wilson was committing himself to the defense of Germany and trying to save her. Other senators were concerned that the president had not consulted them on the matter of participation in an international organization.[53]

The antiwar faction greeted the announcement with enthusiasm. Stone believed that the president's speech now put the burden on the belligerents. Hitchcock introduced a resolution in the Senate which would endorse the principle of the note.

It is not clear whether Hitchcock introduced this resolution at Wilson's behest or did it on his own—more probably the latter. It is similarly not clear whether the president approved of its introduction. The debate was intense, taking basically a partisan turn but reflecting some of the arguments that would later be heard in the debate over ratification of the Treaty of Versailles. Most of the Republicans argued against it, and eventually Hitchcock was obliged to water it down to a point where it merely endorsed the fact that Wilson had called upon the two sides to declare the terms under which they would be willing to talk. Even Borah could vote for this, although Lodge could not. (The Massachusetts senator had once endorsed the idea of a league of nations, but by January 1917 he had reconsidered.)

Only one Democrat voted against the diluted resolution, Martine of New Jersey. Nine Republicans voted for it in addition to Borah. At least two prominent antiwar Republicans, Works and McCumber, were against. The final vote was 48-17; over a third of the Senate did not vote.[54]

Wilson's actions did not sit well even with some of his closest advisers. A few days after the note had been sent, Lansing commented to the press that war was close. Chastized by Wilson for this, the secretary, motivated by a desire to see the United States enter the war on the Allied side, began to maneuver around the president, informing Allied ambassadors that they should not take the proposal seriously.[55]

Neither Germany nor Britain viewed Wilson's proposals with any pleasure. The German government, as noted, had already made the decision to resume unrestricted submarine warfare, and they now fixed February 1 as the date, provided no acceptable offer for a peace conference was received. This point was communicated to von Bernstorff, the German ambassador, in mid-January, and shortly afterward his government sent him another message to be forwarded to the German ambassador in Mexico—the famous Zimmermann Note which was to be the basis of their plan in the event that the United States declared war. Their official replies, and those of the Allies, were unsatisfactory to Wilson.

The president decided to make one more effort. He would attempt to spell out the nature of the peace he hoped to see come out of the conflict, a "peace without victory," one in which neither side would triumph and one which would be followed by an agreement of nations to try to resolve through diplomacy the matters which had been resolved in the past by wars. One of the few to whom he entrusted this proposal was Stone. Perhaps feeling that he needed the counsel of someone more receptive to his idea than Lansing, he asked the Missourian to postpone a return to his state to assist. Stone was more than happy to comply.[56]

On the twenty-second Wilson laid the matter before the Senate. Escorted by Stone to the rostrum, and to the accompaniment of some grumbling by senators who, according to Ashurst, resented his use of their chamber as a forum, he delivered what was probably one of his most widely quoted speeches.[57] The tone of this message was one that few who heard it could forget. "A great state paper," said Stone upon its conclusion. LaFollette said that those present had just witnessed an "important hour in the life of the world."[58]

58

Most members of the president's party were impressed. Tillman said that he thought the speech was the greatest document since the Declaration of Independence. Others called it an "encouragement to peace." There was one interesting negative comment from the Democratic side of the aisle, from Senator James Reed of Missouri, a caustic and abrasive debater, who would emerge as the president's tormentor during the League of Nations fight a few years later. Stone's junior colleague said that he feared that the United States would be drawn into every petty dispute between European nations.

Among the Republicans, only Norris, Clapp, and LaFollette were sympathetic, as most of the others, even members of the antiwar bloc, joined Lodge and the pro-Allied faction in denouncing it. Cummins stressed the theme that once again Wilson had made a major policy move without consulting the Senate or even giving any hint of his intentions. He introduced a resolution to the effect that the Congress would have to be consulted before any further commitments towards a world organization be made. He also called on the president to be more explicit about his plans.

The other Republicans were even more critical. Lodge warned that it would mean the end of American sovereignty, Borah called for a resolution reaffirming the principles of the Monroe Doctrine, and Senator Francis Warren of Wyoming, a Medal of Honor winner from the Civil War and the father-in-law of General John Pershing, snidely remarked that Wilson thought he was "president of the world."[59]

There was no formal debate on either the Cummins or Borah resolution, but other events were to intervene that would cause it to be pushed into the background.[60] Nine days after the "peace without victory" speech, von Bernstorff, who had been conducting unofficial discussions with House even while in possession of the information about his government's intentions, was heading for the State Department to deliver Germany's official reply to Lansing.

4

THE BREAK WITH GERMANY: FEBRUARY 1-7 1917

At four in the afternoon of January 31 1917, Count von Bernstorff arrived at the State Department to present his government's message. His manner was apologetic. Lansing remarked later that the self-confidence that was part of his usual behavior was missing, and he soon learned the reason for it. The ambassador had a note from his government, informing the United States that Germany no longer intended to abide by the *Sussex* pledge and that at midnight she would begin to sink all ships, belligerent and neutral, found in the war zone around the British Isles, France, Italy, and the eastern Mediterranean. There would be no warnings. It would be the ultimate in unrestricted submarine warfare.

Von Bernstorff had regarded himself as a man of peace, and from all accounts he was bitter and disillusioned by his government's decision.[1] Later he would say to newsmen that he was finished with politics for the remainder of his life.[2]

The message from the German government did say that it would permit one vessel to sail each week between New York and Falmouth, in Cornwall, provided that it be plainly marked with a large red and white stripe. At the same time that von Bernstorff presented his government's message announcing the end of the truce in submarine warfare, he also handed Lansing the terms under which Germany would have been willing to negotiate. These were terms that would have been unacceptable to the United States and to the Allies.[3]

Wilson heard the news late in the afternoon. Tumulty reportedly showed him a wire service report on the German government's action

60

even before the information reached the White House from the State
Department. The president is reported to have said that the break he
had hoped to avoid now seemed inevitable.[4]

He shut himself off from everyone, including Tumulty, while waiting
for Lansing's memorandum on his meeting with von Bernstorff to arrive.
When it did, he read it and then sent for the secretary, and the two talked
far into the night about the implications of the message. Lansing wanted
to break relations immediately, but Wilson was more cautious. He told
the secretary to prepare a message announcing the severing of relations,
but said that it was for discussion purposes only.[5]

His other adviser on foreign policy, Colonel House, was at that moment on his way back from New York. He had been summoned by Frank
Polk, now the State Department counselor, who wanted to ensure that
the colonel would be avilable to help convince Wilson that it was time
for strong action.[6] In addition, von Bernstorff, mindful of House's role
in the formulation of Wilson's foreign policy, had advised him of the
situation in a note sent by special courier even before going fo see Lansing.
As it was, the letter arrived after Polk's call, but House had it when he
boarded the train.

He arrived back in Washington as the morning papers were breaking
the story. At the White House he found the president edgy and nervous
while waiting for Lansing to arrive with the draft of the message announcing a break with Germany. Mrs. Wilson reportedly suggested that the
chief executive might work off some of the nervousness by playing a
little golf, but Wilson rejected the idea, believing that it might look bad
to the country—like Nero fiddling while Rome burned. But the White
House basement was out of sight to the public, so the two men relaxed
there for a moment in some billiards.

One of the matters that delayed the secretary of state's arrival was a
conference with Hitchcock. With Stone back in Missouri, working on the
business that he had neglected while helping to prepare the "peace without
victory" address, the Nebraskan was the ranking member of the Senate
Foreign Relations Committee. He suggested to the secretary that the
United Stated might ask both sides for a ten-day armistice—to gain time.
Lansing replied that such an approach would be useless.[7]

After Lansing arrived at the White House, he talked at length with
Wilson and House about the wisdom of breaking relations. He and the
colonel were for taking such a step immediately, but the president was
hesitant. He explained that he wanted to discuss the matter with his
cabinet, even though he could probably predict the reactions, individually
and collectively. Further, he had the problem of Stone. He had sent a

61

telegram to the Missourian asking him to return to Washington, but a conference could not take place until the next day, and he was hesitant about announcing any decision before the conference. Therefore, any action would have to wait.[8]

Whatever Wilson had thought about playing golf on Thursday, he had no such reservations on Friday morning February 2. Before heading for the cabinet meeting that afternoon, he played a round, possibly feeling that the country would not be unduly scandalized.

At the meeting, Wilson reviewed the German note and the overall situation, then asked the cabinet members if they believed that the United States ought to break off relations with Germany. He pointed out some of the things that should be considered—for example, he told them that he believed that a "draw" might be preferable to a victory for either of the two sides. He said that he feared for the "white race" if Germany were defeated and Russia and Japan moved into the vacuum. Pressed as to whether he cared who won, he implied that he did not.

However, many of his advisers did. Houston said that he was concerned only about defeating Germany—he did not worry about Japan, Russia, and China, for they were morally, intellectually, and industrially inferior to the United States. Redfield and McAdoo said that they were for an immediate rupture of relations.

Other cabinet members were willing to take the "long view" that Wilson talked of—Newton Baker, who had succeeded Garrison as secretary of war, Labor Secretary William Wilson, Burleson, and Daniels. The last was still the cabinet member most deeply committed to having the United States stay out of the war.[9]

The president knew of his navy secretary's concern. It was to him that he reportedly had confided his own personal fears about the problems posed by possible American involvement. He told Daniels that should the United States go to war, every reform that the administration had fought for would be lost and the forces that had been uprooted by the New Freedom would come back. He prophesied that neither of them would live to see government returned to the people.[10]

When the meeting finally broke up, there was much grumbling among the pro-Allied faction about Wilson's timidity. They apparently believed that he was not going to break relations but would wait for some overt act at best, or do nothing at all.

With the cabinet meeting over, Wilson headed for the Capitol and his meeting with Stone. The two talked for a while in the senator's office, where the chairman made his views known. He did not believe that the United States should break relations at this time, but should wait until an overt act, perhaps the sinking of a ship, in order to place the onus squarely on Germany. Wilson listened attentively and then told Stone that he felt that he should have the views of some of the other senators, so pages and messengers were dispatched to round up as many as they could.

Friday afternoon is a hard time to find senators around the Capitol, and only sixteen could be located and brought to the President's Room for the conference. All reports of the event, except the one account given by an eyewitness to the meeting, Senator Henry Myers of Montana, say that all were Democrats. He alleges that Senator Knute Nelson, Republican of Minnesota, the "Viking of the Senate," was present.

Myers's accounts of this meeting and of some of the other events of this period are important because they reflect the view of a senator who was not one of the "prime movers" of this time. He was a former judge from Montana, who had been eclipsed by the powerful and influential Walsh, the latter standing in much better with Wilson than he did. Myers might even be listed as one of the critics of belligerent diplomacy; he had voted for the Hitchcock amendment to the ship purchase bill two years earlier.

Those present besides Stone, Myers (and possibly Nelson) included Vardaman, Reed, Hoke Smith, Walsh, deputy minority leader James Lewis of Illinois, Joe Robinson of Arkansas, Lee Overman of North Carolina, and at least two other members, besides Stone of the Foreign Relations Committee—Atlee Pomerene of Ohio, a progressive who was considered to be one of the rising stars in the Democratic party, and Key Pittman of Nevada, a newcomer to the committee and someday to be its chairman at another crucial point in American history.

The senators sat in a semicircle around the president as he outlined the problem. There appears to be some disagreement as to how the discussion proceeded; for Myers, although aware that Stone had reservations about breaking relations with Germany, reports that everyone agreed that it was necessary at this time that the break be made. But the newspaper accounts suggest that both Stone and Lewis did voice concern over rupturing diplomatic ties immediately; both believed that the United States should wait until the "overt incident" referred to earlier had taken place before taking any such action.

Vardaman apparently must have said nothing at the meeting, because when the time came to put the matter of the breaking of relations to a vote of confidence, he was one of a half dozen senators who voted "no." It is doubtful if he would have indicated approval at this time and then have reversed himself radically a few days later. All that the Mississippi senator would say to the press when he left the meeting was that he had told the president to "sit straight in the boat and look ahead."

The meeting apparently impressed Wilson and Stone. The latter could not help but be concerned when he saw his fellow senators, not all of them hard liners on the matter of relations with Germany, give their approval to breaking off diplomatic relations. Whatever view he had of Wilson's position at this time, the reactions of his fellow senators must have displeased him.

As for Wilson, the type of reaction he got from his meeting may well, as Link has suggested, have been the determining factor in convincing him that the time had come to break relations with Germany. No doubt he had been strongly inclined to this course of action before the meeting, and the strong opinions solidified his thinking. After bidding good night to the sixteen legislators, his last words, Myers recalled, were "God help us." He returned to the White House to work on a speech announcing the severing of diplomatic relations with Germany.[11]

The following morning he sent word to the Congress that he wished to address them and sent also for Lansing to inform the secretary that he wanted von Bernstorff given his passport the moment the speech began. Although it was Saturday, news that he was going to speak spread fast and the House gallery filled up quickly; by the time the president arrived, most of official Washington was present.

The speech was probably not so bellicose as Lansing and others would have wanted. Wilson indicated that he did not think the Germans would carry out their threats. He spoke of waiting for some overt act before assuming that Germany meant to harm American shipping by resuming unrestricted submarine warfare. However, he announced that he was "direct[ing] the Secretary of State to announce . . . that all diplomatic relations will be immediately withdrawn."[12]

With this, Ben Tillman leaped to his feet, leading the applause. Among the first to rise was Henry Cabot Lodge, showing more enthusiasm than anyone had ever seen him display towards any remark of Wilson's. Stone was applauding quietly, but with a sense of foreboding. It was, in his opinion, "a blunder," as he told LaFollette.[13]

LaFollette was also deeply upset. As soon as Wilson had finished his address and left, to the enthusiastic cheers of the legislators and the gallery, the Wisconsinite went to his office, where he told his staff that he wanted to be left alone for a while. He brooded a bit, convinced that Stone was right and that the whole thing was a colossal blunder and now there was no way to avoid war. He reflected bitterly on how he had just seen some senators who had taken strong stands against belligerency for over two years, cheering lustily as the chief executive announced that he was going to give von Bernstorff his passport.[14]

The same concern was felt by William Jennings Bryan, who was still traveling around the speechmaking circuit, preaching against war and for Prohibition. He had been addressing a peace rally in New York when he got word of Wilson's intentions and immediately set out for Washington, where he checked into the Lafayette Hotel and sent messages to his friends to come over.[15]

Whether or not he called LaFollette is not clear; probably the latter got word he was in town and decided that the two should meet. He left his office and headed for the Lafayette, where he found the former secretary of state agitated and excited. Bryan wanted to call a huge rally, with all the leaders of the peace movement present, but LaFollette said that such a move would be ineffective. He suggested instead that each try to contact as many antiwar legislators as necessary and see if they could put together a resolution that would permit a rational discussion of the issue.[16]

Each worked independently over the weekend, but without any apparent success; Bryan's experiences with Ashurst, one of those whom he summoned, are perhaps typical. The Arizona senator also found the Commoner excited and nervous and talking about generating an avalanche of telegrams against the war. However, by his account, he was unmoved by the former secretary's plea for support.[17]

LaFollette had no more luck with the Republican antiwar senators. He found that they were worried that breaking relations could lead to war, but were not ready at the moment to rush into a confrontation with Wilson. He believed that they were afraid to do anything.[18]

Over the weekend the majority of the Congress came out solidly behind the president. Lodge, measuring his words carefully, said that he approved the president's move and supported him in it. He believed that it was the correct thing to do under the circumstances and was demanded "by the honor and safety of the American people." Warren G. Harding, whose reputation for statesmanship was not particularly high in the chamber, commented that it seemed nice for a change to applaud the president out of more than just courtesy.

In fact, there was only one statement from any senator that could be called overtly hostile—at least, of those released to the press. This was from Vardaman, who simply said, "I wish the president had waited." Others who would be critical, such as LaFollette, kept silent.

The speech provoked flights of patriotic oratory in the Senate. John Sharp Williams said that it was excellent—the only people who could object to it would be those whose loyalty to their country of origin (German-Americans) or whose hatred of another country (Irish-Americans) was paramount.

Paul Husting, a Democratic senator from Wisconsin, undertook his usual responsibility in matters such as this. Since LaFollette typified Wisconsin to many other Americans, it became this young progressive's self-designated task to set the record straight and assure the nation that his state was behind the president. Majority leader Kern, defeated for reelection and soon to leave the Senate and his battles on behalf of Wilson, took care of the other forty-seven states by declaring united support.

Among the other senators who had been counted as being part of the antiwar bloc, there was support from Hardwick, who was in complete sympathy with the president, suggesting that the United States might even use its battleships to convoy commerce. Two progressive Republicans, Cummins and Kenyon, both issued statements admiring the tone and the substance of the speech. Stone also "endorsed" the idea, but his comments at this time did not betray his real feelings.

Probably the most amusing statement about the situation came from Ben Tillman, who could always be counted on for a quotable comment, saying in this case that von Bernstorff should be told to "pack his duds and go back to his barbarians."

Other comments followed in the same style, from men who had been uniformly behind a hard line towards Germany, and those who had not. "Inevitable," "Best speech I ever heard," "Strong, timely, well-justified," "The nation would have stultified itself . . . if it did otherwise," "In the spirit of Washington," "Has stilled the Republican fire eaters . . . disarmed [his] critics . . . so he can pursue peace."[19]

It was in many ways as enthusiastic a response as Wilson ever received from any major speech; he could not help but be pleased. LaFollette on the other hand, consoled himself with the thought that once the first flush of emotion was out of the way, there might be some "second thought," and he hoped to see a resolution introduced into the Senate that would either express disapproval or at least permit a full airing of the issues.

He was both surprised and disappointed when Stone did introduce a motion dealing with Wilson's action. For the Foreign Relations Committee chairman's resolution endorsed the president's decision completely. To LaFollette, this was incredible; he remembered the Missouri senator's initial condemnation of the move as a "blunder." He hastily conversed with several antiwar senators and found that the majority, although reluctant to support the resolution, actually would vote for it. He thought

Stone's action "unnecessary" and feared that it would only add to the pressures pushing the United States toward war.[20]

Perhaps Stone's motives were vague to LaFollette and to other anti-war senators who might have been aware of the Foreign Relations Committee chairman's feelings, but his resolution had a purpose. He was not introducing it, as most believed at the time, at the behest of Wilson—in this instance, he was not the "president's man." In fact, he had not even discussed it with the president. What he was doing, according to his biographer, was making the point that the Congress was a partner in foreign policy making and was asserting its rights. Although the matter of breaking relations might be exclusively an executive act, declaring war was not, and that surely could be one of the next steps. Stone wanted Wilson to know that Congress was watching him and was mindful of its constitutional responsibilities. And this was his way of reminding him that he should take no further moves that might lead to war without first discussing it with the legislators.[21]

It would appear that Stone did not discuss this point with LaFollette, whose earlier statements clearly indicated that he, too, was concerned about this matter. However, even had the Missourian done so, it is doubtful if the Wisconsin senator would have been able to support the resolution. His personality was such that it was impossible for him to endorse something he opposed so violently—even to make a point.

George Norris was willing to endorse the resolution, although concerned about how Wilson had acted. He argued that the severance of relations with another nation ought not to be regarded as purely the prerogative of the executive since the next step might have to be a formal war declaration. Thus, he argued, the president should report more frequently to the legislature and consult on such matters before taking drastic steps.[22]

This position was taken by most of the senators who had previously been identified as being in the antiwar faction. For as LaFollette had discovered, they were reluctant at this time to speak or vote against the resolution.[23] When the matter finally came up for discussion, only five others were willing to go along with him and formally oppose Stone's motion.

Works was the first, calling the act of breaking relations a surrender to the super patriots and the jingoists. Vardaman said that it was foolish and that the United States should demand instead that its citizens stay off the vessels of belligerent nations, rather than break relations with Germany and risk war.

Gronna and Kirby also spoke against it, the latter saying that it was tantamount to a war declaration. Harry Lane was the last speaker against the resolution, saying that the real pity was that Americans were getting a one-sided impression about the European war. He believed that both sides were responsible, but that nobody could get that idea from the way the papers were reporting it. LaFollette was absent from the chamber when the debate began.

Most of the senators who spoke for the resolution were critical of the way in which the matter had been handled, and some of them were also critical of Stone for having raised the question of endorsing the act. Jones said that the resolution was "uncalled for." However, these senators took the view that, despite their misgiving about the way in which the matter had been dealt with, they could support the principle, albeit in some cases with reservations. It is noteworthy that many of those who spoke on behalf of the resolution were legislators who had been frequently critical of belligerent diplomacy; men such as Smith of Michigan, Thomas, Martine, Townsend, Sherman, McCumber, Borah, Hardwick, and Myers, the last commenting that his only criticism of Stone was that the Missourian had not introduced the resolution earlier.

After extended discussion Stone was finally able to get a vote. Only Kirby, Works, Gronna, Vardaman, and LaFollette voted against it. Lane had left the chamber during the debate and did not return in time. He later recorded himself as against.[24]

LaFollette returned just in time to vote. Typically, he announced that he smelled a rat; there had been a conspiracy to keep him from speaking on the matter, and the vote was called when it was to prevent him from having his say. He had prepared a speech for the occasion. Vice President Marshall said that the call for a vote had come without warning and that there was no conspiracy. LaFollette was not mollified.

The outcome pleased Lodge. Writing afterwards to Theodore Roosevelt, he commented that the resolution was just the first step, dismissing the importance of what little opposition there had been. Vardaman and Kirby were "rabid Bryanite pacifists," Gronna, "dull" and doing what might be expected of a senator from a state that was soft on preparedness. As for LaFollette, he refused to characterize him.[25]

Roosevelt experienced no difficulty on the latter count. He termed the Wisconsin senator, in his reply to Lodge, as being inferior in morality and capacity to Robespierre. He also told the Massachusetts senator that he did not believe that Wilson would go to war unless he was kicked into it, but that when war came, he (Roosevelt) would serve willingly.[26]

LaFollette was downhearted. Writing to his family, he said that he was worried and distressed about the turn of events. He dreaded the possibility of some new sinking, the "overt act." that might well trigger a war. And he could not help but notice that the peace bloc in Congress was getting smaller and smaller each day in the face of mounting public pressure.[27]

5

THE PRELUDE TO DEBATE

February 26 1917

The sinking of several ships and the refusal of most of America's merchant fleet to move, heightened tension in Washington during the weeks following the severing of relations with the German government. Wilson began to look around for some method of resolving the matter short of war and became attracted to the concept of armed neutrality as an alternative. This plan, whose chief advocate was Professor Carlton Hayes, would put the nation on a virtual war footing but would stop short of a formal conflict. One aspect of this would be the arming, by the United States, of its merchant vessels for the purpose of self-defense.

The proposal was viewed favorably in some quarters, even in certain of the peace groups. However, among the more intervention-oriented spokesmen, including members of his own cabinet, Wilson found that it was regarded as an insufficient response to the German threat.[1]

By February 22, after much debate, Wilson had decided that he would attempt to see how far armed neutrality would go by asking the Congress for the power to arm merchant ships and to give him "other instrumentalities" that would permit him to ensure the protection of American lives and property.[2] However, the cabinet meeting on the twenty-third reflected an even stronger and more belligerent approach. Some of the cabinet members spoke so harshly that Wilson was obliged to caution them for appealing to the *code duello*. Lansing solemnly verified for them the rumor that the wives of American diplomats were being obliged to strip at the German border in order to ensure that secret messages were not being written on their flesh. Franklin Lane ridiculed Daniels for his reluctance to advocate the convoying of merchant ships, suggesting that this was a very unusual attitude for a secretary of the navy.[3]

It was over this weekend that Wilson learned of the existence and the contents of the Zimmermann Note, the details of which will be discussed more fully in a subsequent chapter. It is mentioned at this point because, contrary to what some believe, his decision to arm merchant ships did not come about as a result of his knowledge of the existence of the note. He had already decided to try armed neutrality and had already decided to press for it before Congress. He planned to go to speak to them about it on Monday February 26.

Once again news that he was coming to talk was not received with too much grace at the other end of Pennsylvania Avenue. Not so the public, for once the word got around on the twenty-sixth that he was coming to address the Congress on armed neutrality, the galleries filled up quickly.[4]

The Armed Ship speech was only thirty minutes long, containing no significant quotes such as had come from the "peace without victory" or breaking of relations addresses. It was straightforward and plain. When he had finished and the legislators returned to their chores, there were 142 hours and 40 minutes left in the life of the Sixty-fourth Congress.

He spoke[5] of his desire for legislation that would permit the arming of merchant vessels and for the need for the "other instrumentalities" that might permit him to "have the authority to safeguard the practice and right of a great people who are at peace." He also added:

I have asked the privilege of addressing you because we are moving through critical times during which it seems to be my duty to keep in close touch with the houses of Congress so that neither counsel nor action shall run at cross purposes.

He went on to discuss the events subsequent to January 31: the breaking of the *Sussex* pledge, the effect of the resumption of unrestricted submarine warfare on American commerce, the reluctance of insurance companies to insure cargoes, and the unwillingness of the shipowners to go to sea. In stressing the economic aspects of the situation, he was, of course, opening up the door to those who believed that any move that might lead towards war had an economic motive.

He acknowledged that the message was late—in the sense that the Congress had only one week to go before adjournment. However, he said, the move was necessary because the legislation was essential and it would be "difficult" to assemble the new Congress during the remaining nine months of 1917. "I wish to feel," he said, "that I have the authority and power of Congress behind me. No doubt, I already possess the authority without the special warrant of law by plain implication of my Constitutional powers and duties. . . . We must," he concluded, "defend our commerce and our people."

At this point LaFollette, chewing gum as he usually did during moments of crisis, threw up his hands in an "all is lost" gesture. Nearby, clasping and unclasping his fingers, but reflecting very little emotion, sat Lodge, quite pleased with the turn of events.[6]

I hereby request that you will accord me your vote . . . a definite bestowal, the means and authority to safeguard in practice the right of a great people who are at peace . . . war can only come by the willful acts and aggressions of others. . . .

My theme is one of those great principles of compassion and of protection which mankind has sought to throw about human lives, the lives of non-combatants, the lives of men who are peacefully at work, keeping the industrial processes of the world quick and vital, the lives of women and children and of those who provide the labor which ministers to their sustenance. We are speaking of no selfish material rights, but of rights which our hearts support and whose foundation is that righteous passion for justice upon which all law, all structures alike . . . must rest . . . as upon the ultimate base of our liberty. I cannot imagine any man with American principles in his heart hesitating to defend those things.

The applause that greated the conclusion of his remarks was reported by the press to be deafening.

After the conclusion of the speech, the senators went back to their chamber, discussing it as they went. Only Stone apparently had had prior knowledge of the contents of the address; Wilson had met with him earlier that morning and had informed him of his plans. It would appear, however, that he did not tell the Senate Foreign Relations chairman of the existence of the Zimmermann Note. According to reports, Stone told the president of his opposition to the concept of armed neutrality; believing that however noble the idea might sound, it was still an invitation to war. There is no report as to whether or not he suggested to Wilson the amendment that he would offer later in the Foreign Relations Committee.[7]

Interest in the speech was sufficient to bring about a number of trespasses into foreign policy during the discussion of the revenue bill, then before the Senate. The best example of this came when Warren Harding was going through a rambling discourse that constituted his criticism of the measure. He had started his speech by telling the Senate of his trip to Paris, where he had bargained with his wife ("the Duchess," as she would some day be known to the country) for a night on the town alone without her, in exchange for her choice of a Paris hat. ("It was not worth it," he advised his colleagues.) From Paris night life he digressed into foreign policy.

Martine challenged him. "Who," he asked, "is responsible for peace and what would have been the situation if Theodore Roosevelt had been in the chair for the past three or four years instead of Woodrow Wilson? .... Does ... [the Senator] think we would have had peace?"

Harding's reply was a play for the galleries, not an answer to Martine. "I have abiding faith," he said, "that if Theodore Roosevelt had been President, the *Lusitania* would not have been sunk." There was a loud burst of applause from the audience, and the chairman was obliged to issue the customary warning that such demonstrations were out of order.[8]

After Harding subsided, the Senate moved on to other matters. Works wanted to talk about the reclamation of the Sacramento Valley. Ashurst wanted to discuss Indian appropriations, but one of the more interesting moments came when LaFollette insisted that the names of senators who had voted in 1907 to raise their own salaries be printed in the record. One can readily see from this why he was not overly popular with some of his colleagues.[9]

While these matters were being discussed on the floor, legislators from both houses were meeting to draft the bills dealing with the arming of merchant ships. Others were busy preparing statements about why they did or did not like them. Most of the Democrats expressed complete support for arming the ships. Majority leader Kern predicted that the bill would pass with the support even of the Republican members of the Senate, and Lewis likened Wilson's situation to that of McKinley in 1898. Hitchcock called the speech sensible and the proposal reasonable.

But within the ranks of the Republican minority, there was strong opposition. Reed Smoot claimed that it was irresponsible, and John Weeks said that it was unreasonable to give the president the kind of power he sought. It would be better, he said, to call a special session of Congress to deal with a matter as vital as this.

Jones and Townsend also attacked the proposal, the former calling it "a beautifully worded demand for autocratic authority," while the latter said that it was "monstrous, no despot could ask for more." Other senators within the antiwar bloc of the Republican party were even more critical. "It is not specific enough," said Cummins. "There is much sentiment against giving blanket powers." LaFollette believed that it violated the letter and the spirit of the Constitution by taking the war-making powers from the Congress and giving them to the president.

73

Norris believed that passage of the bill would plunge the country into war.[10]

Most of the antiwar bloc, on both sides of the aisle, objected to the bill specifically for the mention of the "other instrumentalities," which they feared would give the president a virtually unlimited right to wage an undeclared naval war that could easily escalate into a declared one. There was not too much concern over the simple question of arming ships, for most of them believed that the president already possessed the power, and if he did not, he should, although they were concerned about the matter of arming munitions-bearing vessels under provisions of the bill. But more than anything else, they feared the implications of the total bill: guaranteeing the president a blank check in the field of foreign relations.

Therefore, as the debate over the revenue bill continued, some of those opposed to the Armed Ship measure met to plan the fight against it. LaFollette became the most important single figure in this activity. He immediately started rounding up senators to join him in organizing a filibuster against the bill. With only a few days remaining in the session, a filibuster would have a good chance of succeeding if enough senators were willing to participate in it to some degree. Apparently, neither LaFollette nor any other senator who was concerned about the implications of the bill considered any possibility of organizing a faction that might amend the proposal, with some clause that would limit the president's powers. The amendments that were offered were apparently put forward independently, and they dealt only with preventing the arming of munitions-bearing ships.

Not all the antiwar bloc was willing to go along with a filibuster, for it would seem that even those who might have been willing to vote against the bill could not bring themselves to block it by talking it to death. Therefore, LaFollette was left with only the hard core of progressive Republican opponents of belligerent diplomacy who would be amenable to filibuster—Norris, Clapp, Gronna, Cummins, and Works. Kenyon, opposed to the bill but not sure about the wisdom of the filibuster, sat in on some of the conferences at which the mechanics of it were discussed, but he did not join them in their efforts.[11]

There is some question as to whether the five Democrats who would oppose the bill and who would be blamed for being a part of the filibuster sat in. George Norris, writing twenty-six years after the event, says that Stone was among the filibusterers. However, it is probable that Norris was taking some license or that he had allowed the passage of time to blur his memory. He probably meant that Stone was one of the dissenting senators, for the evidence is strong, as will be shown, that Stone had nothing to do with the planning of the filibuster and, in fact, was to take steps to get the bill onto the floor and voted on. Both Cummins and Works, during the course of their speeches on the bill, would imply that they were ignorant of any conscious cooperation on his part.

Some other senators did apparently sit down with some of the dissenters to talk about filibusters, even though they had no intention of participating, or even of opposing the bill publicly. They did not want to see the bill pass, but they were not in a position to defy either presidential pressure or constituent anger by taking a position against it, let alone by aiding a filibuster. They knew of the dissenters' plans (for those opposed to the bill had made no secret of their intentions), and therefore, to the extent that they could, these senators came to talk with them, not only to lend moral support, but also to give technical advice on how to conduct the filibuster.

Norris, to whom some of them spoke, said that he and his colleagues who planned to filibuster appreciated the moral support and the advice, but what they really needed was someone to take up time during the debate. The person need not agree with them; he only needed to take up time defending the Armed Ship Bill.

Accordingly, he related many years later, at least two of the senators who had come to him with advice and who had indicated their unwillingness or inability to speak openly against the bill, agreed that they would talk on behalf of the bill at great length. He implies that both these men were Democrats, which would lead one to the conclusion that the reason for their reluctance to oppose was their concern about being shut off from executive patronage or incurring Wilson's disfavor in some other fashion. He also implies that had not the pressure built up in the late hours of the filibuster to get the dissenters to stop talking, some of the others who conferred with him might also have taken the floor in order to consume time.[12]

It is not surprising to find senators behaving in this fashion, agreeing with filibusterers to assist them in their plans by speaking for the bill being opposed. It is not an uncommon practice, particularly when the senators are of the president's party and he is strongly committed to the matter in question.

What is interesting to note is that neither Norris, LaFollette, nor anyone else ever publicly identified these men; either those who allegedly helped out by speaking on behalf of the bill, or those who simply came to give moral support. Perhaps this is understandable in the case of LaFollette—he did not write his own memoirs and perhaps never even told his biographers (his family) who they were. But it is hard to understand in the case of Norris.

The latter survived into the forties, wrote his own memoirs, and certainly knew who they were. He could hardly claim, in 1943, that he might be damaging their careers, because most of them were dead or at least out of politics by then, and, further, the public and most historians were inclined to take a more sympathetic view of dissent back in 1917 as the years passed. If he did not identify them because to do so would violate a confidence, he would be inconsistent, for as will be noted during the debate over the war resolution, he was given an antiwar letter by a senator who was afraid to use it, because of pressure, and by 1943 he had no hesitation in naming that particular legislator.

While reflecting on this, one must also look at the attitude towards the situation at this time of Henry Cabot Lodge. His views on the matter are best revealed in a letter he wrote shortly after Wilson's Armed Ship speech, to Theodore Roosevelt.

He told the ex-president that the Wilson speech was unfortunate. The proposal was not nearly strong enough. Lodge also believed that the Republicans would now have to double their efforts to force a special session of the Congress, for although the Massachusetts senator had very little faith in his colleagues, he thought that it would be better to have them around than to have the president alone for nine months. He was particularly critical of the peace element in the Congress—a few sincere pacifists and an even larger number of "pro-Germans," as he perceived them.[13]

These comments would appear to be at variance with the public statements of some of his close allies, particularly Weeks and Smoot. However, as will be noted, Lodge was able to persuade most of them to abandon their all-out opposition to the bill even before the Zimmermann Note was made public and opposition to arming merchant ships became politically dangerous. Only the progressives in the minority party, who were out of Lodge's orbit, and a few others such as Jones and Townsend, would continue to attack the measure. In the Foreign Relations Committee, all the Republicans would be willing to support a "strong" bill, with a strengthening clause inserted.

Even before the introduction of the Armed Ship proposal, Lodge's desire to have a special session had led him to take an unusual step. He would need the collaboration of all Republicans in order to filibuster several of Wilson's major projects and thus force the president to call the special session. This would mean working with the progressive faction of his party, and that meant dealing with LaFollette, the "radical," whom the Massachusetts senator regarded as pro-German, and worse yet, a disloyal Republican.

The Wisconsinite had been thinking about the possibility of a special session as well, for, like Lodge, he wanted Congress in Washington during the summer months to keep tabs on Wilson. Neither Lodge nor LaFollette, despite their differences on almost every matter that came before the Congress, trusted the president to run the country in his absence. The former feared that perhaps Wilson would allow the war fever to die down; the latter was concerned about the possibility that the chief executive might do something that would provoke war.

The two wings met on February 23, three days before the Armed Ship message was delivered. For the conservatives, it was Lodge, Weeks, Smoot, Brandegee, and Penrose; for the progressives, LaFollette, Norris, and Miles Poindexter of Washington. There was little discussion at the meeting, for each side was well aware of what was needed. They agreed to join forces in preventing votes on a number of key bills before the Sixty-fourth Congress expired on March 4.

Almost as soon as the meeting broke up, they put their plan into action. All eight of them rushed to the floor and began to delay action on the revenue bill, the major item on the agenda at the moment. Democrats looked on in dismay and amazement at what John Sharp Williams called the "unprecedented" sight of LaFollette and Penrose working together.[14]

This particular delaying action lasted until Saturday morning, when the Republicans agreed to call it off until the following Wednesday, February 28. There would still be enough legislation pending to put pressure on Wilson to call Congress back into session. However, once the president made his announcement that he wanted the power to arm merchant ships and antiwar groups gave evidence that they were going to filibuster this proposal, Lodge and his allies quietly withdrew from any active participation in efforts to delay legislation.

The specific planning of the filibuster against the Armed Ship Bill appears to have been left largely to Norris. While LaFollette had rounded up the volunteers, the Nebraskan was the best man to deploy them, for he was a much better parliamentary tactician than his Wisconsin colleague. The latter may have been the spiritual leader of the dissenters, but it was Norris who was responsible for their success by his efforts in coordinating the fight.

Norris knew that only a few senators would actually help in trying to block a vote, with a few more willing to help by consuming time speaking either for or against the measure. Therefore, he arranged a battle plan which would save the strongest and the least vulnerable speakers till the last—LaFollette and himself—and let those who might be likely to be pressured go first. This would probably explain why the first anti-bill speech was made by Kirby, who, although committed to the antiwar cause, was not really known to the others. One could not know if he would capitulate to White House pressure. The other Democrats also spoke early in the debate; only Harry Lane was available on the last day. Fatally ill, Lane knew that he had a short time to live and would be immune to any sort of White House threats.

Norris's plan envisioned some seventy-two hours of debate on the bill, since he could not at this time imagine that other matters would intervene and actually leave only a little more than half of that for the dissenters to fill. With this figure of seventy-two hours in mind, he arranged a schedule so that at least three of those who were actively trying to prevent a vote would be on the floor at all times.[15]

The *Laconia*

While Wilson was speaking to the Congress on his proposal for arming merchant ships, news was being received in Washington about the sinking of a British ship, the *Laconia,* with two American women among the dead. This information was being passed around the floor during the speech.

In his speech breaking relations with Germany, Wilson had spoken of "overt acts" on the part of that nation following her resumption of unrestricted submarine warfare. In his Armed Ship message he said that there had not yet been any such acts as might cause the United States to take more drastic steps. However, he decided on the instant that he would consider the sinking of the *Laconia* as that act. Burleson, conferring with members of the Congress about the Armed Ship Bill, informed the members of the Senate Foreign Relations Committee and the House Foreign Affairs Committee of that fact in the afternoon. It is Link's contention that Wilson believed this incident would be enough to push the Congress to pass the bill in the way he wanted it.[16]

The newspapers also tended to think that this incident was enough. Almost uniformly the larger papers in the country came out in favor of the Armed Ship Bill. However, rather than focus on the *Times* and other major journals, this writer has picked out a sampling of opinions from papers in states represented by senators who would oppose the passage of the bill. It should be pointed out that these are extracted from a compendium of opinions collected by the *Times*, which favored the bill, and they do not reflect the disapproval of such as the Hearst press. But there is some significance.

In Nebraska the *Lincoln State Bulletin* and the *Omaha Bee* said that Wilson had expressed the mood of the country. There would not be war, said the *Bulletin,* unless Germany wanted it. The *St. Louis Globe* applauded the action and lamented the possibility that Wilson might not move swiftly enough. The *Pioneer Press* in St. Paul, Minnesota, said that not to support the president would be to deny the cause of the nation. The *Milwaukee Sentinel* said that for Congress to refuse the president would be to show that America was a divided nation. In Bismarck, North Dakota, the *Tribune* said that Congress owed its support, and in Grand Rapids, Iowa, the *Herald* endorsed the president and his action; and the *San Francisco Chronicle* argued that arming merchant vessels was the only way to ensure respect for American rights.[17]

But probably the most telling comment, as peace groups began to rally in Washington to protest the bill, and as William Jennings Bryan once again prepared to come to the capital to confront another crisis, calling passage of the Armed Ship Bill a sure sign of war, was that of the son and brother of the victims of the *Laconia:* "When is our government going to do something?"[18]

February 27-28 1917

By the twenth-seventh it was apparent to all of Washington that a split had developed in the Senate Foreign Relations Committee over the Armed Ship proposal. Four members of the committee opposed the bill as the president sought it, favoring instead one with an amendment attached that would have prohibited the arming of merchant ships which had munitions aboard. They were Stone, who indicated that he would take his fight to the floor and not attempt to obstruct the bill by bottling it up in committee; O'Gorman, who the *Times* implied was motivated by anti-British feelings; Hitchcock, whom they labeled as pro-German; and Republican William Alden Smith of Michigan.

Lodge and his faction opposed this idea, as did most of the Democrats, men such as Williams, Swanson, Pomerene, and Pittman, who rarely went against Wilson on foreign policy matters. However, the committee did approve another amendment to the bill, this one proposed by Lodge.

As noted in the Massachusetts senator's letter to Theodore Roosevelt following the introduction of the Armed Ship proposal, he not only was anxious for his party to back the arming of merchant vessels, lest it be charged with dragging its feet and not being responsive on the matter of protecting American rights, but, moreover, he wanted to strengthen it beyond what Wilson had proposed. Therefore, he persuaded a majority of the committee, including the Democrats, to add an amendment which would repeal an 1819 statute that prohibited American merchant vessels, armed against pirates of that era, from firing on the ships of nations with which the country was not at war. He argued, and apparently most persuasively, that without this repeal the Armed Ship Bill would be worthless, for American law would make outlaws out of the seamen. Some of the Democrats were probably hesitant at first, for there was no word on this from the White House or from the State Department. The Republicans no doubt accepted Lodge's interpretation without question; they were mostly Lodge men, such as Fall, Brandegee, Weeks, and Wadsworth. Borah, also a member of the committee, was not, but in this instance, he was completely in sympathy with Lodge. Smith, the lone minority member to oppose the bill was, as previously noted, frequently aligned with the antiwar faction. He subsequently ceased his opposition and backed the bill.[19]

Some Republicans indicated on the twenty-seventh that their initial opposition to the bill when Wilson first asked for it was not so much opposition to the idea of arming merchant ships as it was an expreesion of their concern that, no matter what powers they might give him, they could not rely on Wilson to use them in the full defense of American rights. It is probable, however, that most of them, members of the Foreign Relations Committee and others, were sincere in their original condemnation of the bill and that Lodge, some time between Wilson's speech and the twenty-seventh, had persuaded them that supporting the bill and strengthening it was much better than using the opportunity to take a few more shots at the president by criticizing and opposing it.[20]

Therefore, the bill that emerged from committee was as much the work of Lodge as anyone else, and the coalition behind the bill was clearly more his work than any other senator's. The senior Republican defended the idea of repeal of the 1819 statute on the twenty-seventh during a colloquy with LaFollette over some matters associated with the naval appropriations bill. The latter had broken into a defense of the appropriations bill by Swanson (once again shouldering the burden in place of Tillman), by asking if any items in this measure related to the president's message of the previous day.

Lodge also defended the position that the Armed Ship Bill was necessary because, while vessels could defend themselves, it was only under certain conditions, as against pirates, and the government could not loan or give them arms without new legislation. LaFollette, beginning on a theme that the antibill forces would use frequently in the debate, said that the government already possessed this power and thus the bill was unnecessary. Fall and Norris continued the argument, with some time being spent over the definition and present-day application of the word "pirate."[21]

LaFollette's first effort to hold up debate on the Armed Ship Bill came when Stone went before the full Senate and asked for the niceties of a first and second reading. After the introduction James Watson of Indiana, new to the Senate, but soon to be one of the Republican stalwarts, took up some time heckling the Missourian by asking if the committee was unanimous in its support of the bill. Stone would not verify the matter for him. The Wisconsin senator then claimed that the Senate Foreign Relations chairman, in asking for unanimous consent, had not specified which bill he was talking about; therefore, there had been no objection. Now that it was clear that he had been talking about the Armed Ship Bill, he (LaFollette) was objecting to unanimous consent. Further, he charged that Stone had not even asked for unanimous consent but that the presiding officer had taken it for granted. He wanted the whole matter reopened.

The debate over whether the chair had made a valid ruling was a very complicated one, with even Smoot taking up the defense of LaFollette, and Stone admitting that he had not asked for unanimous consent. Finally, after considerable wrangling, Stone conferred with some other senators and agreed to withdraw his request for a second reading. This seemed to satisfy everybody.[22]

LaFollette claimed afterwards that he was opposed to any business being taken up until the revenue bill, which by unanimous consent was to be before the Senate until voted on, was out of the way. In addition, he told a reporter that he wanted the public to know about the Armed Ship measure before it was voted on. His actions were not unnoticed by the press, which began to suggest that perhaps this was the beginning of a filibuster.[23]

The twenty-eighth was the day for the senators to vote on the revenue bill. However, before they could get around to it, they had to wait for other matters to be disposed of. First, Oscar Underwood of Alabama wanted to discuss oleomargarine; then, Wadsworth wanted to talk about diversion of the Niagara River; and finally, Ashurst insisted on bringing up the matter of Indian appropriations.

The debate and vote on the revenue bill went on into the night, as peace groups roamed the corridors buttonholing legislators on the matter of the Armed Ship Bill. The votes on the various amendments offered on the twenty-third by the Republicans as part of their earlier strategy all came out satisfactorily for the administration; in each instance they were beaten down, some by rather impressive majorities. Early in the morning of March 1, the final version of the bill was passed 47–33.[24]

At this point Stone asked for the disposition of any further parliamentary niceties and immediate consideration of the Armed Ship Bill. LaFollette objected. Penrose then moved that the Senate take up the matter at ten the following morning, but they turned this idea down. They then agreed to a ten-minute recess, while they went into little huddles on the floor, deciding how best to deal with the problem. When they reconvened, LaFollette took the floor, asking that the *Journal* be read. Poindexter objected.

The Wisconsin senator said that he would gladly agree to stop, provided that the Senate agree to let the bill lie over till Friday. This would mean, if the body accepted his proposal, that it would not come before them again until approximately forty-eight hours before adjournment.

If the senators who were still on the floor at this hour had any hesitation about cutting off at least a third of the time remaining in the season, they did not show it. Certainly, they must have known about the plans for a filibuster. Perhaps, considering the lateness of the hour, they were just too tired to care. One or two, including Fall, did grumble about the fact that the bill might never see the light of day, but LaFollette's proposal was accepted.[25]

As the senators headed home through the chilly Washington morning, the presses were printing a story that would alter all plans made that evening. Most historians would also agree that it would alter, as well, the course of history.

6

THE ZIMMERMANN NOTE: MARCH 1 1917

As the Senate convened shortly after noon, the front page of every news-paper in the country carried a story that was perhaps one of the most startling in American history. It was an Associated Press release to the effect that the United States had in its possession a note, reported to have been sent by the German Foreign Minister, Zimmermann, to Mexico, proposing an alliance between the two nations (and Japan) if and when the United States and Germany went to war—an eventuality that the sender seemed to feel was imminent. It would be known to history as the Zimmermann Note.

In the view of many historians, this telegram was the most important single factor in persuading a large number of Americans that war with Germany must be faced. It produced alarm, shock, and resentment around the country. The various newspapers published fiery editorials denouncing the note as a threat to all Americans.

The accounts were vague. How had the United States acquired the note? how long had they been in possession of it? why had they chosen to release it now? However, to most Americans, and this included a great many of the legislators, the fact that it existed was all that was important.[1]

Among the antiwar faction in the Senate, there was consternation. Some of them believed that it was a forgery, or wanted to believe that it was, but others, who recognized this to be wishful thinking, concen-trated on the threat to peace. They were most concerned by the fact that all too many of their colleagues were taking it at face value.

The note had reached the United States by way of Great Britain, for British intelligence had intercepted it as far back as January 16 when it had been originally sent, and had decoded it. (They had been able to decode German messages for some time.) Actually, the British had four notes, for they had obtained one from the conventional wireless, one by tapping the roundabout cable that went through Stockholm and Buenos Aires, one from the diplomatic cable, also by tapping, and a final one by "acquisition" in Mexico City. This last one was the one they needed, because they could not foresee how the United States would react to the news of how they had gotten the other three.[2] Further, they did not want Germany to know that they had broken the code.

It was not until the Mexican note was received that they decided that it was time for Walter Hines Page to know about it. Even with his strong pro-Allied sympathies and frequently distorted sense of loyalties, Page would have to be convinced that it was genuine; so significant was the import of the message. He was convinced; then he and some of his aides sat down and worked out a scheme designed to ensure that not only would Wilson be convinced, but that there would be no problem about the protocol involved. When all these machinations had been worked out, the ambassador wired the State Department to be prepared for an important message.[3]

The message arrived in Washington over the weekend and Wilson got word of it on Saturday February 24 or Sunday February 25. Frank Polk was the first one to learn of its existence; he was in charge of the State Department for a few days while Lansing took a three-day weekend, and as soon as he saw it he immediately recognized its importance. He took it to Wilson, who apparently never doubted it for a moment, but exploded with rage and indignation. He was tempted to release the news immediately, but Polk was able to restrain him. He advised the president that it would be better to wait for Lansing to return in order to determine how best to deal with it, and Wilson agreed. But he sent Polk to get the copy of the message out of the Western Union files, no easy matter, since the company was reluctant to violate a federal law concerning the secrecy of its files, and it took the State Department counselor several days to get it.

Lansing returned on the twenty-seventh, the day after the president had delivered his Armed Ship speech. He too advised that they go slow on releasing the news of the message, for it might appear to be an attempt to pressure the Congress. With the mini-filibuster now in progress, and with the antiwar bloc making noises about filibustering the Armed Ship Bill, there had to be extreme caution about just how to handle the explosive piece of information they had.

By the twenty-eighth, however, Wilson felt that he could not wait any longer. He knew that Stone had come out against the bill as he (Wilson) wanted it; Stone was not going to play the role of the good soldier this time, and that put the bill in some danger. Wilson called Lansing and told him to meet with Gilbert Hitchcock, the second ranking member of the Foreign Relations Committee, and show him the telegram.[4] Obviously, Hitchcock was not the best person to be invited to see the note, for as we have seen, not only was he a prominent neutralist, but he had supported the Stone amendment to the Armed Ship Bill in the Foreign Relations Committee. However, he was the second ranking member, and protocol dictated that he be the one asked over to the State Department to see the message.

There is an interesting and compelling point to consider here. Why Hitchcock and not Stone? Stone's position on the wording of the Armed Ship Bill, at this point, was no different from that of the Nebraskan, and what was more important, he had put aside his better judgment many times to do the president's bidding, which is more than could be said for Hitchcock. We do know that Wilson had not shown Stone the Zimmermann Note on the twenty-sixth, when the two talked on the matter of the Armed Ship message, so we can rule out the possibility that Stone knew of it and still was obstinate. Therefore, there appears to be no reason for either the president or Lansing to doubt that the Missourian would behave any differently in this instance than he had in the past, putting aside his own doubts and accepting the responsibility thrust upon him by his perception of party loyalty in a time of crisis. It would have been one thing if they had brought in Williams or Swanson, Wilsonian loyalists, but it was Hitchcock who arrived at the State Department at four-thirty on the afternoon of February 28 at Lansing's invitation.

The secretary showed him the note, and the senator from Nebraska's first reaction was one of disbelief. Eventually Lansing was able to persuade him of its authenticity and managed to elicit some rather harsh and critical comments on Germany from him. One writer says that this latter fact was particularly important in convincing the administration of the effect that the letter would have on the American public.[5]

Lansing asked him to take charge of the bill in committee and get it out on the floor. He also asked him to notify Stone of the contents of the note. Hitchcock agreed; as we have seen, he was in concurrence with the concept of armed neutrality, although he preferred it with the Stone amendment added to the bill, so it did not amount to a major reversal of behavior for him to agree to become the spokesman for the committee's proposal. He left the State Department, one of the few men in the country aware of the existence of the Zimmermann Note and the government's possession of it. In all probability, as will be observed, he did inform Stone as Lansing had requested.

Then Lansing took another step which he and Wilson had earlier agreed upon. The time had come for a public release of the note, but in a manner that would not suggest that the administration was trying to "pressure" Congress. This would involve "leaking" it to the press, with instructions not to reveal the source of the information; and so the secretary gave the information to E. M. Hood of the Associated Press, with additional instructions not to let it out until ten that evening.[6]

Writing of this period, Link maintains that Wilson was not trying to pressure Congress, but evidence is strong to the contrary. He believes that Wilson did not think there would be obstacles to passage of the bill, that the *Laconia* incident was enough of a goad to persuade the legislature to pass it. However, the House committee had passed a watered-down version of the original, and the antiwar bloc was grumbling about the possibility of a filibuster, so that it is doubtful that the president could have been sure on the afternoon of February 28 that some additional "push" might not be necessary. It would seem more logical to think (despite Link's view that Wilson simply felt that the public had a right to know of the message) that he was once again trying to make Congress compliant by news that would be hard for it to ignore.[7]

Whatever Wilson's motives, those of Henry Cabot Lodge on the morning of March 1 are quite clear. One can almost see his mind at work the minute he learned of the existence of the Zimmermann telegram.

He regarded the note as an unexpected opportunity. Writing afterwards to Theodore Roosevelt, he said that he believed that it was the one thing that would arouse the country to demand war and would put the president on the spot where he could no nothing to prevent it. However, he first had to verify the authenticity of the note and tie Wilson to it.[8]

So, when he arrived at the Senate that morning he had a resolution to introduce.[9]

Resolved, that the President be required to inform the Senate whether the note signed 'Zimmermann' published in the newspapers the morning of March 1st, inviting Mexico to unite with Germany and Japan against the United States, is authentic and in the possession of the Government of the United States, and if authentic, to send to the Senate, if not incompatible with the public interest, any further information in possession of the United States Government relative to the activities of the Imperial German Government in Mexico.

It is probable that almost every other senator had been framing a similar resolution in his head that morning over breakfast, but to the Democrats the fact that it was Lodge who introduced it was a cause for alarm. To them, anything that he proposed was something to be concerned about. Immediately Claude Swanson left the chamber to telephone Wilson as to what had happened and was no doubt surprised when informed that the president had no objections at all to furnishing an answer. Swanson told this to Lodge before notifying the whole Senate, but the Massachusetts senator wanted to press his resolution.[10]

The Republican leader told his colleagues that there was no danger to the national security, since the resolution stressed the fact that information "incompatible" with the national interest could be held back. However, the Senate continued to haggle over the wording of the message and even the desirability of sending it. Ardent Wilsonians protested that to ask for information would imply a lack of confidence in the president, while Republicans, and some Democrats from the antiwar bloc, argued that some sort of inquiry was warranted. Among those most eagerly seeking an answer was LaFollette, who was concerned about the timing of the release of the note—with the Armed Ship Bill about to come to the floor.

Stone suggested that the best place for the resolution was in his committee, since it involved a foreign policy matter. But Norris objected to this and declined Stone's unanimous consent request, saying that he was afraid that the matter would die in committee. Whatever impression the Nebraskan may have had about the Foreign Relations chairman a few days later, as the two stood charged with obstructionism in the Armed Ship debate, he seems not to have trusted him at this time. He offered a timetable for release of the resolution, but the Missourian declined the offer.

Lodge agreed with Norris—if the resolution was going to be killed, he wanted it done on the floor, not in committee. Williams grumbled something about the fact that nobody was going to kill anything.[11]

Finally Stone got unanimous consent to have the resolution referred to his committee, which immediately went into session to consider it. In committee Stone and O'Gorman broke with the others in insisting that Wilson be asked to reveal his sources. The other Democrats objected to this out of loyalty to the president, and Lodge demurred as well. However, his reservations had nothing to do with loyalty. As he noted in his letter to Roosevelt, he believed that he knew where the letter came from; he thought that it had arrived by way of Mexico, not England, and that this nation had somehow or other managed to "purchase" it there.[12]

87

The discussion in the Foreign Relations Committee did not take much time, and the members returned shortly with their report. With Stone in the minority, insisting on adding an amendment about sources to the resolution, it fell then to Gilbert Hitchcock to assume the responsibility for presenting the majority position. It would be the first but not the last time that the senior senator from Nebraska would be obliged to do so.

For a man who played a major role during a significant period in history, Gilbert Hitchcock has received remarkably little attention from historians, and some of what he has received is not overly flattering. The image of him that one gets from the Armed Ship debate is that of a Wilson loyalist; however, he was anything but that.

Further, he was not even one of Wilson's favorite senators. The president is reported to have been very upset that the Nebraskan succeeded Stone as chairman of the Senate Foreign Relations Committee a year later.[13] For apart from the fact that Hitchcock had frequently been critical on a number of matters related to foreign policy, there had also been opposition on the ship purchase bill (as noted previously), the Federal Reserve plan (which he eventually backed), and most important of all, the conflict created with Bryan over politics in Nebraska.

The relations between Hitchcock and Bryan were such that Wilson had to be careful in distributing patronage, but he generally favored the latter; even after the Commoner left the cabinet the president worried about offending him. In 1916, when Hitchcock was up for reelection, Bryan was sufficiently resentful of the senior senator that he reportedly hoped that Wilson would not even endorse him. The main area of difficulty between the two was Prohibition, with Hitchcock representing the "wets" and Bryan the "drys," and so great was the ex-secretary's feeling about the issue that no compromise was possible.[14]

Although there is some evidence that Hitchcock's behavior on certain issues may well have been due to his resentment of Wilson, this was not true in the area of foreign policy. Here he tended to follow his own path, one which would lead him to support the president on matters where he found himself in agreement, and to oppose him on others. Of particular note is the fact that he was a supporter of the league of nations concept, a highly unusual position for a senator from a state that tended towards isolationism.

It is unfortunate that Hitchcock was involved with men whose biographers choose to use him as a villain or a knave.[15] Writers focusing on the battle over the Treaty of Versailles usually dismiss him as a small-town prairie editor (his papers were anything but small, and he had the advantage of a European education), who was overmatched by Lodge and could not stand up to Wilson. However, in retrospect one must wonder if even a masterful politician such as Kern or perhaps Stone would have been any more successful in dealing with the matter.

The image created by Norris's biographers is even more critical. They see Hitchcock as an opportunistic politician who had gotten support in Nebraska for his neutralist posture; who then, having been reelected, switched over when he saw that national prominence might accompany his becoming the president's spokesman. He makes a convenient villain for them to counterpose to Norris. What they do not explain is why a man who would behave this way would then turn around and oppose the president during the war on a number of issues. If he switched because of an ambition to become president (Hitchcock did flirt with the idea at times, but his bids were never very serious), his behavior is extremely strange.[16]

He was not the ambitious turncoat that Norris's biographers would have him be, nor was he the incompetent that might be gathered from his losing fight to get the United States into the League, nor was he, certainly, a blind Wilson loyalist. But at the moment he was the "acting" chairman of the Senate Foreign Relations Committee in the lack of Stone's ability to act in that capacity.

The report from the Foreign Relations Committee endorsed the Lodge resolution, with minor technical changes. Stone had an amendment which followed the main body of the resolution:

And also to inform the Senate whether this information he has in his possession regarding the letter signed "Zimmermann" originated with any governmental official of any government engaged in the present European war and if so to inform the Senate as to the facts relating to it.

Stone's motives in offering the amendment are obvious: he was responding to the oft-expressed concern of many antiwar spokesmen that the Allied nations were fabricating facts and incidents in order to stir up war sentiment in the United States. What is most interesting about his behavior during this debate is the fact that he was behaving as though he had just heard of the note that very morning. In fact, as has been mentioned earlier, Lansing had instructed Hitchcock to inform him of the note's existence the previous day, and it is unlikely that the Nebraskan would not have done so. Further, it was after Hitchcock returned from the White House and presumably told him, that Stone attempted to "force" the Armed Ship Bill on to the floor.

In addition, one ought to study the nature of Stone's remarks during the course of the debate over the future of Lodge's resolution. While everyone else seemed to be reacting to the information and did not know quite what to make of it, the chairman of the Foreign Relations Committee was taking a much more reflective course, all the while maintaining that the whole thing was news to him. He was acting, not reacting.

We are passing through strenuous and dangerous days just now—a publication of this nature is calculated to excite public opinion and inflame the public mind . . . and . . . develop a tendency towards working up a spirit of belligerency on our part.

He indicated that he saw a distinct possibility that the British press—a frequent scapegoat for antiwar groups—and Lord Northcliffe, the British press lord, had been responsible. And if this were true, no validity could be attached to the note as far as he was concerned. "I want to know the facts before I am swept off my feet by the clamor of the jingoes."

Hitchcock was impatient with this line of questioning. He said he believed that pressing the president too closely might impair his work, and he did not feel that it was appropriate to cross-examine the chief executive. "I am opposed to war also," he said, "but a government must have its secrets."

Stone received some support for his arguments. Hardwick was concerned about the source also, arguing that if it could be shown that the note came from one of the belligerents (in this case, England), he would be leery of it. Kirby was even more direct. He said that he was not so much concerned about the source as he was about the way it had come to light. He charged that Wilson had released the note when he did by leaking it, in order to pressure the Senate into passing the Armed Ship Bill.

Thomas was not sure about authenticity, either. He was concerned about the timing: just how long had the United States been in possession of it before the public heard about it? Williams impatiently answered him that once authenticity could be proved, all other matters were irrelevant.

Smith of Michigan, suggesting that he had some background in international affairs and thus was qualified to make a judgment on the matter, said that he doubted that the note was of any value at all. He would support the Lodge resolution, but he was of the opinion that no sophisticated and intelligent diplomat would commit such a stupid blunder. The whole thing was just too impossible for him to believe.

Williams was growing impatient with those who would not believe the note to be authentic and a threat to the United States. He complained that this dialogue was becoming a rehash of the conversations in the

Foreign Relations Committee and that only Chairman Stone remained unconvinced of the note's validity. O'Gorman challenged him on this, stating that he, too, was a member of the committee and that he was not convinced either.

The New York Democrat used the opportunity to make one of his last statements as a senator on behalf of the Irish attitude toward Britain. He said he believed that the British press had inflamed American attitudes to a point where senators were reacting to the note without thinking. He said that the British had been flooding the United States with propaganda so as to draw it into the conflict, and he sensed another trick here. He implied that any note that came to the United States by way of England was suspect, and therefore he wanted to find out if they had any hand at all in the American procurement of the message. If it could be shown that they had, then, as far as he was concerned, it would destroy the validity of it and would be further proof of their intentions.

Lodge spoke again on behalf of his resolution. He pointed to the XYZ affair as an example of the necessity of secrecy in diplomacy. He dismissed the allegations of Kirby with the comment:

I am no blind follower of the President [one of the biggest understatements in American history], but I am a blind follower of the interests of the United States. I think it is in our interest to know whether or not the document is authentic and not to ask questions which might convey false implications or embarrass the President of the United States.

Smith of Georgia offered a substitute resolution which he hoped would cover the Lodge proposal and the Stone amendment:

That the President be requested to furnish to the Senate whatever information he has concerning the note published in the press of this date, purporting to have been sent Jan. 19, 1917 by the German Secretary for Foreign Affairs to the German Ambassador to Mexico, which is in his opinion not incompatible with the public interest.

This seemed to satisfy everybody. Fall and Brandegee, who had been supporting the original, immediately concurred, and Stone was willing to drop his amendment. He did get in a few remarks, however, in his speech withdrawing it. He was particularly caustic about Lodge's motives, suggesting that there was something odd about the Massachusetts senator objecting to his (Stone's) amendment. He wondered aloud about Lodge's sudden support of Wilson when an amendment probing deeper into the matter was presented.

His other comment was apparently aimed at Hitchcock and would seem to support the point that the latter complied with Lansing's request and informed the chairman of the Foreign Relations Committee of the nature and contents of the Zimmermann Note.

I shall use such powers as I have to prevent this country from entering war until I find that vital interests and honor are assailed and that there is no honorable escape. I have been frank with the President, I talk to him as I would to another Senator [how Wilson viewed this, if it is true, is questionable]. I do not go on to the White House like some other people and immediately proclaim my admiration and approval of whatever the President suggests.

Stone appeared more alarmed at Hitchcock's defection from the neutralist ranks on this issue than at that of any other senator. Unanimous consent was granted and the resolution agreed to, but not before Ben Tillman entered the chamber to make another of his colorful contributions. "The note is obviously a forgery," he said, "because the plot is so monstrous. Why, everyone knows that such an alliance is impossible. The Japanese hate the Germans like the devil hates holy water."[17]

Lodge was exultant. He had, as he wrote Roosevelt, connected the message to the White House.[18]

The reply to the request arrived before the senate adjourned. Knowing that some sort of request would come, and having no reservations about furnishing some sort of answer, Lansing had begun the preparation of a reply. It was completed after he left his office, brought to him at the Italian embassy where he was dining, and he signed it. The note then went to the White House, where Wilson signed it in turn, and sent it on to the Senate.[19]

The reply stated that there was little doubt as to the authenticity of the note and that it had been in the possession of the United States for about a week. However, it added, questions of national security forbade any disclosure of sources.

The House Vote

The House passed the Armed Ship Bill on the afternoon of March 1. It was not what Wilson wanted, for the measure omitted the "other instrumentalities" clause and included another amendment which prohibited the War Risk Insurance Bureau from insuring munitions-bearing ships. But this form passed by a large margin, no doubt swelled by news of the Zimmermann message, 403—13. The president was not happy with this and pinned his hopes on a strong, unamended bill from the Senate, which House leaders believed they could eventually get through.

For an analysis of how the lower chamber felt about the matter, one might look at the way it handled an amendment similar to Stone's introduced by Cooper of Wisconsin. One hundred twenty-three congressmen voted for this proposal, including most of those from the Middle West and Pacific coast areas. This is a much clearer index of antiwar sentiment in the House than the final vote on the amended bill.

Voting "no" on the measure, which ultimately passed, were Cooper, Cary, Stafford, Nelson of Wisconsin, Lindbergh of Minnesota, Helgesen of North Dakota, Benedict of California, Wilson of Illinois, and Davis of Minnesota, Republicans; Sherwood of Ohio, Shackleford and Decker of Missouri, Democrats; and London, Socialist, of New York. For Lindbergh, who had been defeated in the primary the previous year, it was the last act of his political career.[20]

7

THE DEBATE

March 2 1917[1]

Shortly after the opening of the Senate on March 2, Stone called up the Armed Ship Bill for discussion—labeled, for official purposes, Senate Bill 8322. After a series of motions and roll call votes, the upper chamber agreed that it would be scheduled for debate at four that afternoon after conclusion of the debate on naval appropriations.

Some of the group that planned to filibuster objected even to this—the longer the delay, the better—but one must avoid using this roll call on the procedural problem as a means of assessing sentiment against the bill. Some senators certainly not in sympathy with the dissenters voted with them, concerned primarily with the timing of the debate on the naval bill and on other matters. Similarly, at four when the time came to begin the debate on the Armed Ship measure, George Chamberlain, as chairman of the Military Affairs Committee, moved to delay it even further so as to be able to discuss army appropriations. However, the Senate overruled this suggestion, support for it coming only from the opponents of the Armed Ship Bill and a few others who were apparently more interested in the procedural problem than in blocking debate on armed ships. This defeat of Chamberlain's motion meant that when the Senate formally began to discuss the bill, exactly forty-four hours remained of the life of the Sixty-fourth Congress.

Stone introduced the matter and then explained that since he could not personally support the majority report of the Foreign Relations Committee, he would withdraw from his position as committee spokesman.

He indicated that he would want to push for his amendment and that, therefore, the floor manager for the measure would be Hitchcock. He made it quite clear, prior to turning the bill over to Hitchcock, that he would work to bring the matter to a vote.

For his part, Hitchcock's introduction could hardly be called a ringing endorsement. He conceded that it did not represent his best judgment, but that he preferred to trust Wilson under the circumstances. A number of antiwar senators would later take particular delight in fixing on this statement; the bill's own sponsor was not particularly enthusiastic, indeed, almost hesitant.

The text of the bill read:

That the commanders and crews of all merchant vessels of the United States and [those] bearing the registry of the United States, are hereby authorized to arm and defend such vessels against enemy attacks and the President of the United States is hereby authorized and empowered to supply such vessels with defensive arms, fore and aft; and also with the necessary ammunition and means of making use of them; and that he be and is hereby authorized and empowered to employ such other instrumentalities and methods as he may in his judgment and discretion deem necessary and adequate to protect such vessels and the citizens of the United States in their lawful and peaceful pursuits on the high seas.

That the sum of $100,000,000 is hereby appropriated to be expended by the President of the United States for the purpose of carrying into effect the foregoing provisions, the said sum to be available until the first day of January, 1918.

The next two sections dealt with financing.

That the President be authorized to transfer so much of the amount herein appropriated as he may deem necessary, not exceeding $25,000,000, to the Bureau of War Risk Insurance, created by act of Congress approved September 2, 1917, for the purpose of insuring vessels, their freight, passage monies, and cargoes against loss or damage by the present risks of war.

The Stone amendment is an addendum following the first paragraph.

Provided: That nothing therein shall authorize the President to employ or direct any person to manage or operate any arms placed on any merchant ship of the United States as herein authorized and

Provided: That it shall not be lawful for any merchant ship, supplied by the President with arms as herein provided, to carry or convey as part of the cargo, any munitions or other supplies of war destined for delivery to the armed forces of a belligerent nation engaged in war with another nation with which the United States is at peace, and

Provided further: That it shall not be lawful for any merchant ship which may be under the convoy or immediate protection of any public vessel of the United States to carry or convey as part of her cargo any munitions or other supplies of war destined for delivery to the armed forces of a belligerent nation engaged in a war with another nation with which the United States is at peace.

Hitchcock defended the need for the bill by pointing to the nature of the problem, while conceding that the lateness of the hour would necessarily leave little time for consideration. The president, he said, had asked for this authority only for the purpose of maintaining neutrality, for it was the purpose of this legislation, he added, solely to protect citizens and vessels on the high seas. He explained that part of the bill (section one) which gave the armed merchant vessels the right to fire on submarines, something which, he argued, they would have been forbidden to do otherwise, because of the 1819 statute.

The Nebraska Democrat agreed that the bill held out the possibility of war, but he said that he believed armed neutrality was a better course of action than doing nothing. He indicated that he had no reservations about trusting Wilson, for in the past he believed that the president had shown himself committed to the cause of peace, devoted to keeping the United States out of the war in Europe, and capable of using his powers in a statesmanlike manner. He could be counted upon, Hitchcock assured his colleagues, to do so in the future.

Wesley Jones was skeptical. He was worried, he said, about the matter of the "other instrumentalities" mentioned in the first paragraph. It seemed to him that such a vague phrase would put entirely too much power in the hands of one man. What, for example, he asked, would prevent the president from ordering, under provisions of this clause, American warships to escort British merchant vessels bearing war goods?

Hitchcock had just a few more remarks, and then it was the turn of Lodge to speak on behalf of the bill. However, the Massachusetts Republican did not merely indicate his support (and with it, the support of the majority of the members of his party); he defended it with all the resources at his command. And those resources were being used in support of a measure proposed by a man he considered to be his enemy.

He dismissed Jones's concern, stating that the matter clearly applied only to American vessels. What the bill was all about, he said, was the assurance that Americans could enjoy their rights on the seas without infringement by German submarines. He read a letter from the young man whose mother and sister had died on the *Laconia*, and spoke at great length on how such tragedies should not be allowed to recur.

LaFollette was not impressed. He asked Lodge if, indeed, the president already had such powers as he was asking for—if the legislation was necessary. Lodge replied that he did not; he might arm the ships, but without this bill repealing the provisions of the 1819 statute it was useless.

The gunners would be in jeopardy if they fired on any German submarine while the United States was at peace with that nation. American law would consider them outlaws if they did; therefore, it was imperative that the bill be passed if American shipping was to be protected.

Wouldn't an armed ship be tempted to run the blockade? asked Clapp. He was thinking of the British blockade, which had also had an effect on American commerce. To the Minnesotan, the act of arming merchant vessels and ensuring that they had the right to fire their guns gave them the right to act aggressively against anyone or anything restricting their activities.

No, Lodge assured him, because that would be an act of war. Blockades, he impatiently pointed out to Clapp, start with visitations and confiscations, not with abrupt sinkings without any sort of warning. He then changed direction and began to discuss the Stone amendment. He ridiculed it and the Missourian as well for refusing to trust the president not to arm ships carrying contraband. To do so would be an act of war, said the Republican foreign policy spokesman to the Democratic chairman of the Senate Foreign Relations Committee, and the Democratic president of the United States could be relied upon to avoid such an act.

Lodge's comments were not so impressive to O'Gorman who favored the amendment. This would be the last public utterance of his Senate career, and it would be brief. He suggested that the clause in the Stone amendment would protect the chief executive. For the latter could be deceived into offering protection to ships whose owners had disguised the contraband. In such a way, the New York senator said, the president would be committing an act of war without realizing it.

Cummins questioned Lodge. "Suppose the merchant vessels spotted a submarine before being spotted themselves. Would they be allowed to shoot?" Lodge answered curtly, "I hope they do," and the packed galleries, including British Ambassador Sir Cecil Spring-Rice, applauded.

The applause over, Cummins pressed the meaning of his question. To him, the implications of the bill were that the United States was sending out ships to sink submarines. The Iowan said that there was no way for an armed vessel to know that the submarine meant any harm. If it did, the ship could fire—but the merchantmen were being armed for defensive, not offensive purposes, and if they fired first, this could hardly be construed as a defensive act.

Lodge's answer was a brilliant exercise in sophistry. If the ship was not carrying contraband, he said, then it had a perfect right to fire the

97

minute it saw the U-boat's periscope, for it knew that any attack on it would be illegal. And the simple sighting of a periscope, he told the Senate, is evidence that the submarine plans to attack.

"It is not an act of war," he added, "for a merchant ship to defend itself." He drew an analogy for those senators who were perhaps more familiar with the laws of self-defense on land than with international law. He likened the plight of the merchant vessel in question with that of a man who, while walking down the street, confronts another man who he knows is planning to shoot him. Therefore, he is within his rights in shooting first.

Lodge made no effort to explain how the submarine could know if the ship bore contraband. His assumption seems to have been that the ship could fire on anything, and if it (the ship) was not carrying the contraband, it possessed the legal right to fire, in light of the fact that it knew that the submarine attack would be an illegal one. He did not discuss the legality of whether a contraband-laden vessel could fire first.

The Republican leader also stated that he preferred that the Congress remain in session to deal with problems such as armed neutrality, but this particular problem was too urgent for any delay. The legislature had no alternative but to give the president the powers he asked for. If anything made it clear what Germany's intentions were towards American shipping, it was the Zimmermann Note, and this was reason enough to pass the bill.

In referring at this point to the Zimmermann Note, he clearly indicated that his resolution of the day before, asking for information about it, was little more than a ploy. For he made no bones at this time about the fact that he regarded it as genuine, declaring his contempt for those who believed otherwise; it is a direct threat, he asserted, from a government that seeks to deny Americans their rights.

This was the single most important speech of the debate, first, because it indicated just where the bulk of the Republicans would be in the event that there was a vote on the matter. Second, there was the irony involved— Lodge defending Wilson and urging some hesitant members of the president's party to give him all that he desired.

With the Massachusetts senator's address out of the way, it was the turn of some of the probill Democrats. The first of these was Walsh of Montana, who maintained that it had long been the practice for neutral nations to defend themselves thus against unprovoked attacks by belligerents. They could arm their vessels and convoy their ships, he said; this is a right that is as old as the seas themselves and understood to be a point of international law.

Stone interrupted to point out to Walsh that the law of the sea and the points of international law to which he was referring were designed to deal with pirates at an earlier time in history. Walsh accepted this, but indicated that he believed that the principle remained, even if the pirates did not. It was still, the Montanan reminded the Senate, an extremely effective and perfectly legitimate way of fighting belligerents and blockades. Williams broke in to suggest that there whould be some differentiation between the types of blockades employed in the war. There are, he said, legal and illegal blockades, an example of a legal one being the one Britain was conducting: stopping ships, seizing them, and confiscating their cargo. It could not be compared to the way the Germans were conducting theirs.

Walsh agreed with Williams. He continued, talking about the proper method of enforcing blockades, the right to confiscate contraband seized in a lawful search, and suggested also that it would appear to him that under the terms of the proposed bill it might be legal for the United States to convoy ships as well as to put guns on merchant vessels. Perhaps, he surmised, that was what Wilson had in mind when he referred to the "other instrumentalities."

That was exactly what the dissenting senators were concerned about; that, given such a grant of authority, Wilson could assume that he was empowered to let the navy escort merchant vessels into the war zone and possibly be forced into a fire fight with a German submarine. There would be no question about a state of war if that happened.

Walsh was willing to acknowledge that either of these conditions, arming merchant vessels or allowing the navy to escort them, constituted a threat of war. For once shots were fired, he admitted, war was a matter of hours away. In his analysis of the bill, published in his magazine, LaFollette would place great emphasis on Walsh's speech in making his contention that the Armed Ship Bill meant war and that its supporters well knew it.

Reed asked Walsh if there was any difference, from a legal point of view, between convoying ships or arming them, as was proposed under this bill. Walsh said that the question was largely one of strategy, and Reed replied that it appeared to him that convoying them might be a much more effective way of doing it. He hastened to add that he did not want it to appear that he was not supporting the bill—he was merely seeking information and his line of questioning should not be interpreted as a lack of confidence in the president.

Ollie James took the floor to scoff at the senators who thought that arming merchant ships and letting them fire on submarines was an act of war. A vessel of the United States, he said, had as much right to sail the high seas and defend its rights to do so as "I do to walk down Pennsylvania Avenue."

Hitchcock broke in on him to request the presiding officer to enforce the rule on brevity. The chairman agreed, and James protested. "This is not a filibuster," he said. "It's very interesting."

Brandegee got the floor for a few minutes to discuss what he believed to be the handicaps that would be imposed by the Stone amendment. No one had been pressing that point, but the Connecticut senator wanted all to know why the whole principle of the bill would be imperiled if the amendment was added to the original. After he finished, the Senate briefly turned away from the matter of armed neutrality to deal with a couple of other items.

After this short diversion, the debate on the Armed Ship Bill resumed, with Miles Poindexter speaking for it. He spoke at some length; his speech was less belligerent than that of others, but he was still very much in favor of arming merchant ships. He, too, had no illusions about the potential of the bill; he recognized that it presented a very clear possibility for war and admitted that the moment a submarine was fired upon by an armed vessel, it meant war.

He was the only one of the progressive Republicans favoring the bill to speak for it. Borah did not.

The Washingtonian pointed out to the Senate that the matter of war or peace would hinge, if the bill became law, on the actions of the captain of each armed merchant ship. But despite this rather perilous situation, America, he believed, had no choice. The old standards of morality in naval warfare had become outdated as a result of the development of the submarine, and new methods would have to be found to combat the new situation. He contended that the arguments of those favoring the Stone amendment were irrelevant. The Germans would sink anything, regardless of cargo, he said, and would not stop to inquire if there was contraband aboard. Therefore, the restrictions on the arming of one particular type of merchant ship served no useful purpose at this time.

Clapp asked him if he believed that the bill might allow American warships to escort merchant vessels into the war zone—particularly those with American citizens on board. Poindexter answered that he believed that such an activity might be possible through a broad interpretation of the "other instrumentalities and methods" clause.

But this interpretation did not sit well with Brandegee. He took the floor to disagree with Poindexter, telling him that no interpretation of the proposed measure could possibly suggest that American warships could be used for this purpose. After this answer to the Washington progressive, the Connecticut conservative then devoted a few moments to indicating why he believed that the United States had no real alternative but to risk war by taking the step of arming merchant ships. He admitted that it would heighten the probability of war, for if one merchant ship armed under the provisions of the bill fired on a German submarine, it was war on the spot. But there was nothing else for the United States to do. The ports on the east coast, he pointed out, were tied up, America's merchant fleet paralyzed. Arming merchant vessels was necessary in order to avoid a serious economic crisis.

Now Thomas of Colorado spoke for the bill. He said that he did not believe that a defensive act, such as firing on a submarine attacker, was an act of war, although he admitted that Germany would probably not see it that way. However, he said, regardless of the risk, it had now become necessary for the United States government to ensure its rights as a neutral, and to do this it would have to take the chance of war. He said that he had always opposed war and had frequently voted against measures he thought would bring it, but he believed at this time that the future of the United States as a nation precluded the possibility of letting Germany "get away with it" by intimidating the American merchant fleet out of the seas.

If the reader is somewhat confused at this point about whether or not the bill meant war, whether or not the "other instrumentalities" included the possibility of having the navy convoy merchant ships, and other points raised in the debate, he is not alone. For the senators themselves, as the antibill legislators would point out, did not seem to know just what the bill was all about. There was a considerable degree of confusion even among the bill's advocates as to just what it did mean; all that they could agree upon was that it was necessary to give Wilson the power.[2]

Kirby followed Thomas to the floor with the first antibill speech. He started out by stating that since the president already had the power to arm merchant ships, the bill was superfluous, and represented merely an effort on the part of the administration to create the illusion that the whole nation stood behind the president.

The rest of his speech dealt with what he believed to be the cause of the war fever. He talked about the commercial interests, how they were the only ones who could profit from American intervention. If the people could have their say, he argued, they would reject war by a large margin. For the people knew, he maintained, that they would be the big losers in any American involvement in the European war, while the business interests who were shouting loudly for it would reap a harvest.

He was not sympathetic to Americans who took rides in the war zone.

Citizens who did so, he argued, cannot expect the government to protect them from attacks, and if these incidents continue, the United States is under no obligation to respond by declaring war.

This bill, he added, means war, no matter how it is phrased. At one point, as he neared the end of his speech, he became so carried away with his own oratory, that he blurted out, "Fellow citizens, gentlemen of the convention," and the Senate chamber rocked with laughter. The *Record,* which can be amended, omits his error.[3]

At 10 P.M., after the Arkansan finished, Porter McCumber was recognized. He indicated that he was concerned about the Armed Ship Bill primarily because of the enormous amount of power that it would give the president—power that he believed rightfully belonged to the Congress. He would vote for the bill, he said, but he would prefer that the Congress adopt instead a resolution which recognized the rights of merchant vessels to sail without being threatened by submarines and which also recognized the necessity of arming these ships.

McCumber was being cautious, and to some extent his arguments seem to be in contradiction to his assertion that he would eventually back the president's bill, if and when it came up for a vote. This was very representative of his political style, and he pressed his point in a very deliberate and long-winded manner, probably to the consternation of many of the probill advocates.

As the North Dakotan finished, Hitchcock again got the floor with a request for the unanimous consent of the Senate to drop the Senate bill and to take up the House proposal (HR 21052) as a substitute. This action would obviate returning the matter to the House and would send it immediately to a conference committee. Since administration sources were convinced that the House would accept the Senate substitute, Hitchcock proposed that upon taking up the House bill, the Senate would amend it by striking out everything after the enacting clause and then substitute its own version—including the "other instrumentalities."

However, LaFollette objected to the request for unanimous consent. As he did, Vardaman obtained the floor and the dissenters met to confer on the implications of Hitchcock's request. Although the proposal was designed to shorten the time necessary to secure passage of the bill, it could be turned to the advantage of those seeking to delay it. If they could get Hitchcock's promise that the unanimous consent request would be coupled with an adjournment until the following morning, it would cut down on the time that they would have to consume, virtually by a third.

Vardaman spoke for a relatively short period of time, but his speech was, as usual, impassioned, flowery, and liberally dotted with biblical quotations and literary allegories. He said that he hoped that the United States would retain its sanity in spite of the irrationality in Europe. War, he said, was horrible and he was opposed to the United States becoming involved in any way. That, he said, was why he had consistently refused to vote for appropriations to increase the size of the military and naval forces.

War, he said, would bring a heavier tax burden—a burden that would fall mostly upon those least able to bear it. Specifically, he referred to the poor farmers, such as those in his state, who were already suffering from the impact of the British blockade. Is it less of a crime to rob farmers than it is to inconvenience munitions makers? he asked his colleagues.

Vardaman also said that he opposed the bill because it gave away Congress's power to declare war. The implications of the measure, he added, were such that the warmaking power would now repose in the hands of the president, and in this respect it would be unconstitutional. It was too great a concession of power and would leave the legislature completely out of any participation in deciding the fate of the nation.

After Vardaman concluded, Hitchcock again asked for unanimous consent to have the House bill substituted. Norris, speaking for the dissenters, had informed his fellow Nebraskan that there would be no objections, provided that the resolution also stated that the Senate would stand in recess until ten the following day. Hitchcock agreed, and while a few probill senators were somewhat hesitant, fearing the consequences of a delay, none of them voiced any serious reservations.

Norris and LaFollette walked from the chamber together. It was now early morning of March 3, and less than thirty-six hours remained of the Sixty-fourth Congress and barely twenty-six for the dissenters to take up in debate. Norris told LaFollette that he believed they had won.[4]

March 3 1917[5]

At ten in the morning the Senate met for what would be its final session. The success of the filibuster seemed to be assured, for at least six men who wanted to talk against the Armed Ship Bill were yet to take the floor, and if there were others who were willing to use up time by speaking for it, they as well were possibly still available. Only Norris, despite his prediction in the late hours of the previous session, was worried; he could see the level of anger that was being accorded those who were known to be filibustering against the bill.

The galleries were fuller than usual, for news of a filibuster travels fast in Washington. There was a general stir of excitement; the *Congressional Record* contains more than the usual number of admonitions for silence by the presiding officer, with the customary threats to clear the chamber if they were not heeded. On the floor there was an atmosphere of tension that grew in the last hours to complete chaos. As the time slipped by, ties were loosened, nerves tightened, and tempers grew short. The cloakrooms were cluttered with senators sneaking brief naps, not wishing to be too far away when quorum calls were requested or votes taken. The sense of drama was not lost on anyone—the press, the spectators, the senators themselves, or even the president, who was busily preparing his inaugural address.[6]

Among the proponents of the bill, there was anger and frustration. It was most apparent in Williams and Reed, neither of whom had ever been noted for patience and tolerance of those with whom they disagreed. Hitchcock, not unmindful of his responsibilities, tried to maintain a cool and calm appearance, but eventually gave way to nervous fidgeting. Other senators were even more outspoken in the cloakrooms than Williams and Reed would be on the floor.

The session opened with the usual spate of minor matters that certain members of the Senate were anxious to have dealt with before the Sixty-fourth Congress passed into history. Hardwick wanted a private bill put through for a constituent who had lost money in a post office robbery, Overman had a variety of problems on his mind, Myers wanted to talk about Glacier National Park, and Norris and Smoot were concerned about post office appropriations.

When all this was concluded, Frank Brandegee got the recognition of the chair, asking that the *Record* be read for the senators so that he could show them how the bill proposed in the Senate and the one passed in the House differed. Most of the senators were already well aware of the difference. Brandegee was particularly concerned about stressing the importance of the Lodge addition in the Senate version, allowing merchantmen to fire on U-boats.

Norris challenged him on this, stating that vessels already had the right to arm and to fight. In fact, he added, if that was what the bill was about, then the matter could be dropped, since the president already possessed the power to arm ships on his own authority. As for the right of defense, that was written into international law.

Brandegee was not ready to concede this point, referring to the case of Belgium, where civilians, in defense of their homes, were summarily executed on the spot by the German army. He conjured up a picture of American seamen being tried at drumhead tribunals for defending their rights as neutrals and then shot. The only way that this could be prevented, he said, would be if the German government knew that the sanction of American law lay behind the actions of seamen defending their rights on the seas.

He admitted that arming ships raised the possibility of war. But this did not intimidate him in the least, for he announced that as far as he was concerned, war would be welcome. For the first time during the course of the debate over the arming of ships, a senator made the flat statement that he favored the prospect of war; he thought that war was inevitable because of the course that German-American relations had been traveling.

"I am for peace," he conceded, "but liberty is more important." Now, he insisted, liberty and national honor were at stake. He derided the "pacifists" and their ilk, stating that if they had had their way in 1776, the United States would still be a British possession, the revolutionary war would have been a dismal failure, and George Washington a traitor. America, he said, is threatened by the possibility of a German victory.

LaFollette, writing after the debate, would lay particular stress on Brandegee's speech, as he had with Walsh's, as testimony to the fact that many senators who were for the bill believed that it would be likely to produce war. And he would specifically cite the fact that Brandegee said that he would welcome the possibility.[7]

Warning of the consequences of a German victory, the Connecticut senator said that the "Teutonic and Ottomanic powers" were on the verge of triumph and that America was next. Lest anyone be deceived on their threat to America, he reminded his listeners that the morning papers had carried a story to the effect that Zimmermann had admitted the authorship of the controversial telegram. How else, he asked, can one interpret their intentions?

He wanted war, he admitted, because of the fact that he could not tolerate seeing the United States standing idly by while the "Frankenstein" monster trampled on its honor. "I would vote today for war and would have for the last month. Let us face up to it without equivocation and apology."

Applause greeted his remarks, and the chairman had to admonish the galleries. The general state of confusion there, crowded as they were with diplomats, families of legislators, and the curious, was a matter of concern for some senators. Overman addressed the chair and said that he was disturbed over the fact that he had seen unauthorized persons sitting in places reserved for senator's families. Some additional time was used up while a number of senators solemnly agreed that this was a regrettable situation and should not be repeated.

Most of the senators were on the floor now, with one notable exception—LaFollette. He was in his office, resting and working on the speech that he planned to deliver. His eldest son, Robert Jr., and his personal secretary, John Hannan, would bring him messages from time to time on the progress of the debate, and once in a while he would venture out on to the floor. but for the most part he remained in his office. He believed that the speech he was preparing would be one of the most important ones of his career, and he wanted it to be one of his best.[8] While he rested, his colleagues Norris, Gronna, Clapp, and Cummins watched the floor in order to ensure that the filibuster would not be broken.[9]

Albert Fall was the next speaker. Less gifted as an orator than Brandegee, less polished than Lodge, described in some accounts as being harsh and abrasive, he stated that he favored the bill because he believed in giving the president the instruments he desired. In a few years he would be the chief spokesman for those senators who questioned Wilson's sanity following a stroke, but for now he indicated support for and confidence in the president. He talked about Jefferson and the Barbary pirates, quoted the third president of the United States to antibill senators on how to fight buccaneers, and teased Democratic dissenters about not trusting their own president and not taking advice from the founder of their party.

He agreed to most of the criticism aimed at the bill by its opponents. But still, he believed the measure to be necessary. While it was not a formal declaration of war, it was very close to being one, and that was all right with him. As far as he was concerned, he said, war was necessary and desirable, and if he had had his way, America would have been at war for some time.

Cummins challenged him on the right of merchant seamen to fire on submarines. Even if the United States were to repeal the statute of 1819, he argued, the Germans would still regard their action in firing as illegal and would hang the sailors if they could catch them.

Fall dismissed this, saying that any court would uphold the right of Americans firing on potential attackers. He did not indicate how this would help those men already swinging on the gibbet.

Jones wanted to know about the possibility that the bill might permit armed ships to feel that they could run the British blockade. Like Clapp earlier, he felt that now that the ships had arms, they might be emboldened to try this maneuver. Fall replied that any blockade defiance would be wrong by all standards of international law.

The New Mexico senator continued. He had disagreed with Wilson in the past (and vehemently), he said, but in a moment of crisis, partisanship was out of the question. Convinced that war was imminent, he said that he would vote to give the president the maximum degree of latitude with which to fight. Arming merchant vessels and giving the president his "other instrumentalities" was the least that the Congress could do.

Never before, he said, had America shrunk from a crisis. He then read into the *Record* some one hundred incidents in which the United States had gone to the defense of its citizens and their property rights. American rights were no less precious on the high seas than they were on land. Fall recalled that even Stone had approved of the punitive expedition to Mexico in order to "vindicate" rights there. Stone protested, but Fall, reading from the *Record*, assured the Missourian that he was on record as having approved of it.

He concluded that it was the constitutional duty of the Senate to help the president, and that it could not deny him the power to perform what he felt needed to be done.

I do not want an attempt to be made to force an extra session to be held immediately if that is what my colleagues intend. I say to my friends that I think they are grievously in error, for they will be held responsible to the special session by the people of the United States ...

Not far away from where Fall was speaking, Norris checked his watch. There were less than twenty-four hours remaining in the life of the Sixty-fourth Congress, and most of the morning had been taken up by two men who favored the Armed Ship Bill and also, by their own admission, war with Germany. LaFollette, catnapping in his office, would add Fall's name to that of Brandegee and others who admitted that the Armed Ship Bill meant war.[10]

It was now Stone's turn to deliver what would be the longest individual speech of the debate. He spoke for nearly five hours, the most interesting point being when, during an exchange with one of Wilson's ardent supporters, the Irish-born Democrat from New Jersey, William Hughes, he gave away what some regarded at the time to be confidential information about the navy's plans to fight submarines. He said that they had "submarine chasers," which could be carried on merchant vessels and put into the water in the war zone.[11]

Although he had crossed the Rubicon and now opposed him openly, Stone took great pains to indicate that he still trusted the president. He

praised him for having avoided war until that point, but said that the
chief executive might not be able to continue to do so if the bill passed
in the form that he had asked for. The president was a man of peace, he
added, but the Armed Ship Bill presented too great a danger, not only
to the cause of peace but to the American political system.

The bill, he argued, gave Wilson the power to declare war, a right
reserved by the Constitution to the Congress. Thus, it was contrary to
the spirit of the Constitution and entirely too much for one man to cope
with. Further, he said the United States would be making auxiliaries of
its merchant vessels, thus making the first exchange of shots a de facto
declaration of war.

But the gist of his amendment was the fact that by arming merchant
vessels that were carrying munitions, the government was collaborating
in the shipment of arms to belligerents. He favored free trade, he said,
but not to the extent of aiding it by supplying private munitions-bearing
merchant vessels with government arms.

Hitchcock challenged Stone by asking him if he thought that the
United States would escort or arm ships that it knew were carrying contraband.

Stone answered, "Unless you adopt my amendment, you will. Do you
think that if we pass this bill, the President will not arm those vessels
[the ones carrying munitions] by putting guns and ammunition aboard?"

Hitchcock replied, "I do not believe that it is the President's intention
to arm . . . or convoy ships carrying munitions of war to belligerents."

"I didn't ask about his intentions," said Stone. "I asked if the Senator
believed they could be armed . . . ?"

"They could not be armed without violating our neutrality," said
Hitchcock.

"Then," said Stone, "why are we authorizing the president to arm
[them]?"

Hitchcock virtually repeated himself. "We are not authorizing the
President to arm [merchant ships carrying contraband]."

"I am not talking about munitions ships," said Stone. "I am talking
about arming ships. And surely the Senator must know that the Bill
would authorize the arming of merchant vessels without regard to the
character of the cargo." He went on to discuss with Smith of Georgia
and with Underwood the point that if the amendment he sought was
adopted, the danger to other ships was lessened, since the Germans would
know that if a ship was not armed, no contraband was aboard.

The debate between Hitchcock and Stone points up one of the major
concerns of the opponents of the bill: the fact that it would be virtually

impossible to prevent the arming of munitions ships unless some specific provision made it illegal to do so and required some sort of inspection before a ship bearing arms was allowed to leave port. As O'Gorman had claimed earlier, without some specific provision, the president could not prevent the arming of vessels bearing munitions.

For a lengthy period of time, Stone replied to Fall's case histories of incidents of intervention, with his own list of situations in which the United States had replied with negotiations instead of action. He then went into the background of the European war, the clamor for it in many parts of America—a clamor that he said was the direct result of misleading information put out by the British press—and the way the United States should respond. He said that the war was a lawless and a brutal one, with no profit accruing to the United States should it intervene.

Who would profit? Stone had an impressive list. American investors in British firms, holders of British bonds, the shipping trust, J. P. Morgan —all these, he said, would be the beneficiaries of American intervention. "I stand unmoved on the subject of neutrality," he concluded. The tradition, he went on, was as old as America itself and a legacy of the past that America ought not to discard so lightly. If war came in spite of his effort, he would support it, he said, but he would use all his energies to help the nation avoid it.

It was the greatest effort of his life. He nearly collapsed following his speech and had to be helped from the chamber by Moses Clapp who had been sitting nearby.[12]

It was nearly dusk when he finished. The lights were being turned on in the streets outside and in the corridors of the Capitol. The personnel in the gallery was changing, but the audience was still rapt with attention. Now any serious doubt that a filibuster existed had been removed by Stone's five-hour oration, and people flocked to watch it. Elsewhere, the House of Representatives, angrily waiting for the Senate to wind up its business, adjourned until the following morning.

Norris, Cummins, and Gronna were watching the floor when Hitchcock, following Stone, moved for a limitation on debate. First, he asked for a cut-off at nine o'clock, then ten, then one in the morning, and finally four, all with a fifteen-minute limitation on talks. Norris said he would object to all of these.

"Let's have the names of the objectors," said Ashurst, and the presiding officer assured him that they would be printed.

Hitchcock again moved for a cessation of debate, and when frustrated, said he wanted to develop the fact that there was a filibuster and to identify those responsible.

"I wouldn't hesitate to kill the Bill if I could," said Norris. "But I should point out that those who want it [the bill] are taking up the time. I may not get a chance to talk and I object to those who want the Bill taking up the time and then gagging the rest of us." He then proceeded, with the assistance of Gronna, to take up some more time with a long and rather complicated debate concerning the mechanics of considering unanimous consent rulings, without which there could be no cessation of debate. The two even went to far as to propose that roll call votes had to be taken to determine if the Senate was ready to vote.

Now Hitchcock, seeking to respond to Norris's complaint that the bill's advocates were taking up too much time, proposed that all debate end at three the following morning, but with two-thirds of the remaining time going to one party and one-third to the other. He accepted an amendment from a supporter that it be two-thirds for the opponents of the bill and one-third for its adherents. Cummins objected. He then offered ten hours for the dissenters to make their case. More objections.

Weeks broke into the discussion. He accused Hitchcock of aiding the filibusterers by filing futile motions that he knew had no chance of success. Since the dissenters had made it plain that they would not accept any unanimous consent rulings, the majority was holding up its own proposal.

But the senators continued to press procedural matters, with Harry Lane getting the attention of the chair to chide Hitchcock for taking up time and also for his rather tenuous status as the spokesman for the Foreign Relations Committee. When all the procedural wrangling had been concluded, George Sutherland of Utah, an English-born Republican who would one day sit on the Supreme Court, took the floor for his final speech as a senator (he too had been defeated for reelection). Eighteen hours remained.

It was now clear to everyone, particularly to the leadership, that the dissenters had enough speakers to last out the session. Therefore, it would be necessary to change tactics and try to persuade them to abandon their filibuster, and failing that, at least to get into the *Record* a statement indicating the sentiment of the Senate on the Armed Ship Bill. Hitchcock and Furnifold Simmons of North Carolina met with two Republicans, Brandegee representing the regulars and Kenyon, the progressives.

Kenyon's inclusion is interesting, because not only was he clearly opposed to the bill, but he had sat in on some of the early meetings at which the filibuster was being planned. He, no doubt, made his feelings known at the session with Hitchcock, Simmons, and Brandegee, but they

110

probably informed him that they only wanted him to try to get his colleagues to stop talking—how he voted was his own business. There is no evidence, one way or the other that he tried to, but if he did, he obviously met with no success.[13]

The statement that would reflect the sentiment of the Senate was to be in the form of a round-robin or manifesto, which would indicate that the signatories favored the bill and desired to vote on it. The inspiration probably came from Lodge and some of the Republicans, for they had to be concerned with the fact that some people might not be able to distinguish between the Armed Ship filibuster and their own mini-filibuster of a few days previous. If this is the case, it was probably Brandegee who proposed the idea at the meeting with the other three.

There is some disagreement on who actually drafted the wording of the manifesto. One source suggests that it was drawn up by a bipartisan committee consisting of Lodge, Fall, Sutherland, Nelson, Simmons, Hardwick, Hughes, and Pomerene. Against this idea is the argument that it is unlikely that such a diverse group could agree on the wording in such a short period of time.[14] More to the point is the view of Link that it was drawn up by Lodge, Brandegee, and Borah, with the specific view of exonerating the Republican leadership. If this is true, it was no doubt done with the very close scrutiny of the Democratic leadership,[15] which would always be very careful to watch everything that Lodge had a hand in. They would not want him sneaking something into the petition that would imply a lack of confidence in Wilson.

After Sutherland had finished his address to the Senate, Wesley Jones obtained the floor. He was as critical of the demand that the dissenting senators cede the floor and allow a vote as he was of the bill itself. He said that he resented the contention that those who wanted to have a full and open debate were unpatriotic. He said also that the members of the Senate had a right to debate any subject as long as they chose to do so. In fact, he added that for the lawmakers to do otherwise would be for them to deny their responsibilities.

As for the bill, Jones said that he regarded it as tantamount to a declaration of war. In fact, that was what made it all the more imperative that the Congress remain in session and why the plea for haste was so insidious. He saw all of this as part of a pattern whereby many senators were simply rolling over and giving the president what he wanted without inquiring into the consequences of their action. In reply to one of his questioners, Thomas Sterling of South Dakota, he said that he thought that the practice of investing large amounts of discretion in the hands of the executive was becoming the rule in government, and he would like

111

to see it stopped. He felt that Wilson was trying to "force the Senate out of town," in order to do the job himself.

"I am willing to stay here all summer," he said. "And others are willing to do the same."

He was critical of the British blockade. To him, it was just as inhuman as was the use by Germany of the submarine, for while the U-boat provided a quick, watery death, the blockade slowly strangled the people of the other side. He read into the *Record* excerpts to show the suffering and hardships that resulted from the British blockade.

Nelson, who had been born in Norway, interrupted Jones to inform him that the British did not sink ships. He told him also that over three hundred Norwegian vessels had been stopped by the Royal Navy, searched, and allowed to pass.

Upon regaining the floor, Jones continued his criticism of the bill, although indicating that he would vote for it, but he would prefer it if one of the amendments that had been offered could be added. On the surface, Jones's conduct seems to be rather strange; his language in criticizing the bill was as strong as that of any of the "willful men," yet he was not unwilling to vote for the measure. For an explanation of what appears to be a contradiction in his behavior, one must look at the general nature of the Washington Republican's career—that of a middle-of-the-roader who usually avoided getting caught in embarrassing political positions. He had criticized the bill, thus catering to the antiwar sentiment in his state, he had commented on the rising tide of executive usurpation, but then had stepped back when the threat of a filibuster was raised and avoided getting trapped and branded as an obstructionist.

He concluded his speech. "I am for maintaining rights, but I think that if citizens had done their part and had not insisted on traveling . . . they owe it . . . to help keep us out of the way, so when it ends we can be a factor in the peace."[16]

Behind the scenes, in the cloakrooms, offices, and corridors, the real drama of the debate was taking place. The first names were being scrawled on the petitions, and senators were being deployed by both sides in accordance with their strategy. For the majority, it required that there be enough available in case there was a quorum call; for the dissenting senators, it was necessary that there be someone on the floor to block unanimous consent requests. The galleries were still fairly full and would not begin to thin out until much later in the evening.

Townsend spoke next. He agreed with Jones that there should have been some efforts earlier by the administration to keep citizens off the vessels of warring nations, and reminded everyone that he had always been an advocate of this. He believed that it was the failure of the administration to do this that had created the clamor for war. As for the bill, he worried about the fact that it appeared to give too much power to the president, but felt that given the circumstances of the moment, he had no choice but to vote for it. He indicated, however, that he would prefer to see the Stone amendment added. "If it should mean war, I would hesitate," he said. "But in this solemn hour, I should vote to give notice that Congress is behind the President."

Hardwick announced that he was anxious to get on with the vote and did not want to take up much time, but proceeded to do so anyway. "This is the greatest crisis in our history," he proclaimed. "The President is our Commander-in-Chief in it. We cannot refuse to give him the powers necessary to the execution of his task."

Freedom of the seas and the defense of neutral rights were the issues, the Georgian announced. He did not think the bill would mean war, for he claimed that he trusted Wilson to use his powers wisely. (Statements by Hardwick at other times suggest that he rarely trusted Wilson to use any powers wisely.) He warned the dissenting senators that the prestige of the country would suffer if the bill was defeated and America was shown to be a divided country.

When he had finished, Albert Cummins took the floor. For some time, the senior senator from Iowa had been trying to get the attention of the chair, but without success. He had an amendment which would have forbidden the clearance of any vessel armed under the provisions of the bill from any American port if the vessel was carrying arms or munitions destined for one of the combatants in the European war.

Without this proviso, or one very similar to it, Cummins said, he could not vote for the bill. The other bill (the original) was war-provoking, and while he decried the evil of the German military and the German government, the evil was not such as to bring about a war. He argued that since many of the supporters of the bill admitted that the arming of merchant vessels was an act of war, the question should be given much more serious consideration than it had been thus far. What would be the result, he asked rhetorically, if a formal declaration of war was being posed instead of this bill, which heightened the possibility of war? No one chose to try to answer that question.

He rejected the idea that patriotism, or standing by one's country, precluded a senator's thinking for himself about issues. He rejected the standard of loyalty that many of the supporters of the bill had attempted to impose, that of accepting the president's perception of the international situation and giving him everything he wanted. He objected to the idea

113

that all morality in the European conflict rested with Britain and im-
morality with Germany; British mines had been just as deadly as German
submarines. England, he said, was no less guilty than Germany in the
conduct of the war.

As for the bill, Cummins had no objection to arming the ships, nor did
he see any reason why the 1819 statute ought not to be repealed. The
two things that bothered him were the points that concerned the other
antibill senators: he wanted a provision that would prevent the arming of
merchant ships bearing munitions, hence his amendment; and he objected
to the unlimited grant of power to the president contained in the bill.
Its passage in its present form, he told his colleagues, would mean the
"kaiserizing" of the United States. It was wrong, he said, for one man
to have the power of life and death over millions of Americans.

When Cummins finished his speech against the bill and for his amendment, the debate on arming merchant vessels was suspended for one of
those amenities that are part of the lifestyle of the United States Senate.
Several senators were finishing their terms in the upper chamber within
hours, and the custom is that when any lawmaker is leaving, he says his
farewell and then hears himself eulogized by his colleagues—no matter
how pressing the business before that body at the time. So, at this point,
the debate was put off for a while as John Kern, the Democratic leader,
who had been strangely silent through all these discussions, said good-by.

Only eulogies to senators who are deceased exceed in language those
to senators who are merely deceased politically. The departee is praised
as a noble and wise statesman, a paragon of wisdom and tact, one of the
greatest legislators in the history of the Senate, a man whose departure
is a great blow to the country. Some of this might have been true in
Kern's case—he was certainly one of the more effective leaders the Democrats had—but even had it not been, it would have made no difference.
At this crucial juncture in American history, as millions waited for the
outcome of the debate, politics was suspended while John Kern delivered
his valedictory.

Then came the eulogies. "Parting is such sweet sorrow," said Lodge
for the Republicans. When the senior senator from Massachusetts had
concluded, Watson of Indiana took up even more time in praise, as did
Clapp and Smith of Michigan. Moses Clapp was also going to be leaving
the Senate in just a few hours, so he too bade farewell to his colleagues,
and Thomas and Townsend lamented his going. Works then made reference to his own departure, and Stone took up even more time, commenting how much poorer the Senate would be for his absence.
Valedictory speeches are generally mawkish in nature, but these were

even more so, since departees were using up time to say good-by, and
two of them were opponents of the Armed Ship Bill.

Midnight was approaching, and at least six antibill senators were
still to speak. It was now obvious to supporters of the measure that the
filibuster was likely to succeed. Hitchcock again moved for unanimous
consent. Objections came from some of the dissenters.

Now the leadership tried a new approach. They proposed that there
be a thirty-minute limit on speeches, but both Works and Clapp objected
to this. They were both about to finish their careers in the Senate and
their last speeches were lying on their desks in front of them, and they
did not wish to be limited. Hitchcock angrily charged that they were
frustrating the will of the majority of the Senate, and Works replied that
he was not speaking for the majority of the Senate, but for the majority
of the nation and would not be limited to thirty minutes.

Reed, who had been bristling with anger through the valedictory
speeches and unanimous consent requests, denounced Cummins for his
"kaiserizing" remark. The Iowan replied that it was aimed at no one
in particular and that he had great faith in and admiration for Wilson.
Reed, not satisfied with this, then devoted another half-hour to the bill's
defense, calling it an exercise of the protection of rights and a defense
of the country's honor.

After Reed finished, the Senate moved back briefly to the Naval
Appropriations Conference Committee report, with Swanson once again
speaking for the committee. Among other things, he read a letter from
the chairman, Tillman, urging passage of the bill and boosting appropriations for naval facilities in his home state. There was an interruption in
this, as Ashurst wanted to talk about the need to establish a Grand Canyon
National Park in Arizona. As he finished, the clock struck midnight.
There were just twelve hours left in the life of the Sixty-fourth Congress.

March 4 1917[17]

As March 4 dawned, and as senators resting in the Democratic cloakroom
were being entertained by Senate Chief of Pages Joseph O'Keefe with
his impersonation of several of their fellows,[18] Swanson was again
talking on the Naval Appropriations Conference Committee report.
Finally the Senate approved it, and then followed a series of other
reports and announcements, including Vardaman's mention of a pending
"Blue-Gray" meeting in Vicksburg.

At one-thirty Senator Ellison ("Cotton Ed") Smith of South Carolina insisted on bringing the Agriculture Appropriations Committee report before the Senate. Immediately Gronna, who was watching the floor, jumped up to discuss it. The leadership, which had been trying to keep extraneous matters off the floor, had apparently been caught off guard by Gronna's action, and Smith, in vain, tried to retract it. He said that he had simply wanted to bring notice of it to the Senate, but when he asked for unanimous consent to have it laid aside, Gronna refused, saying that he would discuss the report.

Gronna's biographer, Phillips, writing of this event, suggests that Smith might have been in collusion with the dissenters and that this effort to have the matter laid aside was simply a little play-acting. However, there is not much evidence to suggest that Smith was one of those senators who were in sympathy with the dissenters and would risk being identified with them by such an obvious act. Rather, it is probable, as Phillips also suggests, that Gronna had cleverly seized upon an error on the South Carolinian's part and the brief lapse on the part of the leadership. After refusing to yield his right to discuss the report, the North Dakotan proceeded, with the help of friendly questions from Clapp, to spend a great deal of time talking about wheat, barley, corn, and other matters that were irrelevant to the Armed Ship Bill in what was probably the most boring speech of the three days. The floor was almost empty as he spoke in his usual dull, rumbling, monotone, made all the more so by the nature of his subject.

One might, by using a little imagination, see the frustration of the advocates of the Armed Ship Bill as Gronna stumbled over the figures and statistics in front of him while the clock ticked away the last hours of the Sixty-fourth Congress. Once in a while he would look up from his figures to enlighten the Senate about rural poverty. "This is a mighty dry subject to go into—some of these statistics, and yet I am going to try to make an impression, not only on the members of the Senate, but on the Agriculture Department also. I think [they] need some of this information."

He paid tribute to the farmer as the noblest of yeomen and continued to pour out the statistics over the demands of the probill senators that he conclude his speech. Finally he subsided; it was two-thirty, and less than ten hours remained of the session.[19]

Myers of Montana wanted to talk about the conference committee report that would authorize the secretary of the interior to sell certain public lands and coal deposits. If forces favoring the Armed Ship Bill were upset with Gronna taking up time with his recitation of agricultural data, they were furious with Myers, who presumably favored the proposal.

Hoke Smith and Williams both asked him to yield the floor; Williams was exceptionally caustic when he refused. Myers persisted in discussion of the report in the face of this pressure until three, when Hitchcock asked for and received the floor.

As he began to speak, almost as if by magic, senators began to appear on the floor. During the debates on the two conference committee reports, few save the discussants were present; now at least three-quarters of them were in their places. Hitchcock held a petition, signed by seventy-five senators, expressing support for the Armed Ship Bill and expressing also their desire to have a vote taken on the matter. He asked that Robinson of Arkansas read it to the Senate. The petition reads:

The undersigned United States Senators favor the passage of S 8322, to authorize the President of the United States to arm American merchant vessels and to protect American citizens in their peaceful pursuits upon the sea. A similar bill has already passed the House of Representatives by a vote of 403 to 13. Under the rules of the Senate, allowing debate without limit, it now appears impossible to obtain a vote prior to noon March 4 1917 when the Congress expires. We desire this statement entered into the *Record* to establish the fact that the Senate favors this legislation and would pass it if a vote could be had.

/s/ Furnifold M. Simmons, Henry Cabot Lodge, William E. Borah, G.M. Hitchcock, George Sutherland, Hoke Smith, George T. Oliver, John W. Kern, J.W. Wadsworth, Thomas Sterling, James H. Brady, William P. Dillingham, L.B. Colt, Frank B. Brandegee, Clarence D. Clark, P.J. McCumber, Morris Sheppard, Atlee Pomerene, Willard Saulsbury, C.E. Townsend, Bern M. Fernald, Albert B. Fall, John K. Shields, George P. McLean, Joe T. Robinson, Duncan U. Fletcher, Reed Smoot, Ollie M. James, Claude A. Swanson, Thomas S. Martin, N.P. Bryan, Thomas W. Hardwick E.D. Smith, Charles Curtis, Knute Nelson, W.G. Harding, T.B. Catron, John Sharp Williams, J. Hamilton Lewis, T.J. Walsh, J.S. Beckham, H.L. Myers, Paul O. Husting, Henry F. Hollis, James D. Phelan, Miles Poindexter, O.W. Underwood, John F. Schafroth, F.E. Warren, Carrol S. Page, W.L. Jones, James E. Martine, Charles S. Thomas, George E. Chamberlain, Lawrence Y. Sherman, William Alden Smith, W.E. Chilton, John H. Bankhead, Henry F. Ashurst, Lee S. Overman, Ed S. Johnson, Blair Lee, William Hughes, John W. Weeks, James A. Reed, John Walter Smith, Luke Lea, Key Pittman, Robert F. Broussard, James E. Watson, H.A. duPont, Robert L. Owen, Francis G. Newlands, William H. Thompson, Joseph E. Randsell.

Senator Lippitt is out of the city. Senators detained from the Senate on account of illness include Nathan Goff, Jacob H. Gallinger.

The following Senators have not had an opportunity to sign this agreement: Mr. Gore, Mr. Tillman, Mr. Smith of Arizona, Mr. Stone, Mr. Johnson of Maine, Mr. Culberson. [20]

Robinson had some difficulty reading all the signatures, since many of the signers had scrawled their names illegibly.[21] As he stumbled through the list, the dissenting senators, like so many unruly schoolboys, hissed and hooted at the names.[22] LaFollette wrote a note to himself that revealed his anger—particularly at Lodge. He was resentful of the "Tory" Republicans for having first planned an extra session of the Congress, then having abandoned their filibuster because they believed, in his opinion, that the Armed Ship Bill would bring war. [23]

There does not appear to be any particular sequence to the list of signatures, so the first names on the petition were probably those who were around when it was completed, and the last ones those who were not on the floor at the time. There is no indication that the final names were those of senators who were hesitant about signing. Two men who were hesitant signed with reservations—Jones, subject to any of the three amendments that had been offered, and Townsend with specific reference to the Cummins amendment. Martine later announced that he would have signed subject to amendments if those who circulated the round-robin had told him that this was possible. Apparently, the circulators of the manifesto did not let their colleagues know that they could indicate reservations and put their names down subject to amendments, as had Jones and Townsend. It might be noted that the petition reads in such a way that the signer indicates support for the original bill without any amendments. Therefore, some of the dissenters, who might well have signed the statement had they known that they could sign subject to amendments, refused because of the fact that it was presented on a take-it-or-leave-it basis. Many of them said on the floor—or would say later—that they would have voted for the measure with certain amendments added.

There were two senators who did not sign the manifesto immediately, but who would subsequently. (Some others indicated, through friends, lest anyone get the wrong impression, that they too would have signed had they been present.) One of the late signers was Tillman, who it has been noted was rarely on the floor during this period. The other late signer was Penrose, who was on the floor and who refused when the manifesto was initially presented to him. He favored the Armed Ship Bill, but said initially that he would not sign because he felt that circulation of the petition was a mistake.

It is probably that some of the Republican regulars talked to him when they discovered that he had not signed, pointing out that the round-robin was their idea, and that it was necessary for all of them to sign it so as to absolve the party from any blame that might be attached as a result of their earlier delaying tactics. Penrose had been an important part of this effort to hold up legislation. [24]

Penrose was not the only member of the Senate who signed despite certain misgivings about the situation. Borah's biographer reports that the Idaho senator was not at all happy about the late introduction of the bill, believing that Wilson should have brought the matter up right after breaking relations with Germany. However, his reservations about tactics did not lead him to protest by refusing to sign the manifesto.[25]

There were eleven senators unaccounted for—Stone was listed as having been unable to sign, whereas he did have an opportunity and refused. Reed had been pleading with him to do so, but the senior senator from Missouri would not listen. Otherwise, the eleven who were "given a chance" but did not choose to take it, were Norris, LaFollette, Clapp, Cummins, Gronna, Works, Kenyon, O'Gorman, Lane, Vardaman, and Kirby.

Lane had been specifically approached to sign by Chamberlain but brushed the petition from his desk by way of indicating his attitude. Norris had been personally visited by Hitchcock and had pointedly refused.[26]

As soon as the reading of the names had been completed, the Senate chamber erupted into a crescendo of noise. Wesley Jones was one of the angriest, even though he had signed the paper. He said that the use of the document in this manner was not only unprecedented, but improper and unethical, and added that it was being used as a coercive device by the leadership. He said that he had signed it as a means of expressing his views and not in the expectation that it would be made public. He said that the effect of its release would be to place the dissenters in an unfavorable light and would cast reflection on their right to debate. He added that he personally did not feel that there had been unreasonable and undue debate thus far.

While Jones was speaking, Robinson left the rostrum and charged over to him, waving his fists. The two stood chin-to-chin, screaming at each other with charges and countercharges. LaFollette strolled over to the scene and made a point of laughing in Robinson's face.[27]

Williams, having left a sickbed to be present,[28] was more short-tempered than usual. He told Jones that he was naive if he thought the document was not going to be made public. He charged that the dissenters knew exactly what they were doing; namely, trying to kill the bill by filibuster. Jones said that it was their right, and Williams replied that it was an improper use of the right of unlimited debate.

Robinson was not impressed with this argument. "Let men of courage rise to speak," he said. "The hour has arrived," he told them, when members of the Senate ought to be afforded a chance to say where they stood. "It is a fateful hour, an important issue, gentlemen."

Hitchcock, noting that it was three-thirty, asked for unanimous consent for a vote at six. It was denied. Weeks then rebuked him for having

119

employed the round-robin in debate, charging that this was unethical. This took up more time.

Gronna rose to complain that he was being "bulldozed." He objected to the use of the petition and was proud that he was not on it. He objected to a vote. This prompted Williams to complain about the humiliating spectacle taking place on the floor, one that could only please the Kaiser and the military class in Germany. The Mississippian could not tolerate what he regarded as insults to American honor, and he chafed under the restraints of not being able to strike back by passing the Armed Ship Bill. The country, he said, cries out for the protection of its rights, and a few men refuse to heed its call. Is this the role of the United States? Is not honor more important than the rules of the Senate?

"Can we get an agreement for nine?" asked Hoke Smith.

Williams immediately jumped in to endorse this proposal. It would, he said, give the Senate time to pass the bill and get it over to the House of Representatives which had been waiting for the upper chamber to act. Works, however, objected to this call for consent; he had been waiting patiently, he said, for a chance to speak on arming merchant ships and he resented the fact that such people as the senior senator from Mississippi were consuming time and then demanding that others cut their own remarks short. Williams grumbled something about the fact that he had spoken very little, considering that he was a member of the Foreign Relations Committee, but Works's objection blocked unanimous consent, and so Hoke Smith's request was denied.

As the Californian began the last speech of his Senate career, a counter-filibuster began. It was not a filibuster in the traditional sense, for a filibuster usually means that senators are planning to block a vote. This move was not designed to prevent a vote, but rather to keep one of their colleagues off the floor.

The object of this maneuver was LaFollette, whom they knew to be the inspiration for the Armed Ship filibuster and who was scheduled to close the debate. The Wisconsin senator had wandered onto the floor once or twice during the evening, smiling and telling all who would listen that he had a "great speech" to deliver. His manner had destroyed the code of genteel fairness and equity with which senators generally treat each other—even someone whom they personally dislike, such as LaFollette.

Just when the decision to deny him the opportunity to speak was made is not clear, nor is it clear who originated the idea and how many senators were in on the plot. But what is clear is that sometime during the morning of March 4, when it became apparent that the filibuster was

120

going to succeed, some senators decided to extract a measure of revenge against LaFollette by denying him the floor. Norris is a bit kinder to his old colleagues than others who have written about the incident, for the Nebraskan partially ascribes their motives to a desire to give their side of the issue a better airing than it had been getting. But time and age had, no doubt, softened Norris's view of their motives, for it is noteworthy that they decided to block the Wisconsinite alone from talking—none of the others.[29]

Earlier, when the dissenters were making their plans to filibuster, they had made up a list and presented it to the vice president, with LaFollette's name last among speakers against the bill. Therefore, all of them believed throughout the early hours of the debate that the presiding officer, be it Marshall or anyone else in the chair, was following the list.

However, Marshall had told LaFollette late on Saturday evening, the third, that he was not keeping any lists and had thrown the old ones away. Apparently, LaFollette presumed that he would have no difficulty getting the floor when Norris finished. But the senators who decided to block him had drawn up a new list of speakers to pick up the debate when the Nebraskan finished.[30]

Works had to undergo a number of interruptions, first by Hitchcock, who corrected him on his denunciation of probill senators who had signed the round-robin after talking a great deal. The Californian believed that Stone had signed, whereas the Missourian had had a chance to do so, but had refused. Works also attacked Hardwick, saying that the junior senator from Georgia had taken up a great deal of time and still signed the paper; the latter complained that he had only consumed about thirty minutes.

Eight hours remained. Pomerene asked Works if he would agree to a vote. If he would, the Ohioan was certain that everyone would be happy to hear what it was that the retiring senator had to say. He could not understand this compulsion to talk, since everyone "knew" that debate rarely changed votes or minds. Works agreed with him, saying that the majority had already made up its mind, upon orders from its leaders. As a judge, he said, he had given both sides equal time and he expected that, the majority having now had its say, the minority could have its.

James broke in. He said that he would be happy to give the dissenters all the remaining time if they would only allow the Senate to have a vote. The Californian ignored this suggestion and proceeded to the main theme of his speech. He was critical of the president for his release of the Zimmermann Note, charging that it had been done in order to pressure the Senate. George Oliver of Pennsylvania, a member of the Foreign Relations Committee, said that the committee had approved the bill even before they knew of the note, and defended the position that they had taken. Works responded that he was ashamed of the committee for what it had done, and for that matter, ashamed of the senator from Pennsylvania for defending it.

Brandegee attacked Works's standard of judicial fairness. He said that since the proponents of the bill outnumbered its opponents, it was only reasonable that they get the lion's share of the time for debate. Works said that this response was only further proof of his assertion that the majority was trying to stifle the minority by limiting their time.

He also criticized those who claimed that the dissenters were pro-German. He said that they were not speaking for Germany, but for the truth, and that the war that Wilson was foisting on America was not a war that anyone wanted, except those few who stood to gain from it. Real courage, he reminded the Senate, is moral courage, and not that which promotes the idea of war. What had happened between 1914 and 1915 had not called for war; the fact that a few citizens had chosen to sail on the ships of belligerents was not an excuse to commit millions to battle.

In an effort to suggest that peace is unpatriotic, he said, the majority had compared the dissenters to the Tories of the revolutionary war. Would Washington or Jefferson have counseled war in 1917? The war was favored only by a small number of people—women did not want it, labor did not, the people who "matter" did not—only a limited few. False appeals to patriotism at this time were "hollow," he concluded.

"I am leaving government service at a critical time . . . . Perhaps I might be of no service here. . . . I pray to God that those who do remain will be reminded of their grave responsibilities."

Six hours remained. The rain was coming down hard on a still sleeping Washington. Suffragettes were getting ready to take up positions around the White House to press their cause. Most of the Senate was still present, surly, rumpled, bleary-eyed, and short-tempered.

Moses Clapp began his final speech. He regarded Wilson highly, he said, but not enough to give him a blank check to wage war at his own discretion. As a believer in the principle of separation of powers, he said that he could not accept the surrender of the Congress to the president in a craven fashion such as this. He further charged that the cry for war was stimulated by those who had an economic interest in the conflict.

The only difference between England and Germany, he said, was that England is a better customer. The United States had become obliged to support her, because that was where the money had been invested. Patriotism was being used to justify an attempt to redeem that which had been bet on a British victory.

He decried the fact that the United States had done nothing to keep civilians off belligerent ships. Even the British keep their citizens home under such circumstances, he said. "If some consider the proposal that we do so cowardly, what does that make England?"

We have sold ourselves to commercialism he concluded, and we are going to war to protect it. His last words were, "I cannot, in the last hours of my Senate life, vote for such a bill." The Senate career of the "Black Eagle of Fergus Falls" was over.

Then came Harry Lane, coughing and wheezing through what would be his last speech. He denounced the round-robin, saying that he only desired a logical discussion of the issues without a time limit imposed by the majority. He indicated that he had not even bothered to read the manifesto before refusing to sign it, decrying the arrogance of those who "waved the document in my face."

He said that he was not filibustering; he simply could not support the bill as it stood, because it would give to the president entirely too much power—power that went beyond that which any one man ought to have. In doing so, he said, Congress would be giving him the authority to declare war when he chose, because arming ships was but a prelude to war. He would not mind the war quite so much, he said, if only he could be certain that, at the same time millions were spent on it, more was given to feed the starving people of the United States. This was where he believed the American legislators ought to be focusing their attention.

He did not believe that the rights of Americans as neutrals were any less than those of other nations. He could not accept the argument that American citizens could go into a war zone and expect not to be under fire and that a government could consider this shooting to be a possible provocation for war. However, Lane indicated that he did not believe most of the senators and other prominent war advocates took the matter of neutral rights very seriously but only used it as an excuse to stimulate public opinion. The real cause of war was the desire of the munitions makers to make a profit and the willingness of many to go along with them.

Lane was particularly disappointed that America had abandoned its role as a mediator in order to take sides in the war. He believed that America had no interest that would be served by a victory for either side, but that it did have an interest in peace. But now, he lamented, the die had been cast for participation in war. With a grim note that may well have been an almost fatalistic prediction, he concluded: "I would not be at all surprised if the next thirty days should not bring about a great calamity for this country."

It was seven-thirty when Lane ended. Most of the Senate was breakfasting, but the galleries were filling up again. Further down Pennsylvania Avenue Woodrow Wilson was preparing to leave for the Capitol, where
he would sign some last-minute bills and take the oath of office.

Wilson had been getting periodic reports about the progress of the debate, probably from Daniels, who was in the Capitol through most of the
night. Sometime during the last day of debate, Daniels, Burleson, Franklin Lane, and Baker suggested to him that he try to alter the situation by
going to the Senate floor to make a personal plea for passage of the bill.
The dramatic setting, Daniels stated, appealed to them.

Whatever Wilson's love of innovations in presidential dealing with the
Congress, this idea did not appeal to him. He told the four cabinet members that he did not believe that he could alter the determination of the
Senate not to act. Further, he argued, it was already too late—if he were
to go to the Senate chamber for this dramatic confrontation, he should
have gone much earlier.[31]

The president's reaction was an intelligent one. The move could well
have backfired, since many senators were already openly resentful of his
methods and of the fact that a bill as important as the Armed Ship measure had been introduced as late as it was. Some might have seized upon
his appearance as an opportunity to criticize him for meddling in legislative business, and he might have suffered long-range consequences.

Further, as he noted, there was no problem about getting a positive
vote for the bill. The problem lay in the unwillingness of some senators
to act, and no assessment of their attitudes on the morning of March 4
would suggest that they could be moved by some presidential message.

George Norris was the next speaker. While he was talking, LaFollette
received a note scrawled on Senate stationery. It told him that the writer
had learned that there was a plot being hatched to have the presiding officer refuse to recognize him when he sought the floor. The note was un-
signed, but the Wisconsin senator alleged that he knew who had sent it.
He never revealed the name.

Shortly before eight-thirty, accompanied by his son and his secretary,
Hannan, LaFollette entered the chamber bearing volumes of material
that he planned to use in his speech. As he did, he noted that Luke Lea,
the young senator from Tennessee, who was concluding his service in the
upper chamber, was in the chair and beckoning to him.

Lea told him that he had a list of speakers to call on after Norris—specifically, Owen and Hitchcock. This shocked LaFollette, who had been
proceeding under the information he had received hours earlier from
Marshall about there being no lists. Lea said that he would have to en-

force the list, but that if the Wisconsin senator objected, he would refuse to have any part of it and would leave the chair. LaFollette, apparently thinking at this time that neither speaker would take up much time and preferring that Lea be in the chair, simply added his name to the list.

The Tennessee senator also warned LaFollette about the talk he had been hearing in the cloakroom—some senators were talking about violence on the floor. LaFollette left the rostrum and went to talk to Owen, asking him how much time he would take. The latter was noncommittal and refused to talk about the matter. Aroused now, LaFollette sent for his gun.

The role of Lea is an interesting one in this incident. The LaFollette account says that the Wisconsin senator was "beckoned" to come to the rostrum to be told of the new list. In short, Lea volunteered the information; LaFollette did not go there seeking it. What makes the incident surprising is that the Democrats had put someone like the young Tennessean in the chair at a time like this, when they were plotting a maneuver to keep the leader of the filibuster off the floor.

The rumors of trouble apparently also reached Harry Lane, who had been resting in the cloakroom. He sent word to LaFollette's secretary of what he had heard and said that he was ready to help. However, this information was not communicated to the Wisconsinite until later.

The gun that LaFollette sent for never arrived at his desk. His son brought the bag supposedly containing it to the chamber and left it there where his father could see it. However, for some unknown reason the young man had removed the weapon, so that if LaFollette, during the hectic hours that followed, thought that he had some sort of protection at hand, he was mistaken. [32]

Norris's speech might have been the highlight of the debate, had it not been for the fact that almost everyone else in the chamber was more interested in the machinations to block LaFollette. The Nebraskan had obtained a copy of Woodrow Wilson's *Congressional Government* and planned to quote liberally (but out of context) from it, in order to demonstrate that there were words of the president's that would belie his actions of the moment.

Norris reminded his colleagues that he wanted no interruptions, citing the fact that in the past hours senators speaking against the bill had been interrupted several times by their colleagues, who then accused them of taking up too much time. He called attention to the fact that as a result of the deliberations during the past two days, proponents of the bill had taken up more time than had those opposed to it.

He wondered aloud if there was not something unusual in the attitude

125

taken by the Senate at this point. In the past the Senate had applauded the idea of unlimited debate and had clung to this right jealously. Most senators were in favor of the concept. Why was this time, this issue, different?

He criticized Wilson for having descended upon Congress with "must" legislation at the last minute. He said that Wilson did not want the Congress to debate the issues, but, rather, to serve as a rubber stamp, to simply capitulate and give him what he wanted. He was afraid of criticism and wanted only subservience. The next step, he predicted, would be muzzling of the press. The press in Nebraska, at the moment, was far from mute. It had come out favoring the bill, as had the Nebraska legislature. Norris was aware of this as he spoke. [33]

Patriotism, he said, lies in a man doing his duty and discharging his oath of office. It would be unpatriotic for the Senate not to debate the bill but to swallow it without examination. If the bill was as important as the president thought, all he needed to do was to call a special session of the Congress and let it deal with the matter.

Then he turned to the Wilson book. Although not the dramatic and flamboyant orator LaFollette was, Norris was not above a little theatrics, if the situation demanded it. He did not initially identify the author, simply telling what few of his colleagues were on the floor (and probably not listening very closely) that he was going to quote on the matter of executive-legislative relationships from the work of a prominent political scientist. After reading a few passages from the book that talked of the duty of the legislature to look into the actions of the president, the Nebraskan said that if the people of the United States feared tyranny, they should insist that the Congress perform its role and examine presidential proposals very carefully. He wondered why the author, whom he now identified, had "changed his mind" about the matter.

As for the bill, Norris indicated that his chief concern was that part which would give the president unlimited power in the field of foreign affairs—the "other instrumentalities." He said that he did not object to the idea of arming merchant ships, although he would oppose it if the measure did not contain a clause preventing munitions-bearing vessels from being armed. He even stated that he had no reservations about repealing the statute of 1819.

He also had a word for those who took what he regarded as a one-sided view of the international situation. He argued that the proponents of the hard line were perverting international law by winking at British violations and were stressing only the German offenses. He got in a blow at Wilsonian diplomacy in Latin-America by repeating his criticism of how the president had, in his view, risked war with Mexico over the incident in Tampico by insisting that the dictator Huerta salute the flag.

There were less than three hours remaining when the Nebraskan finished. Lea recognized Owen, and LaFollette became visibly agitated. He now noted that the president pro tem, Willard Saulsbury of Delaware, had replaced Lea in the chair and he went to ask him if the new list was going to be enforced. Saulsbury did not even want to talk about it, and LaFollette warned him that if he did not get a chance to talk, there would be trouble.

The spectators in the gallery were stirring as rumors of the plot began to spread. Senators who had been breakfasting now came back to the chamber to enjoy the Wisconsinite's discomfort. Norris was alarmed at the way LaFollette was acting; he was afraid that the angered senator might do something that would get him arrested and removed from the floor.

When Owen finished, Saulsbury recognized Hitchcock, in a fashion that struck LaFollette as being incorrect. He began to scream irately. The long night of tension and the importance of the issue had caused him to lose control of his emotions. Hardwick called for a quorum, and the senators on the Democratic side of the aisle glared vindictively at the quivering figure of the Wisconsinite, who demanded a "parliamentary inquiry," stating that he would not sit down until he was satisfied that his rights were not being violated.[34]

During the quorum call several Democratic senators, including Ollie James, got up and set out across the hall towards LaFollette. Lane, noting that James was armed, allegedly took the rat-tail file from his desk and followed them. The ailing Oregon senator told LaFollette the next day that he was never so far from James that he would not have been able to put the file down the Kentucky senator's collarbone and into his heart, if necessary. Lane later gave the file to LaFollette, who kept it in his desk for years. The Oregon senator would obviously have little more need for it. [35]

This incident is not corroborated in the newspapers—all that they and the *Record* show is considerable chaos at this time. LaFollette continued to scream at Saulsbury and the Democratic leadership, and the noise on the floor reached an almost deafening pitch. The Wisconsin senator insisted that he wanted to make a point of parliamentary inquiry concerning the propriety of the chair's ruling in calling on Hitchcock, adding that he would not recognize any ruling until he could be heard. At one point he cried that he would go on until he was carried off, and would like to see the man who tried to do it.

Now Robinson entered the debate. He argued that LaFollette had not made a valid point of inquiry. Saulsbury agreed and LaFollette appealed the ruling.

"Ayes and nays," called Ashurst.

The vote to uphold the chair was 52–15.[36] Therefore Hitchcock retained the floor, speaking slowly and deliberately so as to ensure that the session would end without LaFollette speaking. In the other chamber, the House of Representatives had assembled for a nostalgic binge of valedictories, songs (including "How Dry I Am," by Prohibitionists), a brief appearance on the floor of a congressman's wife impersonating the newly elected (and first) congresswoman, Jeanette Rankin.[37]

Wilson, with his wife, Tumulty, his physician Dr. Cary Grayson, and other officials, was leaving for the Capitol.

At ten-fifteen Hitchcock told LaFollette that he would be willing to let him talk; he offered him the chance, provided that he would consent to a vote. The latter said that he could not "conscientiously" accept this, since the issue was so important. In fact, he said, if it is as important as Wilson claimed, then the best solution would be for him to call a special session. Boos and catcalls greeted this remark.[38]

Still annoyed, the Wisconsin senator told Norris that he was contemplating throwing a spittoon at Robinson, who was now in the chair. Norris was able to talk him out of it.[39]

Hitchcock droned on. As sponsor of the measure, he said he ought to have the privilege of concluding the debate. He was appalled, he added, at the shameful exhibition by the dissenting senators, who would deny the president's wishes. We are reduced to a point of absurdity by the tactics of barely one-tenth of the Senate, he said.

Overman asked if it would be possible to change the rules in order to avoid such a recurrence. Hitchcock agreed that it was certainly time for such a move.

So did Stone. He suggested shelving the Armed Ship Bill immediately and bringing the matter of revising the rules directly to the floor. Hitchcock called this proposal ludicrous.

As Wilson arrived at the Capitol, Williams and Hitchcock were engaged in colloquy concerning the fact that the defeat of the bill was a calamity. It was little more than other presidents had asked for, they agreed. Hitchcock pointed out how armed neutrality had been the policy of such nations as Holland, Switzerland, and Sweden, none of which had gone to war.

At ten-thirty the president arrived in the small room in the Capitol adjacent to the Senate chamber, where he was to sign the bills that would come from the Congress in its last hours. He sat barely fourteen feet from LaFollette, separated by a wall, as the Wisconsin senator broke into Hitchcock's speech to complain that the Nebraska Democrat was speaking twice on the same measure in the same legislative day.

Wilson was not unaware of the drama on the floor, but reports of his demeanor outside the chamber give the impression that his manner was calm. He was chatting with friends, including Chief Justice White, signing bills, and greeting various senators who came out to see him.

Inside, Hitchcock continued. He said that he was personally willing to accept the Stone amendment, but could not support the striking of provisions that some of the dissenters considered to be too great a grant of unchecked authority. There was one hour remaining.

LaFollette was still trying to get the floor, or at least to prevent anyone else from getting it. He jousted with Williams and Hoke Smith ("Hocus Pocus" Smith, in this part of the LaFollette biography), with the latter over the matter of each other's veracity.[40] Again, Hitchcock asked for a vote; again LaFollette refused. By now the noise in the chamber had reached a point where it was drowning out conversation in the room where Wilson was waiting.

Smith of Michigan requested to be allowed to speak, explaining that he had been waiting a long time. Hitchcock, with a glance at LaFollette who was now stretching his legs in the aisle separating the two parties, said that the Michigan senator had a better right than others, but asked him not "to endanger my position on the floor." Smith, a bit nonplussed, left the chamber to greet Wilson, who it is reported, did not receive him cordially.[41]

Norris would comment later that these final moments of the debate were ones that he would remember all his life. He said that the emotion in the room and the anger on both sides of the issue had reached a level the equal of which he could not recall. He described LaFollette as still deeply upset about his failure to get the floor, bouncing up on his feet one minute and back to his chair the next.

Now Williams, who was hard of hearing and who would thus frequently break into the speeches of other senators, charged LaFollette with violating the rules of the Senate, "habitually and continually."

"So are you," retorted LaFollette. "You haven't been recognized yet."

LaFollette continued to deny unanimous requests and to complain about Hitchcock speaking twice on the same matter in the same legislative day. Robinson, still in the chair, continued to rule against him. There was one brief break in the routine; Ben Tillman had returned to the floor and asked for permission to sign the manifesto. As he did, LaFollette glared angrily across the floor at him.[42]

It was all over now, but the Senate had to wait until noon in order to adjourn. LaFollette was beginning to smile a little bit, although internally he was still angry. An unlit cigar was still in his mouth, the crumpled paper that was his undelivered speech still in his hand. Norris, the tactician, watched the clock, lest something go wrong at the last minute.

The remainder of Hitchcock's speech was a variation on the same theme that he and other probill senators had been stressing. He praised Wilson's conduct of diplomacy, blamed Germany for the trouble, read a pacifist poem, "Five Souls" by W. M. Ewer, and pleaded again for a vote— without success. He submitted another request for unanimous consent to have a vote taken—this time written out, as proponents of the bill had requested.

LaFollette objected again, and a quorum call was issued. When it had concluded, eighty-six senators had answered to their names, and LaFollette again repeated his refusal to allow a vote. He tried also to get Robinson to rule that Hitchcock had lost the floor by virtue of the quorum call, but the Arkansan refused to listen. LaFollette objected to this ruling also, but Hoke Smith introduced a resolution that Hitchcock retain the floor, a proposal that was upheld by a division vote, sixty-four in favor, two against.

Hitchcock began his final statement. Across the hall the House was adjourning amidst much hilarity.

The President wants peace, and we have been unable to help him. Twelve men have defeated a request by the President and the will of seventy or eighty men, by resorting to one of the most reprehensible filibusters ever recorded in the history of any civilized country. Mr. President, I am using rather strong language.

"Oh, that is all right," said LaFollette. "It is perfectly safe when no one has the right to answer."

"To the senators who have been so considerate to me— I assure the Senator from Wisconsin that I do not cherish any personal feelings in this matter in any way." He was cut off by Robinson, who announced that the hour had arrived, and the Senate adjourned sine die.

Four minutes later, in the presence of members of his family, Vice President Marshall, and a number of the participants in the recently concluded drama, Woodrow Wilson faced Chief Justice White and took the oath of office. The Bible on which his hand rested was open to Psalm 46:

God is our refuge and strength, a very present help in trouble. Therefore will not we fear, though the earth be removed, and though the mountains be carried

into the midst of the sea;
  Though the waters thereof roar and be troubled, though the mountains
shake with the swelling thereof. Selah.

  Witnesses reported that his finger pointed to the words "The heathen
raged, the kingdoms were moved; he uttered his voice, the earth melted."[43]

8

THE AFTERMATH

The Public Reaction

The last speeches of the Armed Ship debate had barely faded away when
the newspapers and others took up the attack on the filibusters and
those whose opposition to the bill had caused them to be grouped with
the men who had actually tried to prevent a vote. Almost unanimously
the major papers in the country condemned the filibuster and those who
they claimed had participated in it, with particular emphasis on LaFollette and Stone.

Three cartoons seem to be the most descriptive, the most famous of
which was drawn by the noted cartoonist Roland Kirby, who depicted
the "willful men" receiving the "Iron Cross" which he called the "Only
Adequate Reward." Years later Kirby would regret this particular drawing. Another picture showed the filibusterers skulking off into a barren
rocky valley, like a collection of lepers banished from society for their
afflictions—"Men without a Country." Still another drawing showed
Benedict Arnold contemplating them and commenting, "And they called
me traitor." If the ancient cliché is correct, and one picture is worth
a thousand words, these three cartoons tell the story of the criticism of
the dissenting senators far more accurately than do the editorials.

The *New York Times* called them "perverse and disloyal obstructionists," while the *New York World* said that they were "pusillanimous
[wretches] who had denied their country's conscience." The *New York
Herald* predicted that their names would "go down in history bracketed
with Benedict Arnold."

132

This was New York, where one might expect such criticism. Elsewhere the feeling was just as intense. "Political tramps" was the description of the *Hartford Courant.* "A little short of treason" came from the *Providence Journal.* "Should be driven from public life" was the sentiment of the *Portland (Maine) Free Press.*

Feeling was intense in other parts of the country. "Petty and malicious imitators of Benedict Arnold" *(Philadelphia Record);* "The final triumph of the pro-German contingent" *(Montgomery Advertiser);* "The Kaiserbund is already formed" *(Memphis Commercial Appeal);* Stone "has [shamed] the state he so unworthily represents" *(St. Louis Globe Democrat);* "a great outrage" *(Houston Post).*

The papers stopped just short of calling them traitors, but the *Times* expressed its frustration at not being able to do so by saying that "treason in the usual sense cannot be charged against them.... But we are in the shadow of war. Should it come, the odium of treasonous purposes and achievement will rest on their names forever. . . ." And the *Washington Post* added that the "moment the mailed fist of Germany strikes with hostile intent at the American flag, the United States . . . will turn from peace long enough to defeat and destroy the powers that menace liberty. God wills it."[1]

The tone for this denunciation had been set by Wilson's statement. What might appear, by contemporary standards, to be an overreaction stemmed directly from the president's castigation of those who had blocked his bill. This was no accident. Wilson well knew that his words would have some effect and would render ineffective any explanations that the dissenting senators might choose to make. From this point on, all opposition to his proposals, from them or from any other legislators who disagreed with his view as to how American foreign policy ought to be conducted, would be linked to obstructionism.

Wilson might have been more accurate in specifying the number of senators who had filibustered, but he was not—and there was a reason for this. He knew what almost everyone else close to the debate knew— that only a few progressive Republicans had actually collaborated to prevent a vote, but to concentrate only on them would fail to serve a second purpose. He wanted to ensure that those members of his own party who had opposed the measure and thus embarrassed him, would be cast into the same category as the filibusterers. He wanted those men who had dared to defy the head of their party and the majority of their constituents to understand the consequences of going against his concept of "party government." They were all equally guilty in his eyes, those who blocked the bill and those in his party who went against him, and he wanted the country to know this.

In the words of Arthur Link, it was as unfortunate a statement as Wilson ever made in public life. Link points out that it was particularly unfair to Stone (whom the president called "slippery" and vowed never to speak to again). He never mentioned the fact that the bill was introduced at a late hour, nor the possible contributions of the mini-filibuster conducted by Lodge and his cohorts, nor the amount of time taken up on the floor by the bill's supporters.[2] To have done so would have taken the attention away from the point he wanted to make.

One of his cabinet, Interior Secretary Lane, also believed that Wilson should not have singled out the filibusterers alone for criticism but should have pointed up the delaying tactics employed earlier by the Republicans. Lansing wrote that Wilson could hardly have believed that the failure of the bill damaged America's ability to defend herself, because of the fact that the president had worded his request in such a way as to leave himself open to act. He would never, the secretary of state suggests, have depended on Congress.[3]

But politicians leaped to the attack. Governor James Cox of Ohio welcomed back the Ohio Guard from border service with a speech that called the dissenters traitors. Mayor John Mitchel of New York said their actions were a reproach to the American people. A noted political scientist, Albert Bushnell Hart, gravely informed the nation that the demands being made for reform of Senate rules were reasonable, since they (the rules) were antiquated and archaic.[4]

Then, there were the rallies, the most famous of which was the one held in New York by pro-Allied and preparedness spokesmen and attended by much of New York society—perhaps one of the most elegant intellectual lynchings ever staged in the United States. As each dissenter's name was mentioned, the crowd responded with "Hang him!"[5]

Theodore Roosevelt was critical of the dissenters also; but his worst criticism was reserved for Woodrow Wilson. Even as he joined in the ritual of denunciation, he could not resist in his private correspondence to continue to carp at the president's behavior in the conduct of foreign policy. In a letter to Lodge the former president said that if Wilson did not take the nation into war, he would "skin him alive."[6]

Other citizens began to show their outrage. Many state legislatures introduced motions of censure for the dissenting senators. The Arkansas legislature specifically censured Kirby, although most of the states represented by the dissenters stopped short of going all the way with their condemnations. However, some other states, including Colorado and Delaware, did pass resolutions to that effect. A number of effigy burnings were reported in the press, particularly of Stone and LaFollette. Some of the dissenters were shunned in the streets of Washington; one specific incident reported was that when Norris and LaFollette got on a streetcar, the rest of the passengers got off.

Crank letters became commonplace, and some of the dissenters received threats on their lives. This did not affect them nearly so much as did the communications from erstwhile friends who now found it necessary to dissolve their friendships. There were some instances, however, to the contrary. Louis Brandeis, now sitting as an associate justice of the Supreme Court, wrote LaFollette, told him that he disagreed with him profoundly, but invited him to have dinner with him at the Wisconsinite's convenience.[7]

Some citizens cast the debate in the form of a modern morality play and sent Kirby thirty pieces of silver. Someone else sent Norris a likeness of himself wearing a Prussian uniform. Harry Lane got an assortment of German medals from someone in Oregon. From Mississippi came a huge piece of iron beaten into the shape of an iron cross for Vardaman.

LaFollette had been due to deliver a speech in Wheeling, West Virginia, a few days after the conclusion of the filibuster. After the abuse in the press began, the citizens there disinvited him, but the Wisconsinite said that he was going to go anyway, in order to deliver his speech. They warned him not to come, but he was adamant, and it took a great deal of effort on the part of some of his friends to persuade him not to go.

Perhaps the most ingenious proposal for punishment was recommended by some citizens in Oregon for Lane. That state had a provision in its laws for the recall of judges who had delivered unpopular opinions—and only for them. It had no applicability for United States senators, but some Oregonians thought that to circulate petitions for his recall would be embarrassing and humiliating to him. Lane was disturbed at their behavior, although hardly worried that the petitions would have any effect, since he was well aware of the law.[8]

It is interesting to note that the Senate, which is loath to discipline its members for anything save the most serious breaches of senatorial etiquette, held true to form by not doing anything about the dissenting senators. Perhaps some of them might have felt that the almost indecent haste with which they would amend the rules was censure enough, but once the debate was over, they remained, for the most part, silent about the behavior of their colleagues. Only LaFollette, whose relationships with his colleagues was never particularly good, reported any unusual discourtesy; his biographers mention that as he sat in the chamber on the morning of March 5, awaiting his swearing-in for another term, he sat alone, isolated from his fellows.

The Republican caucus did one thing that might be regarded as a form of punishment; they dropped Gronna and Cummins from the steering committee of the Senate Republicans. They had been among the token progressives on it. The other progressives, who regarded this body as irrelevant, since it was dominated by Lodge and his friends, did not seem to be particularly upset. The party caucus probably felt that they ought not to reappoint them because it might be misunderstood if two of the most despised men in the country were on such a high-sounding, if meaningless, committee.[9]

However, when the Sixty-fifth Congress began its deliberations and some of the dissenting senators got up to defend themselves, their colleagues made no attempt at rebuttal. In fact, wherever possible, the Republican leadership made every effort to indicate that they concurred with them in the fact that the real blame for the failure of the bill to pass rested with Wilson.

Some of the dissenters responded on the floor of the Senate, others in press releases. Vardaman, speaking on the floor, called the charges that he had filibustered unfair and false. He said that he disliked filibusters and had not consciously aided this particular one, had never objected to a vote, and had only taken up about fifteen minutes.[10] However, he did not retract his opposition to the Armed Ship Bill and said that this was the reason that he could not sign the manifesto. The bill, he said, gave too much power to the president, and "I never take orders from anyone outside of Mississippi." Needless to say, this last remark angered John Sharp Williams, who decided that his state needed someone to speak on the other side of the issue, and he replied to his colleague. But this was the only real effort on the part of any senator publicly to rebut the "willful men."[11]

In a letter to his townsmen of Lakota, North Dakota, Gronna, defending himself, had no regrets. He said that the bill was a gambit to try to give the president unlimited powers and that he felt that, by helping to defeat it, he had made a major contribution to his country's well-being. It would appear from his biographer's account that he suffered less in his home state for his actions than any of the other dissenters.[12]

O'Gorman, now a private citizen, was back in the practice of law in New York City, where resentment was intense against the "willful men." He issued a statement which emphasized the fact that he had spent little time on the floor speaking on the bill and had not been a party to the planning of the filibuster or its management. He said that he did not sign the manifesto because he could not support the bill without the

Stone amendment attached. Otherwise, he believed that he would be endorsing a declaration of war.

Harry Lane also issued a statement rebutting the assertion that he had filibustered. He had talked at length, but pointed out that he had never objected to having a vote and the only reason that he could not sign the manifesto was that he objected to the bill without amendments. He said flatly that he would have voted for it if certain of them had been added.[13]

Stone came under the heaviest share of criticism because of his position as Foreign Relations chairman. His reply consisted of stating the obvious: that he had attempted to get the bill on to the floor for a vote, had never objected to a vote, and had stated on the floor his desire to vote on it. He said that at all times his actions were designed to give the Senate a chance to act, but that he could not support the bill in the form in which it had emerged from the Foreign Relations Committee.

What made Stone's denial seem rather hollow was the fact the he had spoken for over five hours on the bill—and his remarks were more critical of it than perhaps he was willing to admit. His had been, as noted, the longest single speech of the entire session, the type of address usually given by someone who is consciously participating in a filibuster. It is probable that he would have been blamed even had he spoken for five minutes, owing to the fact that he did not sign the manifesto, for this, rather than the length of speeches, was the criterion.[14]

Also, Stone was vulnerable to any charges leveled against him for filibustering. He was experienced in this activity and apparently notorious for it. Once he reportedly recited *Pilgrim's Progress* to assist in keeping a vote from being taken. Both Penrose and Kenyon had commented earlier about his reputation in this area.[15]

As for Kenyon, he answered charges against himself by pointing out that he had never objected to a vote, never spoken, nor done anything that might be construed as filibustering. He said that he could have voted for an amended bill, but since the measure had not been amended, he could not sign the manifesto as it was presented to him. "I did not see in the document [the manifesto] a test as to whether one was a patriot or a traitor."

Cummins said that he would have voted for an amended bill, but he did not deny being part of the filibuster. He agreed that they were evil, but said that sometimes they were necessary—as when there is the danger of a dictatorial chief executive.[16]

LaFollette did not deny filibustering either and defended his actions in an article entitled "The Armed Ship Bill Meant War," which contained much of what he had wanted to say on the floor. He claimed that he opposed the bill because he believed it to be his duty under the oath of office he took to uphold the Constitution. This, he claimed, he would have stated on the floor of Congress, had not the majority resorted to the measures that it "vociferously condemned" in order to prevent him from obtaining the floor to speak out against the bill.

First, he pointed out, the expiration date of the Sixty-fourth Congress and the nine months hiatus would have left Wilson alone in the Capitol, without the Congress to ride herd on him. This would mean that Congress would have no say in foreign affairs, whereas it should be regarded as an equal partner in this area.

Second, Wilson had brought the bill to the Congress with very little time left to debate it—some sixty-eight hours for the committee, and less than fifty after it got out of committee and was ready to be discussed on the floor. If the bill, he suggested, was so important, why was so little time allowed for the Congress to discuss it? It was a typical ploy of the president's, he charged, for in the past he had kept other important bills back so that by their having to be debated under the gun of adjournment, sufficient examination by the legislature was impossible.

LaFollette also criticized the bill itself for the amount of discretion it would give the president. He was referring to the "other instrumentalities" provision, which, he charged, could even have given the president the power to convoy ships laden with munitions, could have permitted him to order the navy to hunt submarines, and could even have given him the power to send an army to Germany to destroy factories where they were made.

But even the proposal to arm merchant vessels was objectionable to the Wisconsin Republican. He sneered at the possibility that the armed vessels could really cope with the submarines—most of the vessels which had been sunk by the German U-boats had been sunk from a great distance, and all the armaments in the world could not have saved them. How, he asked his readers, could the United States, with a navy inferior to that of Great Britain, do something that the British had failed to do? The British, he said, had realized that they could not stop the submarines directly and had channeled their forces into establishing a blockade to counter the effects of the Germans' actions. Stopping submarines, he suggested, is not so simple a matter as Wilson and the senators who favored the bill might think.

He stressed the point that many of those who favored the bill also favored war—and recognized that the bill could well bring war about. He pointed to a case in international law which he claimed backed up his contention that the bill would lead to a declared war, for it involved the use of force, and the case, he argued, contended that contention by force between two nations is war. In effect, he claimed, arming merchant vessels was war—whether declared or not.

He was also caustic about the way the United States had ignored British violations of neutrality and the law of the sea. He produced a long list of violations of neutrality by the British which the United States, he believed, had allowed to go unchallenged. Why, he asked rhetorically, has the United States not condemned Britain as well as Germany? The answer, he said, lay in the close economic ties between the United States and the former nation.[17]

Norris, too, made no effort to disguise his participation in the filibuster, although he would not, as he indicated in his speech on the floor, have opposed an amended bill. His main objections were, as noted, to the potential problem involved in arming merchant ships with munitions on board and to the granting of "other instrumentalities" to the president. His defense of his actions is best summarized in his autobiography, written some twenty-five years after the event.

He was, by this time, somewhat reluctant to justify the use of a filibuster under normal circumstances, since the instrument was associated with certain causes in the early forties of which he disapproved. But he admitted to having taken part in this filibuster and rationalized it on the grounds that it was the only way to prevent America from being plunged into war. Passage of the bill, he believed, would have given Wilson the right to provoke an undeclared war which would soon escalate into a declared one.

Admitting to the evil of filibusters, Norris said that any senator who participated in one took a heavy responsibility upon himself. Not only did he block the bill that he opposed, but other legislation as well. Thus, he contended, the senator would have to consider that the matter he wished to obstruct was so malicious as to warrant such a course. In the case of the Armed Ship Bill, he felt justified, although not entirely happy with the way that much of the nation appeared to view his actions.[18]

His sensitivity to the criticism that followed his participation in the filibuster led him to the now famous incident that is used as the basis of his inclusion in President Kennedy's *Profiles in Courage,* and on which much of the legend of Norris is based. Noting the antagonism that was being manifested by the newspapers in Nebraska (particularly Hitchcock's *Omaha World Herald*) and elsewhere, he sent a letter to Governor Keith Neville of his state, offering to resign and submit himself to a special election to test the true sentiment of his constituents.

His letter, written against the advice of several other members of what

remained of the antiwar bloc, particularly LaFollette, contained one reservation. He would have to be sure, he wrote the governor, that the election would be honest, for he suggested the possibility that the traditional
archenemies of the Midwest reformers, the corporations and the forces of
wealth, would pour money into the election in order to be rid of him.
This was just what LaFollette feared. Moreover, he was concerned that a
defeat of Norris would be a severe blow to the antiwar movement, coming
as it would in what was considered to be a neutralist state, Nebraska. Even
Borah, when he heard of the proposal, put out a statement calling Norris a
valued public servant, in case the latter's offer was taken up.

There are varying explanations as to why Norris undertook such a risky
move. On one side, there is the conventional explanation—that Norris, like
many reformers, had a deep-rooted belief in the fact that a legislator had
to represent his constituents and that he was, in fact, speaking for a majority of Nebraskans. And in light of the criticism from most of the large papers in his native state, it would be necessary to test this thesis. Against
this argument is the fact that through most of George Norris's career he
displayed considerable indifference to public opinion, in Nebraska and elsewhere, and just as he could not be a rubber stamp for the president, as he
would assert to his fellow Nebraskans, he could not be their rubber stamp,
either. On the other side is the possibility that he believed that the publicity attendant on such a move would give him a chance to get his message
across to the people of his state, and that in the event his offer was accepted, there was sufficient antiwar sentiment in Nebraska to guarantee his reelection. And since the Democratic party in Nebraska was split between
the Bryan and the Hitchcock forces, it would not be in a position to fight
a strenuous battle on such short notice.

By March 25 Norris, still with no word from Neville, left Washington
to go back to Nebraska and tell his story. His reception was probably dis-
appointing, for when he arrived in Lincoln, he found practically no one
there to greet him. What few friends tried to reach him had but one thought—
get out of town in a hurry and forget the idea of trying to talk to Nebraskans
at this time about why he filibustered the Armed Ship Bill to death. Most
of them who did try to see him slipped quietly up the back stairs to his hotel
room, rather than be seen in public with him. The manager of the hall he
rented was fearful of violence and was reluctant to let the meeting go on.

Over the weekend Norris had only one visitor, a young newspaperman
named Frederick Babcock, who represented the *Nebraska State Journal,*
one of the large papers in that state which was hostile to him. Babcock
offered to write the story the way Norris wanted it and publish it, noting
that the editors would be away over the weekend and there would be no

problem getting it into the paper. Norris accepted, for this was the only real chance that he would have to tell his story in the large journals. Most of them were not even telling Nebraskans that he was back in town to tell his side of the affair. He was a deserted prophet in his own land.

His appearance on Monday morning before the state legislature did little to bolster his morale; he found them cold and unfriendly. His own autobiography at this point suggests that he had become disillusioned about his mission, and some of the newspapers were now beginning to pick up on the story of this trip with the suggestion that he had lost control of his faculties and ought to be institutionalized. At eight that evening he finally left for the hall to begin his efforts.

When he walked on the stage of the hall, he was greeted by silence. This was an improvement over what he had expected, for he anticipated a hostile greeting. He had to introduce himself, as he could not get anyone to volunteer for the task.

However, once he got into the body of his talk, he found the audience more responsive. He told them that he had come home to tell the truth, and they reacted with applause. The few friends of his who had come to the hall, packing revolvers in case of trouble, breathed a sigh of relief. George Norris had won his gamble.

He told the crowd (and others during the following week) of the war in Europe and the policies in Washington as he perceived them. He told them that the war was Wall Street's idea, that it was backed by the international money trust, and told them also that it was these groups which had influenced the preparedness program, had caused pro-Allied attitudes to build up in the Capitol, and had eventually led to the arming of merchant ships to protect commerce and investments.

Norris was relying on the populism, the xenophobia, and isolationism of Nebraskans by stressing the theme that the war was not America's, much less Nebraska's. It was strictly for the benefit of the few, the moneymakers who had influenced the administration, an administration that was now trying to get the country into war but did not dare do it directly by seeking a declaration. Instead, it was trying to create some sort of provocative situation that would guarantee that the people would demand war. That was the peril of the Armed Ship Bill.

He told them that the war was popular in the East—in New York, where the Carnegie Hall rally, attended by the wealthy, had called for war. Their poodle dogs, he said, were numerous enough to be a "regiment."

He finished by telling them of his brother's death in the Civil War, of his mother's suffering, and of his love of country and of its flag. He said that he never wanted to see the flag tarnished by having a dollar sign attached. He was greeted by further applause when he finished his speech, a speech he would repeat several times later, with much the same results. The larger papers, however, continued to play down his arguments, charging that he did not discuss the issues and that his arguments were foolish. A few of the smaller journals were somewhat sympathetic.

Governor Neville, possibly on orders from Wilson, but more likely out of a sense of political wisdom, declined Norris's offer, saying that a special election would be unprecedented. Even so, Norris did not have long to wait, for there was only one year remaining in his first term, which expired in 1919. However, by the time the primaries and general election could be held, the effect of the war had settled on most Nebraskans. And when he ran in the primary, the regular Republicans put up Congressman Charles Sloan as his opposition, who had voted against the war resolution—hardly an alternative for those who regarded Norris as a pro-German or a traitor. Norris won.

In the general election Norris had even more luck. The Hitchcock faction won the Democratic primary and put up a man named John Morehead. Bryan, despite his experience in losing, could never do so gracefully and sent word to his supporters to boycott any candidate who was a "wet." Even Woodrow Wilson, in a year in which he made an impassioned partisan appeal for a Democratic Congress, gave Morehead only a perfunctory endorsement, presumably because he still did not wish to offend Bryan and still was not too enthusiastic about Hitchcock. Norris won handily.

To a degree the junior senator from Nebraska was correct in his view that the people of Nebraska were somewhat less enthusiastic about the war than the newspapers would have one believe. He also was correct in assuming that his side of the issue, slanted as it was, had not received much of an airing. Whether his actions in going back to Nebraska to tell his side were "foolish," as LaFollette and others had argued, or courageous, as his biographers assert, at least he was able to provide his constituents with an opportunity to hear that other side of the issue.[19]

Some Questions about the Filibuster

There are some questions about the period immediately prior to March 4 that have been the subject of controversy.

One question concerns the existence of the filibuster and the participation in it of all of those so charged. In the words of Norris and LaFollette, there was a filibuster on the Armed Ship Bill (as distinguished from the mini-filibuster staged by the Republicans on the revenue bill a few days earlier), one in which the participants were aware of what they were doing and had consciously set out to block a vote. Clearly, it would appear that at least three, and possibly four, other senators were a party to this conspiracy; Gronna, Clapp, Cummins, and, in all probability, Works. However, with respect to the other six alleged obstructionists, doubt exists.

All the others specifically denied taking part in a conspiracy to filibuster; and only one of them, Stone, spoke for any great length of time on the bill. And Stone, several times during the period prior to the formal discussion of armed neutrality, went to great lengths to ensure that the bill got on the floor. As chairman of the Foreign Relations Committee, he was in a position to bottle it up in committee as so many committee chairmen have done with proposed legislation that they oppose. Therefore, his actions during the period under discussion have to be viewed in a different light from those of others.

Vardaman and Kirby spoke for relatively short periods of time, and O'Gorman's time on the floor during the debate was very brief. Kenyon, who admittedly did meet with the filibusterers, never spoke at all. Harry Lane spoke for a while, but never took part in any of the efforts to keep the bill from being voted on. In Lane's case there are some inferences that he did meet with the planners of the filibuster and that his lack of help in keeping a vote from being taken was probably due to the fact that, given the state of his health, he could not remain on the floor for any period of time.

Therefore, none of these six took any action that could be called part of a filibuster—if one specifically separates speaking against a bill that others are filibustering from tactics such as objecting to unanimous consent rulings. Their inclusion, along with that of the other six, the Republican progressives, is based largely on the fact that all twelve refused to sign the manifesto which professed support for Wilson's version of the bill.

However, it must be pointed out that those who spoke against the bill, specifically Stone, Lane, O'Gorman, Vardaman, and Kirby, knew that they were "helping" by consuming time. In addition, there is evidence that those against the measure agreed to a speaking order (not an unusual tactic for opponents of any legislation), so these Democrats knew of the filibuster and were not unwilling to have their names bracketed with those senators who were going to do the dirty work initially. They were not so guilty perhaps as they were accused of being, but they were not so totally innocent as they would protest that they were.

The behavior of other senators during the debate raises another question, for, as pointed out in an earlier part of the book, the twelve who stood accused formed less than half of what had been a rather substantial bloc of

143

neutralist senators—Democrats such as Hitchcock, Martine, Hoke Smith, Hardwick, Ashurst, and Thomas, as well as Republicans like Townsend, William Smith, Jones, McCumber, Curtis, and Sherman. (Keep in mind that Gore, previously identified with the antiwar bloc, was not present.) One aspect of this question asks why they chose to support the bill, and another raises the issue of whether some of them might have been among those who reportedly offered to assist the dissenters by taking up time.

On the latter count, there has been only one attempt to identify a possible collaborator, and that is the previously mentioned suggestion by Phillips that Ellison Smith's actions early in the morning of March 4 might have been his contribution to the success of the filibuster. However, Phillips presents a better argument for this being a case of carelessness rather than deliberate, and this writer is disposed to accept that interpretation. There is little, if anything, in Smith's views or in his career that would suggest that he might have felt strongly enough about the Armed Ship Bill to have behaved thus. He certainly (note the list above) was not one of those senators identified during the period prior to 1917 as an opponent of belligerent diplomacy.[20]

If insistence on discussing extraneous material on the floor during the filibuster is a criterion for identifying the "silent partners," then Henry Myers becomes a prime candidate for inclusion. Myers had sometimes sided with the neutralist senators, although perhaps not enough to be listed as one of them. However, Myers wrote a book about his life in the Senate, and in it he does not either mention being one of the "collaborators" or indicate much sympathy for the dissenting senators in his account of these events.

What Myers does do, however, is to suggest another candidate for whatever distinction might come to one of these senators who "aided" the filibuster. For in writing of the fight over the Armed Ship Bill, he lists as opponents Townsend, Jones, Penrose, Gore, and Hardwick, in addition to those most commonly named, minus Clapp, Works, O'Gorman, Kirby, and Kenyon. Some of his inclusions and exclusions can be explained; he probably omitted Works, Clapp, and O'Gorman because they left the Senate right after the filibuster, and Kenyon because of the fact that the Iowan never spoke on the bill. As for the inclusions, Townsend and Jones are probably there because of the fact that they signed the manifesto with reservations, and Penrose because of his initial unwillingness to sign. Gore is probably there because of his reputation; writing many years later, Myers probably forgot that the Oklahoman was ill and away from the Senate.[21]

But in mentioning Hardwick, he might have been repeating what he knew at the time—that the Georgia senator, while a signer of the manifesto, was supporting the dissenters. For even without this account, a good case could be made for him; he spoke for a considerable time, he had a fairly consistent record of opposition to belligerent diplomacy, and talked about "presidential despotism." He continued to talk about the latter even after war was declared.

Hoke Smith and Thomas also took up time on the floor speaking for the bill, and they had been frequently critical of belligerency, although in the case of the former the exchange that he had with LaFollette in the final hours of the debate hardly suggests a man in sympathy. On the other hand, LaFollette reports that on the eve of the debate Smith had told him that he would not object to seeing a special session.[22]

Since Norris specified that the individuals who offered him this covert help were Democrats, speculation on this point has centered only on members of that party. However, it should be noted that three Republicans who had been previously associated with the neutralist position, Townsend, Jones, and McCumber, spoke at length for the proposal (albeit in all three cases with considerable qualification).

Then there is the matter of the specific stances taken by other antiwar senators on this bill. In this respect, they can be divided into three categories. First, there are those who had been converted by this time either to a point of accepting Wilson's lead in foreign policy, or else to a point where they could countenance a more hostile policy towards Germany. In some instances, this could be said to be due to the impact of events; in others, the impact of constituency reaction to these events; and in some, the impact of Woodrow Wilson. Hoke Smith might be said to fall into this category, and so also might Ashurst. In fact, Ashurst's journal reveals what might seem to be a sharp change in direction during this period, beginning with the account of his reaction to the meeting with Bryan in the Lafayette Hotel in February.[23]

Hitchcock would belong in the second category, that of senators who still regarded themselves as neutralists and against war, but who believed that armed neutrality was a risky, though possibly effective, way to keep the United States out of war. As has been noted, even though he would have preferred the Stone amendment, Hitchcock was a proponent of armed neutrality, and as will be shown, he did not abandon his commitment to this until virtually the eve of war.

Finally, there are the hesitators—the most important of whom are Jones, McCumber, Townsend, Martine, and possibly one or two of the others, including Hardwick. McCumber's long-winded resolution betrays the concern of a man trying to keep a foot in each camp, not committed either way, but, perhaps most important at this time, still not committed to belligerence in diplomacy. Jones, as noted earlier, tended to be an equivocator on a number of issues, and his performance on this matter is not too surprising.

There were, of course, no votes on any substantive aspect of the Armed Ship proposal; therefore, one cannot know definitively how the fifteen or so neutralists would have voted, either on the main motion or on the amendments. Possibly some of them, whose position at this time was one of indecision, were anxious to see the filibuster succeed, particularly those who felt that they had divided constituencies on the war-peace issue. If for no other reason than the publication of the Zimmermann Note, anything less than a full defense of American rights might have seemed treasonous to some voters; anything directed towards war particularly odious to others.

Had the filibusterers chosen to stop their tactics and allow a vote, the results might have been interesting. Most of the dissenters said that they would vote for an amended bill, particularly one with a clause that would prevent the arming of munitions-bearing vessels (and probably, in most instances, one that had struck out the "other instrumentalities" provision). Possibly, this claim was made to take the onus of obstructionism off their backs in some cases; in others, it was probably sincere.

Then there is the question of why they filibustered, that is, those who consciously did so. Obviously, they did not do so because they believed that the president could be prevented from arming merchant ships, because most of them had admitted during the course of the debate that they believed that he already had that power. Similarly, it is doubtful that they believed they could really obstruct him in any way from doing what he wanted to do, because he had given every indication upon many occasions that he intended to conduct America's foreign policy as he wished, with no help or hindrance from the Congress.

The answer can be found partially in the fact that they represented constituencies which they believed would understand only this dramatic type of action. They had to be consistent with the faith—they were prisoners, as it were, of their own rhetoric. For if the matter was as grave as they claimed it was, a simple speech against the bill and a "no" vote would not have been sufficient.

But perhaps more to the point was the matter raised by Norris in his defense. The senators had been confronted by a crisis in which they believed that the whole constitutional system was being perverted in order to put Wilson in a position where he would have the dictatorial right, by their definition, to wage war at his discretion. Not only would he have the power to use the "other instrumentalities," but he would have the implied sanction of the legislature to take whatever action he thought appropriate. The filibuster would prevent, for the time at least, the complete acceptance by the Congress of the president's unlimited power in foreign affairs. More cogent than the fear of what might happen if an armed ship fought a submarine was the concern over how the president would act in the nine months before the new legislature was due to meet. There was no alternative.[24]

Those who did filibuster were men who had been obliged to do the unorthodox through much of their political life; they were outsiders, save, of course, for Stone, and he was probably not involved in the filibuster directly. They knew that they were possibly risking political disgrace and calumny (although not to the extent that it came upon them) and were willing to accept the immediate consequences in light of what they believed would be the judgment of history.

Of course, there is the question of the right of a minority to obstruct—a point that some of the senators raised against the dissenters during the debate and that Wilson brought up in his "willful men" statement. This point is perhaps best answered in the defense of his actions made by Norris, noted previously, agreeing that there is a question as to whether senators have a right to obstruct, and the test that must be applied is whether or not that which they are filibustering against is a greater evil than the tactic itself. Obviously, the dissenters believed that the Armed Ship Bill was that "greater evil." Therefore, they regarded themselves as justified in blocking the vote on the bill, as, of course, do many revisionist historians and probably anyone who doubts the wisdom of American participation in World War I.

The problem is that the same argument could probably be made (and has been) by any senator participating in a filibuster. So, the question cannot be definitively answered—only rationalized by each member of the Senate in light of his own perceptions.

The Antifilibuster Move

Even before the Armed Ship Bill's fate was assured, Wilson had planned a special session of the Senate for the purpose of dealing with the treaty he had concluded with Colombia, indemnifying her for certain acts undertaken by the United States during the Roosevelt presidency in connection with the Panama affair. Thus, the stage was set for the Senate to have an opportunity to deal with what the public had viewed to be a grave constitutional crisis—the filibuster.

Most senators did not want to get rid of the filibuster—many of them had taken advantage of the Senate rules in the past—but with an aroused public there was almost as much resentment over the filibuster as there was over the fact that American rights had not been defended to the utmost. When Wilson announced that the rules of the Senate would have to be revised before he would consider a special session of the whole Congress, the fate of unlimited debate was sealed. Within forty-eight hours of adjournment, almost forty senators, including Kirby, Stone, and Lane, had signed a statement agreeing to reform the Senate rules.

What sort of change, no one mentioned at this time. The nature of public opinion was such that most people, who knew very little about the complexity of Senate rules, would accept virtually anything. They equated the filibuster with obstructionism and treason, and that was enough for them.

The official sponsor of this antifilibuster resolution was Owen, although the responsibility rested with the new Senate majority leader, Martin of Virginia, to direct it. Owen was a long-time advocate of cloture, although like so many others who were now for ending unlimited debate, he was not above speaking at length when it suited his purpose.[25]

By the time the Senate got down to the actual business of revising the rules, most of the senators had endorsed the idea and the caucuses were reported as nearly unanimous. A bipartisan committee consisting of Lodge, Penrose, Cummins, Brandegee, Borah, Owen, Hoke Smith, Walsh, Swanson, James, and Reed, drew up the formal proposal.[26]

The committee recommended a two-thirds vote to curtail debate, but Democratic Senator Henry Hollis, a progressive from New Hampshire and one of the first of his party ever to be elected to the Senate from that state, demurred. He suggested that a simple majority would be sufficient. Since the Senate was now under pressure to pass almost anything that would restrict the filibuster, and might have been swayed in any direction, one might speculate that had Hollis's proposal gone through, filibustering in later years would have been difficult. However, Martin persuaded him to withdraw his suggestion.[27]

Only three senators voted against the change: Sherman (who, of course, had not been a party to the Armed Ship filibuster), Gronna, and LaFollette. Vardaman, Stone, and Cummins were among those who spoke in favor of change, the last using some of his time on the floor to emphasize how little time had actually been consumed during the recent debate by those charged with filibustering. Norris, Kenyon, and Kirby also voted in favor of the change.

Some of the senators who spoke for the proposal said that they were doing so with great reluctance. Hardwick, worsening his already bad relationship with Wilson, said that he had reservations. Townsend was critical of the president and his tactics, while Smoot laid out in elaborate detail all the figures which pointed up what the antibill senators had said—had only they spoken against the measure, it would have passed with time to spare.

LaFollette spoke angrily against the change. He called it a first step towards the suppression of free speech in wartime, bitterly denouncing those men who would give the president everything he wanted and relinquish the Senate's sacred right of unlimited debate. He charged that the senators had caved in under pressure.[28]

Under the provisions of the new rule, cloture would begin with a petition signed by sixteen members; then, two calendar days after the submission of it, a vote would be held. If two-thirds of those present and voting approved of the proposal, each senator could speak thereafter for only one hour, and no amendments could be added save by unanimous consent. This change, had it been in effect at the time of the Armed Ship filibuster, could not have stopped it; keep in mind, the debate on the bill did not begin until forty-four hours before adjournment; therefore, the only way to have halted it would have been to circulate the petition before the debate even started—and well before. In fact, few filibusters have ever been stopped by cloture (the ruling of 1917 has been modified since then).

Asle Gronna had one last comment. "Forgive them, for they know not what they do."[29]

The Decision for War

During the period immediately following the Armed Ship debate, the Senate was busy reforming its rules, scuttling the Colombian Peace Treaty, and making belligerent noises. Woodrow Wilson was fighting off a bad cold at this time, as well as the growing demand within his official family that he ask for a declaration of war. And he was losing on both fronts.

Two days after the inauguration he took to bed, reflecting, among other things, on the matter of arming merchant ships. The word was put out that he would not be receiving visitors, but on March 8 Mrs. Wilson telephoned Josephus Daniels, asking him to come around to the White House. In spite of the official story, the president was going to see at least one visitor—him. The subject, Daniels discovered, was the matter of arming merchant vessels, for Wilson indicated that he wanted to take advantage of his position as commander-in-chief and put weapons on them. This, of course, is what the opponents to his bill had always maintained he had the power to do without any sort of legislative approval.[30]

Wilson had conferred previously with Lansing and Attorney General Gregory about the matter, as well as about the question raised by Lodge during the debate over the Armed Ship Bill—the 1819 statute that the Massachusetts senator had argued prevented gunners on armed merchantmen from firing on potential attackers. They concurred that the law in question did not present the problem that the Republican leader thought it did. Lansing continued during these discussions to press Wilson to arm the ships,[31] although, in fact, the president had already made up his mind, and only clear evidence to the effect that he did not have the power to do so would have deterred him at this point.

On March 9 the White House announced that the chief executive had concluded that he did have the power to arm merchant ships, and that he was going to do so. The final orders went out on March 13. Of perhaps greater interest was the fact that Wilson announced that he was going to call a special session of the Congress on April 16.[32]

There were no challenges to Wilson's announcement that he was going to arm merchant vessels, least of all from any of the senators who had opposed the bill in the last hours of the Sixty-fourth Congress. Both Cummins and Kenyon rushed to the press to announce that they favored the move and gave it their unqualified endorsement. Lane was evasive; from his sickbed he sent word that the president had acted and the time for comment had passed. Norris said that he did not approve of the idea, but if the president had the power to arm the ships, there was no way to stop him. LaFollette, Gronna, and Stone could not be reached for comment.[33]

The remainder of the month was spent by the Senate and the nation in debate over whether armed neutrality was a sufficient response or whether the United States should go one step further and declare war. Because of the short time between the final orders to arm ships and the declaration of war, the idea of armed neutrality never really had a sufficient trial to determine just how effective it might have been in ensuring what many regarded as the defense of American rights and keeping the nation out of war. For, each day the newspapers reported a greater degree of eagerness on the part of the nation for a war declaration, or editorialized on the subject themselves.

Public opinion was heightened by the sinking of a number of unarmed American vessels between March 14 and 18. Only in one instance were lives lost, and this the result of a lifeboat accident. However, the impact was no less severe.

Although still reluctant, Wilson was beginning to wonder aloud about a war declaration. A newspaperman close to him, Frank Cobb of the *New York World*, visited him on March 19 and reported later that he seemed fairly well convinced at that point. Some historians are less than persuaded today of the nature of the Wilson-Cobb meeting, so the report must be taken with some measure of reservation; but, in essence, Cobb reports Wilson as saying that he did not believe that he had any alternative but to ask for a declaration. Cobb also reports that even at this point the president had reservations as to whether or not any sort of peace treaty would come out of the war that would have any meaning—an interesting point in light of the later battles over the Treaty of Versailles.

The journalist also reports on Wilson's concern over the consequences of the war at home, where he believed that it would bring about a reversal of liberalism. He predicted that war, if it came, would mean the brutalization of American society, and he feared even the possible demise of the Constitution. It will be recalled that he made remarks of a very similar nature to Josephus Daniels some time earlier.[34]

During the period between the Armed Ship debate and the declaration of war, another event occurred which had a positive effect on many Americans' thoughts about involvement on the Allied side and may also have favorably impressed Wilson. This was the Russian uprising which unseated Czar Nicholas II. It is possible that some historians have exaggerated the importance of the Russian Revolution from the point of view of stirring Wilson, but it was a fact that now all the Allied nations had thrown off "despotism."[35]

On March 20 the president met with his cabinet. All those who were to write of this meeting later would indicate that this was the time at which the decision was reached for a declaration of war. They include Lansing, Franklin Lane, and Houston among the militant faction, as well as Daniels.

According to accounts of the event, the president assembled them in the cabinet room and began to review the situation leading up to the events of the previous week. Then, as he had done prior to the decision to break relations with Germany some seven weeks earlier, he went around the room, asking each to give his opinion. McAdoo, the first to respond, was for war, Redfield said that he was in favor of a declaration also, and Houston said that he believed that the United States was already at war and the time had come to formalize it.

Lansing's position was well known, but he gave his views. Baker, Gregory, and William Wilson also concurred, the latter saying that he was reluctant but agreed that the United States should declare war. Then the president turned to Burleson and Daniels.

If there was to be opposition to war, it would be from either of these. But Burleson, who spoke first, said that he was for calling the Congress together and asking them for a declaration of war. He said, however, that he

151

still harbored personal feelings as to why the United States should not go to war, and that he was speaking the way he did with reservations. But, he added, there was no other way.

Daniels also was reluctant. He wrote afterwards that he wanted to be relieved of the responsibility of having to make a decision in this case because of the enormity of the matter involved. In all probability, had he demurred, or had he dissented from the position of his colleagues, it would not have altered the outcome. But abandoning the position he had been forced to defend alone in the cabinet against such men as Houston, Franklin Lane, Redfield, and Lansing ever since Bryan's departure, the navy secretary indicated in a quavering voice that war seemed bound to come and it would be best to call the Congress into session.

Wilson thanked them for their advice, noting that there was little question as to what it was. Lansing wrote afterwards that he and the other intervention-minded cabinet members were gratified at the result. He and the president conferred briefly after the meeting about the timing of the situation and concluded that it would be best to move the date of the special congressional session up to April 2.[36]

As Wilson began to take steps to prepare his message, the demands for war grew. All the Republican elder statesmen issued statements calling for war, chief among them Theodore Roosevelt, who yearned to lead a division into battle, as well as William Howard Taft, Elihu Root, Charles Evans Hughes, and others. The newspapers of the period report numerous instances of meetings which closed with near-unanimous resolutions calling upon Congress to declare war. There were dissenting views: Bryan continued to urge America to stay out, David Starr Jordan, Jane Addams, and Eugene Debs joined in the cry, but their voices were muted.

To most of the antiwar senators, the news that the special session was being advanced from April 16 to April 2 spelled the end of any hopes they may have harbored that war could be averted. At least one other senator, who had favored the Armed Ship Bill but who still hoped that the United States could stay out of the conflict, was worried. This was Gilbert Hitchcock.

On March 29 he wrote Wilson, urging the president to try armed neutrality a little longer. By this date Wilson had already made up his mind to ask Congress for a declaration. Apparently, feeling that Hitchcock's support for a war resolution would be critical, given Stone's position, he managed somehow to communicate to the Nebraskan that whatever the merits of armed neutrality, the time had passed for that to be the keystone of American policy. As Hitchcock would say later, he was persuaded.[37]

As for those senators who had opposed the bill, only six of them remained to possibly vote against American entry into the war. Three of the dissenters, Clapp, Works, and O'Gorman, had left the Senate, and it would not be unreasonable to assume that the first two would probably have voted against the resolution. Three other men who had opposed arming merchant ships had "shifted" their position.

Kirby, as he would note in his speech to the Senate during the debate over the war resolution, was torn by doubts. But it would appear from the nature of his remarks on the floor that he had finally capitulated to the pressures on him. As for Albert Cummins and William Kenyon, it would seem that they were impressed and concerned for their futures by the reaction to their opposition to the Armed Ship Bill back in Iowa. Cummins was apparently so affected by the criticism that he suffered a physical collapse while addressing a group of Republicans in Washington.

LaFollette was still committed to fight against war until the very end, as were Norris, Gronna, and Lane. The only question about the last was his health and whether he would be able to make it to the chamber to vote when the time came. Stone and Vardaman were under the heaviest pressure to switch. Reed spent a great deal of time with the former, pleading with him to recant and support the president, warning him that it would be political suicide not to.

The senior senator from Missouri reportedly told his colleague that on matters such as this political expediency did not count. He said that he was opposed to the war, not so much because of the cost in lives or in money, but because he feared the consequences to the American political system. He believed that the way of life that Americans had known would be swept away by the war.[38]

Vardaman had miscalculated the feelings of most Mississippians, for he was the target of considerable abuse. Warned by his friends that he was making a mistake, he told them, however, that he was going to stick to his decision in spite of the consequences. Later, in a reply to an editorial in a Mississippi newspaper, he rejected the idea that lack of support for the president was treasonous, by quoting Patrick Henry on the subject.[39]

But for all his bravado, Vardaman was alarmed and saddened. He wrote Bryan, who was living in Florida, that war seemed to be inevitable; nothing could prevent it.[40]

No such feelings were expressed by the other senator from Mississippi. In calling for a war declaration, John Sharp Williams said that he hoped the president would send a million men abroad. And he added that he hoped that for the sake of the South the bands would play "Dixie" as the troops deployed into position.[41]

9

THE WAR RESOLUTION

April 2 1917

April 2 was cool and damp as legislators, members of the executive and the judicial branches, diplomats, most of official Washington, as well as some invited guests, prepared to go to the Capitol, where at two that afternoon the president of the United States was due to deliver a major address, the nature of which practically everyone in Washington believed he already knew. The excitement of the occasion was, however, as if the contents of it were still a mystery; Myers would say later that it was the most thrilling day in his life;[1] Houston, seeing it as the culmination of his efforts to get the United States into the war, would call it the most dramatic scene that he had ever witnessed.[2]

Pacifists and other opponents of war did not find it to be either thrilling or dramatic. They paraded through the halls of the Capitol, accosting legislators, trying to persuade them to see why the war was inconceivable. But they found that the number of lawmakers who were still unwilling to vote for war had dwindled down to a mere handful in the Senate and just a few more in the House. One of the delegations got into a discussion with Henry Cabot Lodge, who indicated that he was going to vote for war, and one of their number punched the senior senator from Massachusetts, only to be beaten in turn by the Capitol police and others. Just who struck first is not clear, but Lodge always maintained afterwards that he had thrown the first blow, even though he obviously had gotten the worst of it from a younger and bigger man.[3]

The president could not begin his speech when scheduled, because of procedural problems in the House of Representatives. The new House had not yet been organized, for the division in that chamber had given neither party a clear advantage. Actually, the Republicans had more, but the Democrats, aided by defectors, were able to organize the chamber and rename Champ Clark as Speaker. Then came the selection of other officers, and the result was the prolongation of the meeting until it became obvious that the president would not be able to speak until after dinner.[4]

There was a certain touch of the macabre to the proceedings: a nation postponing its consideration of a war resolution while some of its legislators wrangled over the petty spoils of office. To the spectators, the wait seemed interminable. Many of them, fearful of losing their places for this history-making event, refused to leave and had to sit through the desultory debate on the floor and through countless rumors as to when Wilson was finally going to come.

Back at the White House, Wilson waited nervously. He conferred with House during the afternoon; Link reports that his adviser was somewhat exercised that the president had written the whole speech himself, with no advice from anyone else. All that he had done was to check out some minor technical points with Lansing.

He had risen early that morning, played a round of golf (remember again his reluctance to play on the morning of the receipt of the news that Germany had decided to resume unrestricted submarine warfare). At ten-thirty he saw Lansing with a copy of the war resolution (not the speech that the president was to deliver asking for its enactment), and suggested that the secretary show it to some legislators. Just whom Lansing showed it to is not completely clear; he did show it to at least three persons, specifically, Chairman Flood, Claude Swanson, and the newly elected Republican senator from Pennsylvania, Philander Knox, a former secretary of state in the Taft administration.[5] Williams's biographer asserts that the president had met with the Mississippian to have him "prepare" his colleagues.[6]

Shortly after eight in the evening, accompanied by his wife, Tumulty, and Dr. Grayson, Wilson set out for the Capitol with a cavalry escort that had been called out by Secretary Baker. Apparently the presence of peace demonstrators in the Capitol had caused a certain amount of panic, although there is no report that the president was worried or even took any notice of it. When he arrived at the Capitol, he found it bathed in light, lending an almost daylight effect to the occasion. At the door, as is the custom when the president arrives to address Congress on momentous occasions, he was greeted by an official escort of senators and representatives.

Inside was what some writers have described as one of the most distinguished gatherings in American history. In addition to the legislators, the members of the cabinet, the Supreme Court led by Chief Justice White (the ex-Confederate soldier who had once confided to Houston that if he were thirty years younger, he would go to Canada to enlist),[7] there was the entire diplomatic corps. Two of these, Spring-Rice and French Ambassador Jusserand, were reportedly unable to control their happiness.

The members of the Congress had gifts for the event. Republican Senator George McLean of Connecticut had presented each of them with a small flag, which they were waving happily as the president came down the aisle towards the rostrum. (The gifts had been given to McLean for the occasion by a manufacturer of silk goods.) Some few of the legislators, however, were not waving flags, in particular LaFollette, who was sitting next to an ailing Harry Lane, the latter having been brought from a sickbed to be present. Nor, for that matter, were the other senators and representatives who had made up their minds not to vote for the resolution. They sat sadly, watching the tumult around them.[8]

One other figure in the room seemed sad and grim. Wilson's face gave testimony to the debate that had been going on in his mind over what he was to do. A friend related afterward that his features were twisted, as if in agony, while he waited to go into the chamber, and only with great effort did he compose himself and assume a grim expression when the time came to enter.[9]

But his voice was clear and crisp as he began.[10] Lodge leaned back, one leg crossed over the other, Stone slumped in his chair, Williams leaned forward to compensate for his deafness, and LaFollette began to chew gum.

Wilson told the legislators that the time had come for them to make a choice. He reviewed the situation since the breaking of relations on February 3 and then talked of the implications. "International Law had its origins in the attempt to set up some law which could be respected and observed on the seas, where no nation has the right of dominion and where lay the free highways of the world. . . ."

He spoke of how Germany had violated the rights customarily accepted as principles of this international law, how her use of the submarine violated the basic canons of decency. He dismissed armed neutrality as now no longer practical for a nation wishing to defend itself and bring peace to the world. "There is one choice we cannot make, we are incapable of making; we will not choose the path of submission."

With that, Chief Justice White rose to his feet and began to clap. Immediately others in the gallery and on the floor rose and continued clapping for several minutes. Only a few on the floor remained seated, or stood with their hands at their sides. LaFollette's jaws worked furiously.

156

With a profound sense of the solemn and even tragical character of the step I am
taking and of the grave responsibilities which it involves, but in unhesitating obe-
dience to what I deem my constitutional duty, I advise that the Congress declare
the recent course of the Imperial German Government to be in fact nothing less
than war against the government and people of the United States; that it formally
accept the status of belligerent which has been thrust upon it. . . .

He talked of the German people, of how the war was not against them
but against their government. He spoke also of his belief that war would
never have come about had all the nations met his test of being truly democratic states, mentioning the "wonderful and heartening" events in Russia.
"A steadfast concert for peace can never be maintained except by a partnership of democratic nations. . . . The world must be made safe for democracy."

Williams caught this last part, and it appealed to him. He began to clap,
and as with the previous incident involving Chief Justice White, this solitary
reaction slowly developed into a crescendo. The flags began to wave on the
floor, and some southern legislators gave out with rebel yells. The sound
was deafening.

Its peace must be planted upon the tested foundations of political liberty. We have
no selfish ends to serve. We desire no conquest, no dominion. . . . We are but one
of the champions of the rights of mankind. We shall be satisfied when those rights
have been made as secure as the faith and freedom of nations can make them. . . .
    There are, it may be, many months of fiery trial and sacrifice ahead of us.

He looked up from his manuscript for a moment at the audience.

It is a fearful thing to lead this great and peaceful people into war, into the most
terrible and disastrous of all wars, civilization itself seeming to lie in the balance.
But the right is more precious than peace, and we shall fight for the things which
we have always carried nearest to our hearts. . . . To such a task we dedicate our
lives and our fortunes . . . with the pride of those who know that the day has come
when America is privileged to spend her blood and her might for the principles that
gave her birth and happiness and the peace she treasured. God helping her, she can
do no other.

The message was over. There was a split second of silence, and then
once again the applause broke out, this time even more enthusiastically
than before. The flags, courtesy of the Connecticut manufacturer of silk
goods, waved all over the chamber in such a way as to make it look like a
sea of red, white, and blue. Wilson still stood in the rostrum, his face set
grimly, one of the few less than joyous-looking individuals in the room. As the

noise began to subside, he slowly descended and began to make his way back up the aisle through the hordes of legislators who rushed over to shake his hand.

Halfway up the aisle he was confronted by the figure of Henry Cabot Lodge. It is hard to conjecture just what went through the minds of the two men at this minute—Lodge, who had told Roosevelt that it was hard even to be civil to Wilson, and Wilson, who had told Ashurst a few weeks earlier that he would not deign to shake hands with the senior senator from Massachusetts.[11]

"Mr. President," said Lodge, "you have expressed in the loftiest manner possible, the sentiments of the American people."[12]

He offered his hand. Wilson took it.

As the president left the Capitol, the two chambers separately convened for the purpose of a perfunctory introduction of the war resolution and the referral to committee. Wilson returned to the White House with a few guests, and they talked for a while about the events of the evening.

After a while, his faithful secretary Tumulty reported, Wilson spoke to him, and to him alone. He said that his message had been one of death to the young men of America and that he could not help but notice the irony of it when men applauded him to the rafters for calling for the conflict.[13]

A sorrowful and troubled LaFollette was in full accord.[14]

April 3 1917

It took the Senate Foreign Relations Committee only a short while in the morning to approve the resolution. The only stand against it in the committee was that of Stone, who after casting his negative vote, turned the meeting over to Hitchcock and left the room. Others present at the meeting included Williams, Swanson, Pomerene, Pittman, Thomas, Saulsbury, Lodge, Fall, McCumber, Wadsworth, Borah, and Smith of Michigan.

Phillips reports that McCumber attempted to amend the resolution by offering a series of points of international law which, if violated by Germany in the future, would constitute a declaration of war. However, the source indicates, this was rejected, with only the North Dakotan voting for it.

As soon as the session of the committee was adjourned, Hitchcock hurried to the floor of the Senate with a copy of the resolution. He asked that the parliamentary niceties be disposed of and that the Senate proceed immediately to a discussion of the matter. LaFollette objected; a bill is not supposed to be debated until all members have a copy of it, and therefore he refused the Nebraskan's request for unanimous consent. Hitchcock argued that the matter was of such importance that it would be ludicrous to hold up debate on it owing to such a minor technicality—and further, copies could be obtained in a very short while. Majority leader Martin agreed, saying that the issue was of such importance that the Senate should proceed without delay.

Such remarks were insulting, LaFollette replied; "I think that I realize that as fully as he [Martin] does."

Vice President Marshall announced that LaFollette's objection was in order (an objection to a bill can force a bill or resolution to lie over one day) and would be sustained. However, Martin announced that he objected to conducting any other matters while the war resolution was pending. With a loud shout of approval, led by John Sharp Williams, the Senate agreed.

Shortly after adjournment the Democratic steering committee went into a secret session to guard against the possibility of a filibuster. They decided that they would hold the Senate in continuous session until the vote, which meant that while there might be a filibuster, it could not delay matters long. Actually, there was no plan on the part of the dissenting senators to filibuster, since there were only six of them and one of those was too enfeebled to assist in any obstruction. Another, Stone, had indicated that he only intended to speak briefly, and neither Gronna nor Vardaman was capable of any protracted oratory. However, against the possibility that some sort of action might be undertaken, the Senate was getting ready, and Martin and Gallinger telegraphed their respective colleagues to be in their places at ten-thirty the following morning.[15]

April 4 1917[16]

Only eight members of the Senate were absent when that body met for formal consideration of the war resolution. The excitement was high, both on the floor and in the galleries, the interest being centered primarily on LaFollette and the others believed to oppose the resolution. For his part, the Wisconsinite had no illusions. He knew the outcome, as did Norris, Stone, Gronna, Vardaman, and Lane, and for that matter, everyone in Washington.

Hitchcock, in charge of the bill, introduced the resolution.

Resolved, by the Senate and the House of Representatives of the United States of America in Congress assembled—That a state of war between the United States and the Imperial German Government which has been thrust upon the United States is hereby formally declared; and that the President be and is hereby authorized and directed to employ the entire naval and military forces of the United States and re-sources of the government to carry on war against the Imperial German Government, and to bring the conflict to a successful determination, all the resources of the country are hereby pledged by the Congress of the United States.

His manner was quiet and deliberate, almost apologetic. "There is no joy on this occasion," he said, "only solemnity. In contrast to others, we have nothing to gain—our only aim is to vindicate our honor and maintain our independence."

This was to set the tone for the debate. While Wilson had stressed America's moral responsibility and its need to extend democracy and make the world safe for it, the senators were talking about honor, vindication, freedom of the seas, defense of neutral rights, etc. Of the dissenting senators, only LaFollette made any effort to rebut the Wilsonian position and argument. The others relied upon an economic interpretation of the war, the role of the press, and the concept of a "false" neutrality.

Hitchcock pointed out that he had until the last been one of the most vocal of the neutralists. But then, he said, the president had persuaded him that the form of neutrality that had been the policy of the United States government was no longer possible. Therefore, he accepted the necessity of America abandoning peace and declaring war on Germany.

Swanson followed with a recitation of ship sinkings, the use of United States territory for sabotage in Canada, and the challenge to the Monroe Doctrine with the issuance of the Zimmermann Note. We cannot submit, he concluded, and remain respected in the world.

Lodge followed Swanson. Although he qualified his remarks with "I speak for myself, and, I believe, my associates," there was no doubting that this was the voice of the minority party. A few other Republicans would speak, Cummins and Kenyon to explain why they had switched, McCumber and Harding because they had particular reasons for having to express themselves personally, and Borah and one or two others. But Lodge was expressing the position of the Republican party, both in and out of Congress.

His speech was not unusually significant. He described the war as being one that was going to be fought against anarchic barbarism which dated back to the dark ages, and against the Prussian autocracy. Then he went on to describe the sort of war that the United States should fight; he wanted no "puny, half-hearted war." He wanted it prosecuted vigorously. There are some things worse than war, he said, and they are national degeneracy and cowardice.

He ridiculed the idea that the war would divide the nation. To the contrary, he argued, war would bring Americans together in a common cause.

The first speech against the war was made by Vardaman, who at one point delivered a parody of Wilson's "little group of willful men" statement by saying:

A large group of little men, with the flame of vaunted patriotism burning on their insincere tongues, will not hesitate to count the cost in sorrow and death which others are to suffer as a result of their foolish, immaturely considered acts.

Vardaman contended that the atmosphere was too charged with emotion for the matter to be discussed rationally. Each senator, he said, signs the death warrant for thousands when he votes for the war resolution. He ridiculed the idea that war could have any effect in bringing about democracy, moral reform, and a parliament of men such as Wilson believed.

He recognized that he and the few who agreed with him were in a minority and that the resolution would pass. However, he said, despite the fact that he would support the war once it was declared, he could not bring himself to vote for it.

Stone spoke for only five minutes, a brief time compared to his five-hour address on the Armed Ship Bill. His speech was quiet and emotional, but direct, as he pleaded with his colleagues to reconsider their course of action. Like Vardaman, he would support efforts to win the war; he would be a "screaming eagle" like the rest, for in a war a nation could not be divided. But, he said, "I shall vote against this mistake, to prevent which, God helping me, I would gladly lay down my life."

His last words were one day to be engraved on his tombstone.[17]

According to the Norris biographers, the one other Democrat who planned to vote against the resolution, Harry Lane, had also prepared a speech. However, he was too ill to deliver it.[18]

Porter McCumber took the floor to offer up his proposal that had been defeated in the Foreign Relations Committee. Among other things, it would place the burden on the Congress to decide when the principles which he said were fundamental to international law and the rights of neutrals had been violated by Germany.

McCumber's speech could hardly have displeased anyone, except for those anxious to go on with the vote, or to hear what it was that LaFollette had to say. He noted that he had been an advocate of keeping American citizens off the ships of belligerent nations and had favored arms embargoes. But he said that at this point in time, to back off from war would be a surrender of American honor. He also indicated that if his resolution did not pass, he would vote for the declaration.

Now George Norris took the floor with what was to be the most dramatic exchange of the session. The junior senator from Nebraska said that he blamed both sides for the war and that the United States had had an option, which it forfeited early in the conflict, to play the neutral. It had chosen to side with one of the participants; had it pressed both equally, the prospect of war would be remote.

Norris read a letter from a Wall Street stockbroker, predicting an upturn of profits when war was declared. The letter had been given to him by Kenyon, who, given his position now, could not use it. Alluding to the letter, Norris gave voice to the reformer's plaint against business, arguing that war would bring profit to the wealthy and death and hardship to the worker. War, he said, profits only the rich and powerful and brings misery to the rest of the nation. It would saddle millions unborn with a huge tax burden that would take an eternity to pay off.

"You shall not coin into gold the life blood of my brethren," Norris said. The war, he went on to explain, was little more than an attempt by the government to preserve commercial profits. Then, in one of the most famous phrases in American history, he said:

"You are . . . to put a dollar sign on the American flag."

While Norris went on in this vein, Reed tried to break in, but the Nebraskan would not cede the floor. He said that he held no brief for Germany, but neither did he for war. For America to join Europe in this conflict would be to join a catastrophe which he felt would never end and would go on for many generations.

After he finished, Reed jumped to his feet. "I trust that the Senator from Nebraska will not leave the chamber," he warned, and then called the speech an indictment of the president and likened it to giving aid and comfort to the enemy. He said that the Nebraskan's speech was close to treason.

"If . . . not treason, it grazes the edge of treason," agreed Williams.

Reed explained that in his opinion the war was over commerce, not money, and was to preserve American rights on the high seas. He and Williams pressed Norris to withdraw or dilute his remarks, but the Nebraskan clung to them and refused to recant.

Reed and James told him that the comments were insulting to Wilson. The Nebraskan agreed that they might be construed as such by the president, but that he (Norris) had a right to his opinion. He was sorry that the language was displeasing, but said that he would stand by his words. James commented that he hoped that the people of Nebraska would hear about this comment and Norris said that he was sure they would.

Pomerene asked him why it was that he claimed the war was so unpopular in light of the great demand for it from so many people. Williams wanted to press home to the Nebraskan the fact that Germany was the real culprit, challenging him to show evidence that the British had ever sunk any ships. Norris cited some evidence to the effect that at least two ships had been sunk by British mines.

Eventually the bitter and intense questioning of Norris subsided, and the time came for more prowar speeches. Ben Tillman was first, saying that war was the only way to crush the German autocracy. Then came Kenyon, noting his opposition to the Armed Ship Bill but now saying that the time had come to get behind the president. His comments were very upsetting to Norris, who knew that he opposed the war but had been pressured into voting for it. He apparently believed that the Iowan had given him the stockbroker's letter as a gesture of propitiation for having deserted the fight against the war.[19]

Then came another antiwar speech, this one from Gronna. It was brief, for as noted previously, the North Dakotan was no orator. It had none of the verbiage of Vardaman's, none of the pathos of Stone's, none of the angry defiance of Norris's. It was direct and to the point; the people did not want war, and if America was truly a democratic nation, it would test the desire of some for intervention with a national referendum. If it did not, he said, it is little better than the Germany it was condemning.

There were more speeches on behalf of the resolution. Kirby traced the history of his opposition to war, told of his personal doubts about the matter, agreed that it was not necessary, and even wrong. But he would "stand by his country" and vote for the resolution. Ashurst, who had observed sometime earlier in his diary that the nature of the war fever was inexplicable to him, was also for the resolution,[20] as was Myers, who years afterwards still seemed to feel justified by his actions.[21]

Now it was time for LaFollette, and the spectators in the galleries leaned forward as the man who had become one of the most hated men in America rose to address the Senate. He started out on a somewhat mawkish note—one of his old allies, Congressman Helgesen of North Dakota, was fatally ill and had requested him to read a plaintive letter from a North Dakota farm woman, asking that the United States avoid war.

It took the Wisconsin senator four hours to present the progressive midwestern answer to Wilson's call for war. He argued that the people would never vote for war if given a chance, but there would be no opportunity for them to do so. He claimed that his mail was overwhelmingly against the conflict and inserted many of the letters into the *Record*, claiming that this, not the editorials of the big papers and calls for war from business leaders, was the true voice of the American people. He derided Wilson's claim that the United States had no quarrel with the German people. Whom did Congress think Americans would be fighting? Perhaps wars are declared by governments on each other, he said, but they are fought by the people of the two nations involved.

LaFollette turned his attention to the matter of preserving democracy at home and spreading it abroad. He foresaw the loss of democracy in America if war came, for he feared that the pressure for unity would cause a loss of civil liberties. We will fight for democracy abroad, he said in direct answer to Wilson, and lose it here at home. As for fighting on the side of democratic nations, LaFollette was skeptical. He did not believe that the Russian Revolution, cited as a positive factor in Wilson's speech, portended any democratic developments in that country.

As to England, LaFollette similarly could not see why she was regarded as a democratic state. He noted her slowness in developing social reform, her imperialistic policy, her hereditary peerage (the House of Lords), her treatment of India and Ireland, both of whom were still "being held in chains." He resented the fact that America had adopted the British position on the war almost from the moment the first shots were fired. By doing so, he argued, America forfeited whatever right she might have had to claim that she was fighting on behalf of neutral rights. Neutrality vanished the moment America made a commitment to British war aims. Whatever faults would be attached to Germany, he said, must also be laid at the doorstep of the British.

It was a long speech that perhaps did not have all the controversy that some had hoped for. After Norris's "dollar sign on the American flag" address, it would have been hard for him to stir the galleries.

It was after seven when LaFollette finished. The antiwar arguments were over. However, there were still a number of senators who wanted to explain for posterity why they were voting for war, and there was John Sharp Williams who had been waiting impatiently to reply directly to LaFollette. His entire speech was a reply.

LaFollette pretended not to listen. He stood at the back of the chamber as the Mississippian went on.

Williams ridiculed LaFollette for attempting to suggest that there were no differences between Germany and England. He scoffed at what he regarded as the Wisconsinite's inability to distinguish between a "prize court and a torpedo." Having waited for over four hours to get an opportunity not only to rebut LaFollette but to excoriate and to deride him, Williams leveled a stream of vituperation at him rarely heard in the halls of the

Senate. He said that the speech he had just heard would have been more
becoming to "Herr Bethman-Hollweg" than to a United States senator.
He said that the speech was "pro-German, pro-Goth, and pro-Vandal. . .
anti-American, anti-American president, anti-Congress, and anti-American
people." He labeled the four-hour address that LaFollette had given "ver-
bal eternity."

"I apologize, Mr. President," he concluded. "I have said too much."

Then it was Husting's turn to reassure America that LaFollette did not
speak for Wisconsin, a state which would do its duty. Cummins indicated
that he was willing, though reluctant, to vote for war, Hardwick announced
that the "sons of Dixie" were behind the president, Borah said that he was
for the resolution, and Key Pittman gravely informed everyone that the
purpose of the war was to stamp out Prussianism.

Warren Harding drifted off into a series of platitudes as he announced
his support. He was less bombastic than usual, and for a reason. One of
his biographers recently uncovered some letters from one of his "liaisons"
and has concluded that his rhetoric was muted somewhat because of a
threat posed by the lady. She was of German ancestry, it appears, and had
allegedly promised him that if war came with Germany, and he voted for
it, she would expose him and drive him from office. Thus, the writer con-
cludes, he was hopeful that a reasoned, less impassioned than usual address
might induce the lady to see his dilemma. While many senators might have
been troubled about voting for war, Harding was perhaps the most concerned. But for different reasons.[22]

Reed Smoot had the shortest speech of all. He decided, as befitted a
Mormon churchman, that he would offer up a prayer, a brief one that
closed with "hasten the day when liberty shall be enjoyed."

The question was called on the McCumber resolution, and it was defeated by a voice vote. Poindexter next moved for consideration of the
war resolution.

The room hushed as the clerk began the roll, starting with Ashurst, who
said "aye." The first "nay" came from Asle Gronna, the second from La
Follette. The third was from Harry Lane, but by the time he cast the last
vote of his Senate career, the resolution already had a majority. There were
more negative votes, from Norris, Stone, and Vardaman. Eighty-two were
recorded for the motion, with eight absent.

When the final count was announced, it was eleven-fifteen. The mood
was somber as the majority of the senators filed slowly from the room.
LaFollette walked grimly past spectators who hissed him; reportedly one
stranger handed him a rope.[23]

April 5–6 1917

The House of Representatives passed the measure in the early hours of April 6, after extended debate. There was some sentiment for putting the matter over until Monday April 9, since April 6 was Good Friday and some did not believe it to be appropriate to declare war on that date. However, the leadership rejected this argument and the debate, with over a hundred speakers, went on.

The final vote was 373–54. Most of the dissenting votes came from the Middle West, with some from the South, some from the Southwest, and a few from the west coast. There was one from the East—the Socialist London from New York. Among the dissenters were Kitchin, Sloan of Nebraska (Norris's rival-to-be in 1918), and such antiwar figures as William LaFollette of Wisconsin, Gilbert Haugen of Iowa, Edward Keating of Colorado, Clarence Dill of Washington, and Jeff McLemore of Texas, and many of those who had voted against the final version of the Armed Ship Bill—Cooper, Nelson, Cary, Stafford, Shackleford, Wilson, and Sherwood. Also against the resolution was Montana's new congresswoman, Jeannette Rankin.

In favor of the measure were some who had been critics of belligerency, including James Slayden of Texas, as well as a number of present and future notables. These included Joe Cannon; Chairman Flood of the Foreign Affairs Committee; a young Georgian named Carl Vinson, who did not leave the House until 1968; three prominent Texans, Tom Connally, one of the architects of the United Nations, Sam Rayburn, and John Nance Garner, both one day to be speakers of the House and the latter vice president; two well-known sons-in-law, Nicholas Longworth (Roosevelt) and Augustus Gardner (Lodge), the latter to die on duty with the military; James Byrnes of South Carolina, a future secretary of state and Supreme Court justice; Cordell Hull of Tennessee, a future secretary of state; future vice president Alben Barkley of Kentucky; Carl Hayden of Arizona, who would go on to the Senate and remain in that chamber until 1968; House minority leader James Mann; and a young representative from New York named Fiorello LaGuardia.[24]

Speaker Champ Clark did not vote. However, Arthur Mullen reports that had there been a tie and had he had the opportunity to do so, he would have voted against the resolution.[25]

The oratory in the House was not distinguished by outbursts such as Williams's against LaFollette and by charges such as those leveled by Norris at America's motives. Some Congressmen did raise the question of the propriety of Kitchin, the floor leader, taking a stand against the president in this matter, but this was all.

The only real drama came during the roll call. In one of the more dramatic scenes of the whole period prior to the outbreak of war, Congresswoman Rankin refused to answer to her name the first time the roll was called. As everyone peered in her direction , the aged former "czar" Cannon quietly edged over to her side and informed her that she had the responsibility of representing all the women of the country and therefore would have to exercise her prerogative.

When her name was called again, she tried to explain her decision, although by custom explanations of votes are not permitted during the roll call. She said that she wanted to support her country, but could not vote for war. Speaker Clark deemed her answer to be a negative vote.[26]

Many years later LaGuardia was asked if the rumors were true—was she crying as she voted? LaGuardia replied that he could not tell because his own eyes were filled with tears.[27]

A short time later Wilson signed the resolution and the United States was at war.

10

AFTER 1917

There were ninety-six men in the Senate when the Armed Ship debate concluded, sixteen of whom ended their service with the fall of the gavel. Within a little more than a year, eight more had died, including Stone, Lane, Gallinger, Tillman, Hughes, and Ollie James.

In 1918 there were even more departures; Vardaman, Hardwick, Lewis, Weeks, and Hollis, and in 1920 Gronna, Kirby, Gore, Chamberlain, Thomas, and Sherman. Harding and Fall left shortly after to assume their positions in the executive branch.

With irony one notes that only two of the senators who opposed the Armed Ship Bill lost their seats either wholly or partially as a result of their actions, Vardaman and Kirby. Of course, the way in which the constituents of the five who left the Senate between 1917 and 1918 viewed their actions could not be ascertained, although, as noted in previous chapters, Clapp and Works had already fallen out of favor at home, and O'Gorman, while he had retired voluntarily, was in a state where pro-Allied feeling was strong. The swing to the Republicans in Oregon in 1918 might have meant that, had Harry Lane completed his term, he could not have won another. As for Stone, in spite of the way the rest of the country viewed him, feeling against the war was stronger in his state, and he was the sort of politician who had survived worse problems than this in the past.

Of the four senators who did win at least one more term, only Norris and Kenyon faced reelection in 1918, and in each instance, as noted in previous chapters, factors worked in their favor. Cummins did not run until 1920, LaFollette until 1922.

As for the two senators who did lose their seats as an aftermath of their actions, Vardaman's defeat is perhaps the more interesting. For he was the target of a Wilson-inspired purge, not only for his opposition to the bill and to a declaration of war, but for a whole litany of offenses against the president. Wilson supported Congressman Pat Harrison in the primary, and Vardaman found that the Mississippians in the back hills failed him this time.

However, he was not completely out of politics; when John Sharp Williams decided to retire in 1922, he became the favorite for the nomination. By now Wilson was gone, and so were questions about the junior senator's behavior in 1917. But Vardaman was to be disappointed, for illness cut short his plans to campaign. He lost all his teeth and with that his greatest asset—his speaking style. He left politics permanently, and shortly afterwards his health began to deteriorate. He died in 1930.

Kirby was defeated by Thaddeus Carraway in 1920, accounts of the campaign suggesting that his antiwar and anti-Wilson politics were a major factor. In addition, Kirby, an appointee, had no real political base in his home state when he went back to seek renomination. He later returned to the Arkansas courts.[1]

Asle Gronna was also defeated for renomination the next time he ran, but not as a result of his stand on the Armed Ship Bill, the war resolution, or much of the wartime legislation. As we saw earlier, he does not appear to have suffered much back in his home state for his views on the international situation. Rather, Gronna lost out because he failed to make peace with the emerging Non-Partisan League that had become a major force in politics, both in and out of the Republican party in North Dakota. Apparently, he had lost some touch with the grass roots and failed to take the new agrarian radicalism seriously.

The league would have been willing to support Gronna, for his record in the Senate was hardly something that they could argue with, but the old progressive would take their support only on his own terms, and the two could not come together. In addition, a third candidate entered the battle, sponsored by the McKenzie machine, and he siphoned away some votes that might have gone to the senator, who was defeated by a narrow margin. By 1922, however, Gronna was ready for a comeback and planned to challenge his old senatorial colleague Porter McCumber (who would eventually be denied renomination). But he became ill with cancer before he could get his campaign going, and died.[2]

As for the three senators who left the upper chamber with the close of the filibuster, O'Gorman had what was certainly the longest and most interesting career. As mentioned earlier, he went back to the practice of law in New York, and there he continued his interest in Ireland and the Irish

169

question, although he insisted throughout the war on a very vigorous prosecution of the conflict. After the war and through the next two decades his was the dignity that becomes an ex-senator who graduates to the role of elder statesman. A student of the classics, as well as of his chosen profession, he pursued these interests and became a mentor to younger attorneys. Unlike Vardaman and Gronna, however, he never made any effort to get back into public life.

He was one of the two dissenting senators to see the outbreak of World War II. He died in 1943, a revered member of the political, legal, and Irish fraternities of New York. His funeral was the occasion for the gathering of almost all political notables in the city. No one, not even the newspapers, remembered that he had been charged some twenty-six years earlier with being one of the "willful men." The *New York Times* forgot that he had "faithfully served the Sinn Fein."[3]

Clapp, whose failure to win reelection was probably due to his infrequent trips back to Minnesota, decided to remain on in Washington to practice law. He might have returned to government when the Republicans came back into power in 1920, as Beveridge sought a position for him in the Harding administration. However, the president never responded, and Clapp remained on in private life until his death some years later.[4]

Works spent the final years of his life in law and his other consuming interest, Christian Science. He died in 1929.

Harry Lane had but a short time to live when the United States entered the war. His last months were filled with increased pain from his illness and the anguish that came from the hostile reaction of many of his constituents who could not understand why he did what he had done. Norris later alleged that Lane's death was hastened by the vituperation that came from critics of his actions, but this is probably too melodramatic, a point that the Oregon senator would have been the first to indicate. What probably caused Norris's reaction was an incident that occurred shortly before Lane left the capital to go back home to die.

Aware of the status of his health, Norris and LaFollette had conspired with members of Lane's staff to "screen" his mail so that he would not see much of the critical correspondence. The Oregonian was confined to his home through much of the period between the conclusion of the filibuster and the vote on the war resolution, so that this ruse worked for the most part. However, one day he decided that he felt a little better and went to his office, where he got a look at some of the uncensored mail that had been piling up. He collapsed and was taken home.

Shortly after the declaration of war, Lane decided that he wanted to die at home, and hopefully, before he died, tell some of his constituents about

170

his motives. But his last mission went unfulfilled, for he died before he could reach Oregon, a little over a month after war was declared. Norris and Gronna attended the funeral, where they were impressed, the former recounted, by the large number of "plain people" who came out to the services.[5]

One year and eight days after the United States declared war on Germany, William Joel Stone collapsed on a streetcar in Washington. He was carried to a couch in Cummins's office, where Ashurst, who saw them bringing him in, recalled later that it was apparent that he would never recover. Four days later the Missourian died. Stone had recovered much of the prestige that he lost in the early days of 1917 and had been restored to some favor with Wilson. He had been faithful to his word that, once war came, he would support it. In the last year of his life, "Gumshoe Bill" Stone was, as he had been for all but a few short months of his life, a faithful and loyal Democrat. He was buried amidst pomp, dignity, and honors back in Missouri, also in a touch he probably would have liked, amidst speculation concerning the future of politics in that state now that he was gone.[6]

Of the four dissenters who were reelected (only Norris was reelected more than once), Albert Cummins was the only one to be admitted into the Senate establishment. He never became president of the United States, but he did become president pro tem of the Senate until his death. He was reelected in 1920 largely through the help of the conservative forces in his state, the same forces that had once been the targets of his attacks.

However, by 1926 the political situation back in Iowa had changed drastically, as a new group of agrarian reformers had emerged, unimpressed by Cummins's long history of reform battles, his titles, his new-found allies, and most of all, his defense of the administration's policies. He was attacked for his conservatism and badly defeated in the Republican primary of that year. He returned to Iowa, a sick and beaten man, who could find little consolation in his past record. He decided to write his memoirs, but after having completed a page of it, he died. Had he completed it, it would have been a significant contribution to the literature of the progressive movement.[7]

His fellow Iowan Kenyon, who had been reelected in 1918, left the Senate before him. But the circumstances of the junior senator's departure were different and much more controversial than were Cummins's. The former had distinguished himself after the war in a number of ways, leading an investigation into the matter of campaign spending, opposing the "buying" of Senate seats in the Newberry affair, despite the fact that he and the newly elected senator from Michigan were both of the same party, and heading a commission that looked into the causes of the famous steel strike. In addition, he and Borah had come to assume the mantle of earlier progressive spokesmen such as LaFollette and Beveridge, becoming the leaders of the "farm bloc," a collection of legislators from agricultural states who harassed the leadership of both parties for insensitivity to farm problems. The future referred to earlier, that might even have included a nomination for the presidency or vice presidency, seemed very bright in 1922.

Then, early that year, Harding announced that he was nominating Kenyon for a federal judgeship. Rarely had a relatively young and prominent politician with national possibilities chosen, at what appeared to be the height of his career, to quit active politics for the bench. The farm bloc took the news hard and were bitter about the appointment. Thinking that perhaps this was the way Harding was going to silence his critics, they took to addressing each other as "your honor."[8]

Harding's appointment of Kenyon, who appears to have been almost a direct opposite of the president, is perhaps understandable when one finds that they had "done the Chautauqua circuit" together while serving in the Senate. Harding enjoyed rewarding old friends, even when they were not so competent or so qualified as Kenyon obviously was. The willingness of the Iowan to accept is best understood by remembering Marshall's comment, cited earlier, that he was never really happy in the Senate and more oriented towards the judiciary. Some of the papers noted this at the time of the appointment.

But even off the bench Kenyon was still a figure of no minor importance in the political picture. Coolidge offered him the position of secretary of the navy in an effort to clean up the mess of the Harding administration; the Iowan declined it but said that he was willing to become attorney general, a post that the president was apparently not willing to offer. The judge's name continued to pop up in presidential and vice presidential speculation, but he indicated that he was through with that aspect of politics. He concentrated on his judicial duties, dying in 1933 at his summer home in Maine, where he wrote many of his judicial decisions in an old wreck of a ship's pilot house that he had salvaged.[9]

George Norris remained in the Senate until 1943, the only one of the dissenting senators to have a chance to vote on the matter of entrance into World War II and the only one to have a public record as to how the United States should view this conflict prior to December 1941. Initially he was, as before, an isolationist, but gradually he began to move more towards an internationalist position, and when the time came for a vote on the war resolution, he was for it. He became more of an internationalist after war was declared and talked in his autobiography of the need for international organization.

172

His record in domestic affairs between the wars is fairly well known, but some aspects of it perhaps warrant telling here. In 1920 Norris voted for and supported the candidacy of Warren G. Harding, but with misgivings. These misgivings were eventually to be justified, and he never again backed a Republican for the presidency. In 1924 he supported LaFollette, albeit somewhat lukewarmly, in 1928 Al Smith, and from 1932 on, Franklin Roosevelt. His support of Smith is especially noteworthy, because the latter was a Catholic wet and Nebraska a Protestant dry state. But he survived this; he even survived the fact that at one point his wife announced that she could not go along with him and would support Hoover.

He also survived a number of plots designed to discredit him or remove him from public life. In 1925 he was charged by the Hearst Press, along with some other senators, including Borah and the younger LaFollette, with being in the pay of the Mexican government: this was the same syndicate that had supported the stand that he and the other dissenters took in 1917. The charges proved to be false, and those publishing them were completely discredited.

He almost did not survive one of the most intriguing bits of political skullduggery ever to be visited on a public figure. In 1930 the Nebraska Republican leadership, which was becoming more annoyed with him each day, thought that they had found a way to remove him. They would put another person named George Norris in the Republican primary, thus splitting the Norris vote and electing the organization candidate. The plan failed, and the subsequent investigation reached right into the Republican National Committee. The bogus Norris, called "Grocer George" after his profession, and one other, spent time behind bars for perjury.

In the thirties Norris was still in the vanguard of progressivism. He was one of the sponsors of the Norris-LaGuardia Act, eliminating among other things the yellow-dog contract; he continued to fight for farm-oriented legislation as a member of the farm bloc; and he was active in the promotion of the concept of a unicameral legislature (Nebraska is the only state with one). He became famous for his advocacy of the Tennessee Valley Authority, trying for twelve years and three presidents before succeeding when Franklin Roosevelt took office. He was also a prime mover in the development of the Twentieth, or "lame duck," Amendment, which, among other things, got rid of the short session of Congress which had been the vehicle for the Armed Ship and other filibusters.

Norris was also a foe of the poll tax, although, curiously, he opposed the anti-lynching bill, which he thought to be unconstitutional. His last years were concerned primarily with foreign affairs, as the issue of involvement in another European war took center stage in American politics.

173

He was finally defeated in 1942 by a Republican, after having success-fully contested one election, in 1936, as an independent. His loss, so he recounts in his autobiography, was attributable to two factors: he had remained on in Washington dealing with legislative business and did not campaign much, and the state was just too conservative to support an in-dependent whose views were increasingly out of step with theirs.

He was the last of the dissenters to leave office, the last to die, and probably the only significant figure, other than Franklin Roosevelt, whose career spanned the progressive era, the New Deal, and two world wars.[10]

Robert LaFollette was nearing the end of his political career in 1917, having only eight more years left in public life, but characteristically for him they were eventful ones. More than any of the other objectors to war, he remained a symbol of opposition to the conflict and to Wilsonian poli-cies for prosecuting it. In many people's eyes during 1917 and 1918, he was the most hated man in America, for he did not give up on his thesis that America had no business in the war and had been led into it by lies and trickery. His charges culminated in an assertion during a speech that Wilson was aware of the fact that the *Lusitania* had carried munitions on her last voyage. The Minnesota Commission of Public Safety then pre-vailed upon Senator Frank Kellogg of that state to initiate action to have LaFollette expelled from the Senate.

There followed one of the more interesting phases of the Wisconsin progressive's career. As we have seen several times previously, he was not liked by many of his associates and most of them would probably have preferred to see him out of the Senate on general principles. However, there was the vexing situation of what would be the precedent if a sena-tor could be expelled for expressing unorthodox sentiments. So therefore, LaFollette, who had always been critical of the clubby "old boy" mores of the Senate, found himself and his seat defended by those same mores.

The Senate dragged its feet for over fourteen months, perhaps hoping that the matter would go away. But during those months two things hap-pened. The first was the end of the war, which took some of the steam out of the patriotic outcry against LaFollette. But more important was the result of the elections of 1918, which resulted in a 49–47 Republican margin. This meant that if LaFollette were to be expelled and a Democrat elected, the count would be 48–48, and vice president Marshall would break the tie in favor of his party, which would then organize the Senate. Thus, Henry Cabot Lodge would not be the chairman of the Senate For-eign Relations Committee. Therefore, LaFollette would have to be saved by his conservative brethren.

In addition to almost unanimous support by members of his own party,

LaFollette had the help of some Democrats who were either hostile to Wilson or else resentful of the forces that had created the outcry for the Wisconsonite's expulsion in the first place. Such men as Hoke Smith, Vardaman, and Reed rounded up votes for him, and when the matter actually came to a vote, the charges were dismissed, 50–21. The merits of the case never did come up; the Democrats were reluctant to let them, possibly because certain revelations might have been embarrassing to the president, so the vote which resolved the issue was on a minor technicality. But the matter was ended.

LaFollette wanted a clearer vindication, but once cleared of the charges, he struck out again as a voice for what was fast becoming less attractive to most Americans. He continued to refuse to support the nominees of his party and to attack its leadership, and also to flirt with various minor radical farm parties (such as the aforementioned Non-Partisan League) that were developing in the Middle West.

In 1924, certain that neither party could ever field a presidential nominee whom he could support, he formed his own party, a collection of old progressives, radical farm groups, and personal supporters, short on money and organization, but long on dedication to the old ideals that LaFollette believed progressivism represented. However, he won only Wisconsin, and Coolidge was able to capitalize on his candidacy by saying that the election was between "Coolidge and chaos."

Still breathing the fire of agrarian democracy, denouncing both parties, and continuing his assault on the forces of wealth, LaFollette died in 1925. He was succeeded by his son Robert, Jr.[11]

As for the futures of the remaining members of the Sixty-fourth Senate, Warren G. Harding became president, and his unhappy experiences scarcely need retelling here. Weeks, defeated in 1918, became his secretary of war, and Fall, his interests still in oil and in Mexico, his secretary of the interior. For his participation in the Teapot Dome Affair, the latter also became the only (as of now) cabinet member ever to go to jail as a result of misconduct in office. He died penniless in New Mexico in 1944. In the investigation of the scandal, Walsh was one of the more relentless probers, and Pomerene, by then out of the Senate, one of the special prosecutors.

Harding's nomination was largely engineered by some of his old Senate cronies in the famous "smoke-filled room" of 1920, including Lodge, Brandegee, Smoot, Wadsworth, Curtis, Watson, and Weeks (Penrose was ill, but conferred by telephone). They wanted to ensure that there would be no question about where the initiative in policy lay, and Harding could be counted upon to leave matters to them. And he would do nothing to move the United States towards the League of Nations. They knew the

Ohioan's limitations, admitting that he was not a stellar candidate, but as Brandegee told a friend, at least he was the best of the mediocrities.[12]

Lodge, who presided over the convention, had most of his battles, in particular his successful battle against Wilson over the Treaty of Versailles, behind him. He would survive until 1924, somewhat frustrated in his later years by the fact that Calvin Coolidge, whom he despised, succeeded Harding, and thus his power and influence waned somewhat. He left behind a rather impressive political dynasty, including a grandson who would play a major role in American foreign policy making.

Frank Brandegee, also a major figure in the defeat of the treaty, died by his own hand in 1924, following a series of business reverses. Smoot remained in the Senate until his defeat in 1932, a spokesman for fiscal policies that had become unpopular, and spent the remaining years of his life in Mormon Church affairs. Sutherland went on to the Supreme Court in the 1920s and was one of the "nine old men" who would dismantle much of the New Deal in the 1930s. Curtis became vice president under Hoover until the landslide of 1932.

Wadsworth of New York, who had been one of the younger members of the Senate, was defeated for reelection in 1926. He returned to Congress in the 1930s, one of the few men ever to go from the Senate to the House of Representatives, and served until 1951, the last of the Sixty-fourth Senate to hold public office. His son succeeded Lodge's grandson as permanent United Nations representative in 1960, and his daughter married Stuart Symington, today a United States senator from Missouri.

Watson of Indiana, a newcomer in 1917, had a long career in the Senate until he too fell victim to the politics of the depression. He became an important figure in the hierarchy of his party. It was he who would remark years later in his memoirs that he could not understand what seemed to him to be a radical reversal on the part of Wilson, and that had he known then what would be the future of America after the war, he would not have voted for the war resolution. He was not the only member of the Senate to say later that the war was a mistake.[13]

As for Boies Penrose, old age and ill health caught up with him in 1922. But at least he could die content in the knowledge that he had helped to create another Republican administration. One of his last bits of political advice was to Harding's managers, counseling them to "keep Warren at home" and not expose his frailties to public scrutiny.

William Borah became a leading Republican spokesman on foreign policy in the 1930s and is associated strongly in many people's minds with the isolationism of that period. It is for this reason that many also assume that he had been close to the LaFollette-Norris position in 1917, which, of

176

course, he was not. However, he would frequently draw on lessons that he believed the nation should have learned from that period, in urging Americans to avoid any suggestion of interest in a foreign conflict. He was another senator who later said publicly that the war was a mistake and he would like to be able to recall his vote.[14]

Wesley Jones left the Senate in 1932, dying after a long and bitter general election, which he lost. In the 1920s he became known as a fiscal conservative and one of the more ardent champions of Prohibition, two causes which by 1932 had become unpopular.

There were a number of Democrats who bridged the gap between Woodrow Wilson and Franklin Roosevelt, although not all of them favored the latter's policies. One of these was James Reed, who sought his party's nomination for president in 1928 and left the Senate when he did not get it. He was an uncompromising critic of the New Deal from the day Roosevelt took office until the day he (Reed) died.

The Missourian was another who appears to have later recanted much of what he said and did in 1917. The man who criticized Norris for saying that America was putting a dollar sign on the flag, was to say in the 1920s that the vote of six senators against the war was one of the greatest acts of political courage in American history. Of course, by this time, all but two of the six were dead, and only Norris was still in politics.[15]

Claude Swanson became secretary of the navy in the Roosevelt administration and when he left that post, he closed out nearly fifty years in national and state government. Joe Robinson became majority leader and the pilot of the unsuccessful "court-packing" bill, after having been a candidate for the vice presidency with Al Smith in 1928. "Cotton Ed" Smith became chairman of the Senate Agricultural Committee, remaining in the Senate until 1944, and Key Pittman, the Chairman of the Foreign Relations Committee.

Walsh of Montana was supposed to be Roosevelt's attorney general. He had distinguished himself by his relentless digging during the Teapot Dome affair and later was noted as a defender of the rights of radicals and dissenters. He was also one of the few old Wilsonians to keep up the fight for the World Court through the 1920s and was even mentioned as a possible presidential candidate in 1928. He had accepted Roosevelt's offer of the position, but before he could take office, he died at the age of 73.[16]

As for those senators who left the chamber early, two returned in the 1930s when the Democrats began to experience more success. Gore of Oklahoma served one term and ended it as an implacable foe of the New Deal. He became increasingly conservative, opposing civil rights and favoring states rights, and in 1948, during the presidential race, identified him-

self as a Dixiecrat.[17] J. Hamilton Lewis also returned to the Senate and
remained until his death in 1939.

Hardwick of Georgia was purged by Wilson in 1918, and his fellow
Georgian, Hoke Smith left in 1920. Henry Myers did not run in 1922 and
went back to the courts of his native state. Both Hardwick and Myers survived into the forties. Henry Hollis of New Hampshire, not a major figure
in the debate, is worth noting because of his future; he left the Senate in
1918, refusing to run for reelection because of his disagreement with many
of Wilson's war policies.[18]

Gilbert Hitchcock became chairman of the Foreign Relations Committee,
then minority leader in 1919. He was defeated for reelection in 1922. In
the interim he had the thankless task of being Wilson's defender before a
frequently hostile Senate during the debate over the Treaty of Versailles.
He was truly the man in the middle as two giants, Lodge and Wilson, resolved to fight it out to the finish. After leaving the Senate he went back
to the newspaper business, making one final try to run for his old seat,
against Norris in 1930, and failing.

John Sharp Williams, disillusioned by the failure of the Senate to ratify
the treaty, declined to run for renomination in 1922. He also is reported
to have become generally disillusioned with life in the upper chamber.[19]

Luke Lea of Tennessee, who left the Senate right after the filibuster,
saw action in the war. He was an artillery officer, winning the Distinguished Service Medal, then returned to Tennessee politics. He had a long and
interesting career, including a jail sentence, but what he is best known for
is something that he did not accomplish. Upon conclusion of the war he
and some fellow officers decided to cap their military careers by kidnaping
the Kaiser out of exile. They failed.[20]

One of the last survivors of the Sixty-fourth Senate was Henry Ashurst
of Arizona. He became chairman of the Senate Judiciary Committee in
the 1930s, having that position during the court-packing fight, finally losing his seat in 1940. As the years wore on, the orator from Arizona became one of the ornaments of the Senate, noted as a speaker who could
regale his colleagues with polysyllabic words. From all accounts, he was
one of the more popular figures in Washington, and his departure was lamented on both sides of the aisle.

Like so many legislators who are defeated for reelection, Ashurst did
not leave Washington. He served for two years on the Board of Immigra-
tion Appeals. In the late 1950s he made a comeback, not as a senator
but as a contestant on one of the quiz shows of that period, and then was
cast as a senator, appropriately, in the Hollywood adaptation of the novel
Advise and Consent. He also was a guest on some television talk shows, a

quaint, engaging figure out of an earlier time in American history.

He too had his doubts about what happened in the spring of 1917. In his diary for March 7 of that year, he noted the abuse that was being directed against the filibusterers by an aroused public. He likened their plight to that of the senators who had voted not to remove Andrew Johnson and recalled that those men were later deemed to have been correct in their judgment. He wondered if the Armed Ship Bill filibusterers were being condemned by an informed or an uninformed public and would be someday vindicated.[21]

NOTES

Chapter 1. A Little Group of Willful Men

1. The full text of the statement can be found on the front page of most daily papers for March 5 1917.
2. For a study of filibustering, see bibliography: Burdette.
3. Bailey, 16.
4. Galloway, 195.
5. Pratt, 146–87.
6. Bailey, 410–14.
7. Ibid., 136–41.
8. Koenig, 271.
9. DeConde, History, 346. For an analysis of antiwar feeling, see also Freidel's article in Morison, 72, and see also Pratt, 233.
10. See Merk's article on dissent on the Mexican War in Morison, 38–50.
11. Russell, 258. The eight senators listed as being perhaps typical were not involved to any degree in the debate. This should not suggest to the reader that some of those who were involved are necessarily of greater stature.

Chapter 2. The Protagonists

1. Link, *Neutrality*, 11–24, and Cooper, 21.
2. Pringle, 405–6.
3. Hofstadter, 258.
4. Ibid., 257. See also Walworth, I, 405.
5. Tuchman, 161.
6. Link, *Neutrality*, 11.

7. For a digest of his book, see Garraty, *Wilson*, 22–24, Hofstadter, 242, and Link, *Progressive Era*, 21.
8. Hofstadter, 237.
9. Garraty, *Wilson*, 5.
10. Link, *Progressive Era*, 35.
11. Fenno, 55, 201.
12. Link, *Neutrality*, 159.
13. For information on Bryan, see bibliography: Koenig, Coletta.
14. Koenig, 534–36. For an assessment of Bryan as a cabinet member, see Fenno, 189–92.
15. Koenig, 536–48.
16. For information on LaFollette, see bibliography: LaFollette, Belle, and LaFollette, *Autobiography*.
17. LaFollette, Belle, I, 503, 590.
18. Goldman, 171.
19. For information on Norris, see bibliography: Norris, Lief, Neuberger, and appropriate chapter in Kennedy.
20. Norris, 107–19.
21. Holt, 133–50.
22. For information on Cummins, see bibliography: Sayre, Hechler, Holt, and Bowers.
23. Holt, 156–58.
24. LaFollette, *Autobiography*, 221–80.
25. Holt, 130, 155.
26. For information on Kenyon, see previous sources in footnote 22, in particular, Holt.
27. Livermore, 147.
28. Marshall, 294.
29. For information on Gronna and Clapp, see bibliography: Holt, Bowers, and Hechler. For specific information on Gronna, see bibliography: Phillips.
30. Phillips, 462.
31. Ibid., 301–19.
32. Bowers, 331.
33. Holt, 76.
34. *New York Times,* June 22 1916, 10.
35. For information on Works, see bibliography: Mowry, Cooper.
36. Mowry, 117–22.
37. Cooper, 101–3. See also *New York Times,* June 27 1917, 20, and July 24 1917, 3, for his later career.
38. For information on Jones, see bibliography: Forth.
39. For information on Vardaman: see bibliography, Holmes.
40. Luthin, 12.
41. It would be superfluous to cite all references to these matters in Holmes, so the reader is referred generally to this work, which covers the matter extensively.
42. Key, 239.
43. Marshall, 302, and Holmes, 270–73, refer to this rivalry.
44. *New York Times,* August 22 1918, 10.

45. There is no biography of Kirby and little reference to him in various works of this period.
46. For information on Smith, see bibliography: Grantham, *Hoke Smith.*
47. Both Smith and Hardwick also served as governors of Georgia, Smith before coming to the Senate and Hardwick after leaving.
48. For information on Ashurst, see bibliography: Ashurst.
49. For information on Tillman, see bibliography: Simkins. For Tillman's activities on behalf of his state, see Daniels, 129.
50. For information on Gore, see bibliography: Billington.
51. Billington, 82.
52. Gore as viewed by his contemporaries in light of his handicap can be found in Ashurst, 67, and Marshall, 319. See also *New York Times,* March 17 1941, 25.
53. Baker, VI, 279.
54. For information on Hitchcock, see bibliography previously noted for Bryan and Norris. See also bibliography: Mullen.
55. For information on O'Gorman, see bibliography: Schlesinger, Freidel. Most information about O'Gorman is secondary and deals only with the early phase of his career.
56. Schlesinger, 333.
57. Freidel, 174.
58. This view is advanced by Mullen, 177. Link, *Progressive Era,* 52, attributes it to a change in New York City politics.
59. Despite his colorful personality, there is no biography of Lane and little secondary information. See bibliography previously noted for LaFollette and Norris.
60. Congressional Record, September 16 1917, 7210 et seq. (65th Congress).
61. For some of these stories, see Neuberger, 56 et seq., and Marshall, 321.
62. LaFollette, V, 620.
63. For information on Stone, see bibliography: Towne.
64. Ibid., 183.
65. Ibid., 173.
66. Ibid., 8.
67. Ibid., 195. See also 182–209 for Stone's views on the matter of presidential prerogatives.
68. Ibid., 227.
69. Ibid., 228–31.
70. *New York Times,* March 11 1917, sec. IV, 1.
71. Ibid., March 8, 9 1917, 1.
72. For information on the character of antiwar dissent, see Cooper, 220–34, Holt, 121–38, and Goldman, 241. See also Graham, 213–17 for a list of those members of the 64th Senate who might be classified as reformers.
73. McKenna, 141–43. See also Cooper, 200.
74. For information on Lodge, see bibliography: Garraty, *Lodge.*
75. Ashurst, 68.

76. For information on Penrose, see bibliography: Davenport; and for Wadsworth, bibliography: Hatch.
77. Garraty, *Lodge,* 305.
78. For information on Williams, see bibliography: Osborn.
79. Osborn, 255–61. See also the article by DeConde in Grantham, *Sectional Image,* 121.
80. LaFollette, I, 583.
81. Osborn, 258.

Chapter 3. The Controversy Prior to 1917

1. Koenig, 535.
2. Link, *Progressive Era,* 151.
3. LaFollette, I, 549.
4. Link, *Neutrality,* 164.
5. Ibid., 143–59.
6. Ibid., 153. Clarke and Camden had left the Senate prior to March 1917. Kirby was Clarke's successor.
7. Lodge to Roosevelt, II, February 4 1915, 453, and February 11 1915, 455.
8. Towne, 189.
9. Lief, 158. See also Link, *Neutrality,* 155.
10. *New York Times,* February 16–19 1915.
11. *Congressional Record,* February 18 1917, 4016 (63rd Congress). Supporting the resolution were, in addition to those named, LaFollette, Norris, Gronna, Cummins, Kenyon, Works, McCumber, Townsend, Smith of Michigan, Jones (Clapp was absent), Borah, and Poindexter. Democrats included the seven rebels, Lane, Ashurst, Owen, Lewis, and Myers.
12. For Bryan see Koenig, 537–40. For LaFollette, see LaFollette, I, 538.
13. Koenig, 539–41.
14. See bibliography: Simpson.
15. For information on this see *New York Times* for several dates in May 1915 following the sinking. See also LaFollette I, 541, Towne, 193, Holt, 127, and Koenig, 542.
16. Koenig, 541–49. For Ashurst's view see Ashurst, 39.
17. Cooper, 41, speaks of Daniels's views. For LaFollette, see LaFollette, I, 543. See also *New York Times,* June 9 1915, 5.
18. Coletta, III, 25.
19. See *New York Times* for December 12 1915, sec. II, 3; December 14 1915, 4; and January 28 1916, 20. See also Ashurst, 45, and LaFollette, 552.
20. *New York Times,* February 24 1916, 2.
21. Mullen, 180.
22. *New York Times,* February 23–28 1916. See also Baker, VI, 170.
23. The letter to Stone is found in the *New York Times,* February 25 1916, 1.

24. *New York Times,* March 3 1916, 1.
25. See Towne, 198; Ashurst, 47; and *New York Times,* March 3 1916, 1.
26. See *New York Times,* March 4 1916, 2, and Ashurst, 48. For Gore's motives, see Billington, 76.
27. LaFollette, I, 557. For Hitchcock's statement, see *New York Times,* March 4 1916, 2. Vardaman also favored the principle of the resolution; see Holmes, 311.
28. Coletta, I, 28.
29. LaFollette, I, 558—60.
30. Lief, 167—69.
31. Link, *Confusions,* 250.
32. *New York Times,* April 20 1916, 1, 4. See also LaFollette, I, 565.
33. LaFollette, loc. cit. For later resolution, see I, 598.
34. Link, *Progressive Era,* 217.
35. Link, *Progressive Era,* 218—22.
36. For an account of the history of the army bill, see Link, *Progressive Era,* 174—88. For a listing of some of the more important antiwar and antipreparedness figures in the House, see Cooper, 88—91, and Link, *Confusions,* 28. For a good study of one of the House antiwar leaders, Claude Kitchin, see bibliography: Arnett.
37. Link, *Progressive Era,* 187—89.
38. Holmes, 307.
39. Morrison, 70. See also Schlesinger, 350.
40. Lodge to Roosevelt, II, July 10 1916, 491.
41. Link, *Progressive Era,* 190, refers to the importance of the Battle of Jutland.
42. Holt, 130.
43. *New York Times,* July 20 1916, 6. For reactions, see LaFollette, I, 576, and Lief, 174.
44. Holt, 130. See also *New York Times,* July 22 1916, 1, for final passage of the bill.
45. See Link, *Progressive Era,* 190, for the result of the conference committee on the naval bill and 195 for the revenue bill.
46. Koenig, 561—69.
47. Morrison, 79.
48. Link, *Progressive Era,* 243.
49. Towne, 209.
50. Link, *Progressive Era,* 247—51.
51. LaFollette, I, 583.
52. Koenig, 561.
53. Link, *Campaigns,* 219. See also Walworth, II, 78.
54. *Congressional Record,* January 5 1917, 897. The nine others were Norris, Cummins, Kenyon, Gronna, Clapp, Jones, Townsend, Curtis, and Sterling of South Dakota. This starts the *Record* for the 64th Congress. See also Walworth, loc. cit.
55. Link, *Campaigns,* 222—26.

56.   Towne, 211.
57.   Ashurst, 53.
58.   *New York Times,* January 23 1917, 2, and LaFollette, I, 590.
59.   *New York Times,* ibid. See also Lief, 181.
60.   Ibid., January 24 1917, 1, 3.

Chapter 4. The Break with Germany

1.   Lansing, 210–12.
2.   *New York Times,* February 4 1917, 5.
3.   Lansing, 210–12.
4.   Walworth, II, 82.
5.   Lansing, 213.
6.   Link, *Campaigns,* 291.
7.   Walworth, II, 83. For Lansing conference with Hitchcock,
        see Lansing, 213–14.
8.   Link, *Campaigns,* 294.
9.   Houston, I, 229 et seq. See also Lansing, 215, and Baker,
        VI, 455.
10.   Morrison, 78.
11.   *New York Times,* February 3 1917, 1. See also Myers, 43.
        For Link's assessment, see *Campaigns,* 298.
12.   *Congressional Record,* February 3 1917, 2578. For his
        instructions to Lansing, see Lansing, 215.
13.   LaFollette, I, 595.
14.   Ibid., 594.
15.   Koenig, 567.
16.   LaFollette, I, 594.
17.   Ashurst, 54.
18.   LaFollette, I, 594.
19.   *New York Times,* February 4 1917, 2.
20.   LaFollette, I, 595.
21.   Towne, 213. For LaFollette's views on the matter of
        presidential-congressional relations, see LaFollette, I, 559.
22.   Lief, 181.
23.   LaFollette, I, 595.
24.   Information concerning the debate on the resolution is taken
        from the *Record* of February 7 1917, 2731–49.
25.   Lodge to Roosevelt, II, February 7 1917, 494.
26.   Roosevelt to Lodge, II, February 12 1917, 494.
27.   LaFollette, I, 595.

Chapter 5. The Prelude to the Debate

1.   Link, *Campaigns,* 340. See also *New York Times,*
        February 27 1917, 2.
2.   Lansing, 224.

3. For information on this meeting, see Baker, VI, 470–72; Link, *Campaigns*, 341; and Lane, February 25 1917, 239.
4. Ashurst, 55.
5. *Congressional Record*, February 26 1917, 4272.
6. Walworth, II, 90, and Baker, VI, 476.
7. Towne, 215.
8. *Congressional Record*, February 26 1917, 4279.
9. Ibid., 4314.
10. *New York Times*, February 27 1917, 1. See also LaFollette, I, 604.
11. LaFollette, I, 603.
12. Norris, 178. See also LaFollette, I, 605.
13. Lodge to Roosevelt, II, February 27 1917, 497.
14. LaFollette, I, 601.
15. Norris, 178.
16. Link, *Campaigns*, 347–53. See also *New York Times*, February 28 1917, 1.
17. *New York Times*, February 27 1917, 4.
18. Ibid., February 28 1917, 1.
19. *New York Times*, February 28 1917, 1. For Smith's withdrawal of opposition, see *New York Times*, March 1 1917, 4.
20. *New York Times*, February 28 1917, 3.
21. *Congressional Record*, February 27 1917, 4381.
22. Ibid., 4399.
23. *New York Times*, February 28 1917, 1. See also LaFollette, I, 603.
24. *Congressional Record*, February 28 1917, 4518–23.
25. Ibid., 4323–25.

Chapter 6. The Zimmermann Note

1. *New York Times*, March 2 1917, 1. See also bibliography: Swanberg, which talks about this period with respect to the attitude of the Hearst press towards this incident and others.
2. The best description of events leading up to the receipt of the telegram (and afterward) is the previously cited work by Tuchman.
3. Tuchman, 160–67.
4. Ibid., 168–74. See also Lansing, 228.
5. Ibid., 174.
6. Ibid., 175.
7. Link, *Campaigns*, 353.
8. Lodge to Roosevelt, II, March 2 1917, 499.
9. *Congressional Record*, March 1 1917, 4569.
10. Lodge to Roosevelt, II, March 2 1917, 499.
11. *Congressional Record*, March 1 1917, 4569–75.
12. Lodge to Roosevelt, II, March 2 1917, 499.

13.	Livermore, 264.
14.	There are numerous references to this rivalry in both Coletta and Koenig.
15.	Mullen is the best source for a sympathetic view of Hitchcock.
16.	Unfavorable allusions to Hitchcock can be found both in Lief and in Neuberger.
17.	Debate on the resolution is found in the *Record* for March 1 1917, 4569–605.
18.	Lodge to Roosevelt, II, March 2 1917, 499.
19.	Tuchman, 180. See also Lansing, 229.
20.	*Congressional Record* (House of Representatives), March 1 1917, 4691.

Chapter 7. The Debate

1.	For purposes of clarity and facility, remarks attributed to the various senators on the floor for March 2, 3, and 4 (as well as April 4) of 1917 will be summarized in one footnote covering the pages of the debate on the Armed Ship Bill of that date. It should be noted that the debate was periodically interrupted for discussion of other matters. For March 2, see *Congressional Record* of that date, 4744–77.
2.	This confusion is noted by Lowitt, who says that the greatest concurrence was among the dissenters.
3.	*New York Times,* March 3 1917, 2.
4.	Lowitt, 40, places great emphasis on the significance of Hitchcock's move. For LaFollette's perception, see LaFollette, I, 609. See also Phillips, 453, and Lief, 184.
5.	Floor comments for March 3 may be found in the *Record* of that date, 4864–919.
6.	*New York Times,* March 4 1917, 1. See also LaFollette, I, 611.
7.	LaFollette's perception of the bill, his assessment of the attitudes of his colleagues and their motives, and his view of the conditions under which the bill was presented can be found in his article "The Armed Ship Bill."
8.	LaFollette, I, 612.
9.	This analysis is based on accounts of the event in the newspapers. It also takes into account those who objected to the calling of the question. It is noteworthy that most accounts leave out Clapp and Works, possibly because they were finishing service in the Senate with the conclusion of the debate.
10.	LaFollette, "Armed Ship."
11.	*New York Times,* March 4 1917, 1.
12.	Towne, 216–20.
13.	Lief, 185. See also *New York Times,* March 4 1917, which suggests that Kenyon favored the bill.
14.	*New York Times,* March 4 1917, 2.
15.	Link, *Campaigns,* 360.

16. It is this speech and his defense of the right of debate that has caused Jones to be listed in some quarters as being one of the dissenters and linked with the "willful men." However, this is not quite accurate. But Jones's biographer tends to hold to the view that he was a dissenter and offers the explanation that he stepped back and "compromised" by signing the manifesto subject to any one of the three amendments. Jones's speech is found on 4898–905 of the *Record* of that date. For the biographer's analysis see Forth, 374–77.

17. Floor comments for March 4 may be found in the *Record* for that date, 4978–5020.

18. LaFollette, I, 612.

19. Phillips, 456.

20. The list of senators may be found on 4988 of the *Record* for this date.

21. LaFollette, I, 612.

22. Ashurst, 58.

23. LaFollette, I, 613.

24. *New York Times,* March 5 1917, 2.

25. McKenna, 142.

26. Neuberger, 84.

27. *New York Times,* March 5 1917, 3.

28. Osborn, 283.

29. Norris, 180, and LaFollette, I, 615.

30. LaFollette, loc. cit.

31. Daniels, March 4 1917, 108.

32. LaFollette, I, 616–19.

33. Kennedy, 195.

34. For the perceptions of Norris, see 180. For LaFollette's, see I, 619.

35. LaFollette, I, 620.

36. Ibid. See also *New York Times,* March 5 1917, 2. The vote on the motion regarding the chair's ruling saw fourteen senators support LaFollette: Clapp, Cummins, Gronna, Husting, Jones, Kirby, Lane, Martine, Myers, Sherman, Thomas, Works, Blair Lee, a Democrat from Maryland, and Carroll Page, a Republican from Vermont. Norris and Kenyon were paired, as was Walsh, who also indicated that he would have voted to overturn the chair's decision.

37. *New York Times,* loc. cit.

38. LaFollette, I, 621.

39. Norris, 181. LaFollette's family was sending him messages, advising him to calm down; see I, 623.

40. LaFollette, I, 622.

41. *New York Times,* March 5 1917, 3.

42. Norris, 181, and Neuberger, 84.

43. *New York Times,* March 5 1917, 3.

Chapter 8. The Aftermath

1. Excerpts from the various papers can be found in the *New York Times,* March 5 1917, 4. Kirby's note of regret is in LaFollette, I, 632.
2. Link, *Campaigns,* 363.
3. Lane, March 6 1917, 241, and Lansing, 224.
4. *New York Times,* March 5 1917, 1, 3, 5.
5. Ibid., March 6 1917, 1, 4.
6. Roosevelt to Lodge, II, March 13 1917, 503.
7. LaFollette, I, 503.
8. *New York Times,* March 6 1917, 1, and March 7 1917, 3. See also LaFollette, I, 626–33, and Holmes, 317.
9. *New York Times,* March 8 1917, 1. The snubbing of LaFollette is found in LaFollette, I, 635.
10. Holmes, 316.
11. *Congressional Record,* March 6 1917, 5. This starts the *Record* for the 65th Congress.
12. Phillips, 460.
13. *New York Times,* March 7 1917, 3.
14. Stone's speech was approximately twice as long as that of any other dissenter.
15. Burdette, 49, 111. See also Marshall, 305.
16. *New York Times,* March 7 1917, 3. See the *Record* for March 6 1917, 7, for Kenyon's statement.
17. LaFollette "Armed Ship" gives his arguments.
18. Norris, 176.
19. For this incident, see Neuberger, 97–104; Norris, 183; Lief, 191–96. The "poodle dogs" anecdote is in Kennedy, 202. Information concerning the 1918 Senate race can be found in Livermore, 194.
20. Phillips, 456.
21. Myers, 72–74.
22. LaFollette, I, 622. See also I, 603.
23. Ashurst, 54.
24. Norris, 176.
25. Burdette, 110. See the list of sponsors, *New York Times,* March 5 1917, 1.
26. *New York Times,* March 7 1917, 1.
27. Burdette, 127.
28. *Congressional Record,* March 8 1917, 20–45. See also LaFollette, I, 637.
29. *New York Times,* March 9 1917, 2.
30. Daniels, March 8 1917 and March 9 1917, 109.
31. Link, *Campaigns,* 372. See also Baker, VI, 475. Link, in addition to being critical of the "willful men" message (see n.2), is also critical of the president's supplementary message put out later on March 5, suggesting that the 1819 statute might prevent him from arming merchant ships, therefore the filibuster which

NOTES

held up its repeal was vital. Link suggests that Wilson should have researched the question more fully, 364.

32. *New York Times,* March 10 1917, 1.
33. Ibid.
34. The source for this story is *Cobb of the World,* a series of editorials and stories compiled by John L. Heaton, 268–71. This version suggests that the meeting took place the evening before Wilson went to Congress with the request for a war resolution, whereas Link, *Campaigns,* 398, makes a stronger case for saying that it was March 19. Heaton notes that the incident was recounted by Cobb to two friends, Lawrence Stallings and Maxwell Anderson. This might account for the discrepancy. There is even doubt as to the authenticity of the meeting; see Auerback.
35. Link, *Campaigns,* 394–96.
36. For information on this meeting, see Houston, I, 241–44; Lansing, 236; Daniels, March 20 1917, 117; Lane, April 1 1917, 242; and Baker, VI, 502–4.
37. See Link, *Campaigns,* 412, and Hitchcock's speech on the war resolution, *Congressional Record,* April 4 1917, 201.
38. LaFollette, I, 654. See also Towne, 225, and *New York Times,* April 1 1917, 1.
39. Holmes, 317.
40. Koenig, 569.
41. LaFollette, I, 665. See also *New York Times,* April 3 1917, 3.

Chapter 9. The War Resolution

1. Myers, 45–52.
2. Houston, I, 253.
3. Garraty, *Lodge,* 333. See also Ashurst, 61.
4. Link, *Campaigns,* 422.
5. Ibid., 422.
6. Osborn, 286.
7. See Houston, I, 253–55; LaFollette, I, 646: and *New York Times,* April 3 1917, 1–3.
8. Myers, 51.
9. Walworth, II, 98.
10. The full text of the speech can be found in the *Record* for April 2 1917, 102–4. For reactions, see Goldman, 238; LaFollette, I, 647, and *New York Times,* April 3 1917, 2.
11. Ashurst, 52.
12. *New York Times,* April 3 1917, 2.
13. Tumulty, 256.
14. LaFollette, I, 649.
15. Ibid., 649–52. See also *New York Times,* April 4 1917, 1. For McCumber, see Phillips, 470.

190

16. The debate on the resolution can be found in the *Congressional Record,* April 4 1917, 201–61.
17. LaFollette, I, 654.
18. Neuberger, 124.
19. Norris, 198.
20. Ashurst, 61.
21. Myers, 54.
22. Russell, 280–83.
23. LaFollette, I, 666.
24. *Congressional Record* (House of Representatives), April 5-6 1917, 412.
25. Mullen, 181.
26. *New York Times,* April 6 1917, 1, and April 7 1917, 4.
27. LaGuardia, 141.

Chapter 10. After 1917

1. See Lowitt, 46. See also Livermore, 231, for analysis of Oregon politics in 1918, and 162–65 for the purge of Vardaman. See Holmes, 350 et seq., for Vardaman's last years.
2. Phillips, 630 et seq.
3. *New York Times,* May 18 1943, 23, and May 21 1943, 20.
4. Bowers, 523.
5. Neuberger, 92–128.
6. Ashurst, 77. See also Livermore, 141, 230, for Missouri politics following Stone's death.
7. *New York Times,* July 31 1926, 1.
8. McKenna, 175, and *New York Times,* February 1 1922, 1. For Kenyon's involvement in the Newberry matter, see the *Times* for January 18 1922, 10.
9. Ashurst, 211. For Harding-Kenyon relationship, see Russell, 303. See also *New York Times,* September 10 1933, 38.
10. The events in Norris's life are given treatment in Neuberger and Kahn, 143–348. For his own explanation of his defeat, see Norris, 370.
11. LaFollette, II, 761–829, covers the events of the attempted expulsion.
12. Russell, 383.
13. Watson, 187.
14. McKenna, 143.
15. Neuberger, 296.
16. Shannon, 331.
17. Billington, 184.
18. Livermore, 144.
19. Byrnes, 47. See also Ashurst, 172, and Smith, 255.
20. *New York Times,* November 19 1945, 21.
21. Ashurst, 59.

BIBLIOGRAPHY

Arnett, Alex. *Claude Kitchin and the Wilson War Policies.* Little, Brown, 1937.

Ashurst, Henry. *A Many-Colored Toga: The Diary of Henry Fountain Ashurst* (ed. George Sparks). University of Arizona, 1962.

Auerback, Jerold. "Woodrow Wilson's Prediction to Frank Cobb: Words Historians Should Doubt Ever Got Spoken," *Journal of American History,* 54 (December 1967), 608–17.

Bailey, Thomas. *A Diplomatic History of the American People.* Appleton, 1950.

Baker, Roy S. *Woodrow Wilson, Life and Letters* (8 vols.). Doubleday, 1927–39.

Billington, Monroe. *Thomas P. Gore: The Blind Senator from Oklahoma.* University of Kansas, 1967.

Bowers, Claude. *Beveridge and the Progressive Era.* Houghton, 1932.

Burdette, Franklin. *Filibustering in the Senate.* Princeton University, 1940.

Byrnes, James. *All in One Lifetime.* Harper, 1958.

Coletta, Paolo. *William Jennings Bryan: Political Puritan* (3 vols.). University of Nebraska, 1969.

Cooper, John Milton. *The Vanity of Power: American Isolationism and World War I.* Greenwood, 1969.

Daniels, Josephus. *Cabinet Diaries of Josephus Daniels* (ed. E. D. Cronon). University of Nebraska, 1963.

Davenport, Walter. *Power and Glory: The Life of Boies Penrose.* Putnam, 1931.

DeConde, Alexander. *A History of American Foreign Policy* (2d ed.). Scribner, 1971.

——. "The South and Isolationism," *The South and the Sectional Image: The Sectional Theme since Reconstruction* (ed. Dewey Grantham). Harper, 1967.

192

BIBLIOGRAPHY

Fenno, Richard. *The President's Cabinet: An Analysis in the Period from Wilson to Eisenhower.* Harvard University, 1959.
Forth, William S. *Wesley L. Jones: A Political Biography.* (Unpub. diss.), University of Washington, 1962.
Freidel, Frank. *Franklin Delano Roosevelt: The Apprenticeship.* Little, Brown, 1952.
Galloway, George. *A History of the House of Representatives.* Crowell, 1962.
Garraty, John. *Henry Cabot Lodge: A Biography.* Knopf, 1953.
———. *Woodrow Wilson: A Great Life in Brief.* Knopf, 1965.
Goldman, Eric. *Rendezvous with Destiny.* Knopf, 1952.
Graham, Otis. *An Encore for Reform: The Old Progressives and the New Deal.* Oxford University, 1967.
Grantham, Dewey. *Hoke Smith and the Politics of the New South.* Louisiana State University, 1958.
Hatch, Alden. *The Wadsworths of the Genesee.* Coward-McCann, 1959.
Heaton, John. *Cobb of the World: A Leader in Liberalism.* Dutton, 1924.
Hechler, Kenneth. *Insurgency, Personalities and Politics of the Taft Era.* Columbia University, 1940.
Hofstadter, Richard. *The American Political Tradition and the Men Who Made It.* Knopf, 1948.
Holmes, William. *The White Chief, James Kimble Vardaman.* Louisiana State University, 1970.
Holt, James. *Congressional Insurgents and the Party System, 1909-1916.* Harvard University, 1967.
Houston, David. *My Eight Years in Wilson's Cabinet: With a Personal Assessment of the President* (2 vols.). Doubleday, 1926.
Kennedy, John F. *Profiles in Courage.* Harper, 1956.
Key, V. O. *Southern Politics in State and Nation.* Knopf, 1949.
Koenig, Louis. *Bryan: A Political Biography of William Jennings Bryan.* Putnam, 1971.
LaFollette, Belle Case and Fola. *Robert M. LaFollette, June 14, 1855- June 18, 1925* (2 vols.). Macmillan, 1953.
LaFollette, Robert. *LaFollette's Autobiography: A Personal Narrative of Political Experience.* University of Wisconsin, 1911, 1913.
———. "The Armed Ship Bill Meant War." *LaFollette's Magazine,* March 9 1917, 1-4.
LaGuardia, Fiorello. *The Making of an Insurgent.* Lippincott, 1948.
Lane, A. W., and Wall, L. M. (eds.). *Letters of Franklin K. Lane.* Houghton, 1924.
Lansing, Robert. *War Memoirs of Robert Lansing.* Bobbs-Merrill, 1935.
Lief, Alfred. *Democracy's Norris: Biography of a Lonely Crusade.* Stackpole, 1939.
Link, Arthur. *Wilson: Campaigns for Progressivism and Peace.* Princeton University, 1965.
———. *Wilson: Confusions and Crises.* Princeton University, 1964.
———. *Wilson: The Struggle for Neutrality.* Princeton University, 1960. 1960.
———*Woodrow Wilson and the Progressive Era.* Harper 1954.

193

Livermore, Seward. *Politics Is Adjourned: Woodrow Wilson and the War Congress.* Wesleyan University, 1966.

Lodge, Henry Cabot (ed.). *Selections from the Correspondence of Theodore Roosevelt and Henry Cabot Lodge 1884–1918* (2 vols.). Scribner, 1925.

Lowitt, Richard. "The Armed Ship Bill Controversy: A Legislative View," *Mid-America* 46 (January 1964), 38–47.

Luthin, Reinhold. *American Demagogues.* Beacon, 1954.

Marshall, Thomas. *Recollections of Thomas R. Marshall, Vice President and Hoosier Philosopher.* Bobbs-Merrill, 1925.

McKenna, Marian. *Borah.* University of Michigan, 1961.

Morison, Samuel, Frederick Merk, and Frank Freidel. *American Dissent in Three Wars.* Harvard University, 1970 (paperback).

Morrison, Joseph. *Josephus Daniels: The Small d Democrat.* University of North Carolina, 1966.

Mowry, George. *The California Progressives.* University of California, 1950.

Mullen, Arthur. *Western Democrat.* Longmans, 1940.

Myers, Henry. *The United States Senate: What Kind of Body.* Dorrance, 1939.

Neuberger, Richard, and Stephen Kahn. *Integrity: The Life of George W. Norris.* Vanguard, 1937.

Norris, George. *Fighting Liberal: The Autobiography of George W. Norris.* Macmillan, 1945.

Osborn, George. *John Sharp Williams, Planter-Statesman of the Deep South.* Louisiana State University, 1943.

Phillips, William. *Asle J. Gronna: A Self-Made Man of the Prairies.* (Unpub. diss.), University of Missouri, 1958.

Pratt, Julius. *Expansionists of 1898: The Acquisition of Hawaii and the Philippine Islands.* Johns Hopkins, 1936.

Pringle, Henry. *Theodore Roosevelt: A Biography.* Harcourt, 1931.

Russell, Francis. *The Shadow of Blooming Grove: Warren G. Harding and His Times.* McGraw-Hill, 1968.

Sayre, Ralph. *Albert Baird Cummins and the Progressive Movement in Iowa.* (Unpub. diss.), Columbia University, 1958.

Schlesinger, Arthur. *The Age of Roosevelt: Crisis of the Old Order.* Houghton, 1957.

Shannon, William. *The American Irish: A Political and Social Portrait.* Macmillan, 1963.

Simkins, Francis. *Pitchfork Ben Tillman, South Carolinian.* Louisiana State University, 1944.

Simpson, Colin. *The Lusitania.* Little, Brown, 1972.

Smith, Frank. *Congressman from Mississippi.* Random, 1964.

Swanberg, W. A. *Citizen Hearst: A Biography of William Randolph Hearst.* Scribner, 1961.

Towne, Ruth Warner. *The Public Career of William Joel Stone.* (Unpub. diss.), University of Missouri, 1953.

Tuchman, Barbara. *The Zimmermann Telegram.* Macmillan, 1966.

Tumulty, Joseph. *Woodrow Wilson As I Know Him.* Doubleday, 1921.

BIBLIOGRAPHY

Walworth, Arthur. *Woodrow Wilson: American Prophet* (2 vols.).
  Longmans, 1958.
Watson, James E. *As I Know Them: Memoirs of James E. Watson.*
  Bobbs-Merrill, 1936.
Wilson, Woodrow. *Congressional Government.* Houghton, 1885.

INDEX

196

TE DUE